THE MARK OF CAIN

THE MARK OF CAIN

The Stigma Theory of Crime
and Social Deviation

by
SHLOMO SHOHAM

Institute of Criminology and Criminal Law,
Faculty of Law   Tel Aviv University

Foreword by
Marvin E. Wolfgang

Israel Universities Press, Jerusalem
Oceana Publications, Inc., Dobbs Ferry, N.Y.

ISRAEL UNIVERSITIES PRESS
is a publishing division of the
KETER PUBLISHING HOUSE LTD.,
a wholly owned subsidiary of the
ISRAEL PROGRAM FOR SCIENTIFIC TRANSLATIONS LTD.
P.O.B. 7145, Jerusalem, Israel.
Manufactured in Israel, by the Keter Publishing House Ltd

For Phillip Rieff

The author wishes to acknowledge with thanks the devoted editorial efforts of Derek Orlans, Chief Editor of Israel Universities Press, and the conscientious help of Mrs. Irene Banit and Miss Shlomit Shtreit in the proofreading and in the compilation of the index.

FOREWORD

by Marvin E. Wolfgang

The social function of branding some segment of a society is as old as our knowledge of man's collectivity. Stigmata have been placed upon one or another group of deviants as a measure of segregating them in the minds of men in whose midst the branded are still permitted to dwell. The process of stigmatization can be physical, quick in time, permanent; it can also be subtle, informal, slowly developed. From branding of the flesh to oral derogation men have known the consequences of being denoted a deviate. Stigma may be a form of retribution, of an untoward social classification that substitutes for more rigorous restraint of deviants, that replaces incarceration as a means for retaining social distance. Those in control of defining the status of others find labels pejorative for those outside the social matrix of familiarity. The label became a convenient shorthand of language that clusters to its simplicity a plethora of adjectival attachments that quickly become stereotypes for the lazy minds of men.

The Mark of Cain is written at an important historical moment in the development of these ideas. In studies of criminology and social deviance, the labelling process has become an increasing concern of theorists and surely will be employed soon by the empiricists. Sociology and social psychology have begun to provide theoretical flesh to the idea and have drawn attention to the social agents of response to behaviour as important ingredients in the meaning of deviance. A label by a response agent can be sewn to the biography of a child such that he cannot successfully rip it away and find a new identity. The political deviant, even with respect for the system under which he lives, may nonetheless be placed in a social category with a publicly displayed label that results in his being institutionalized for his utterances. Such is the symptomatic power of stigmatization through which an individual may be processed.

Drawing attention to these matters is not new. But *The Mark of Cain* has amplified this discussion with embellished theory, a typology that should attract many comments and an empirical case illustration of the application of the author's theoretical analysis. There is wide erudition in this volume and a synthesis of surprising quality. It is not uncommon or unexpected to join Kierkegaard and Jaspers in a discussion of existential features, or to use Erikson to contemporize Freud. But to bring together the powerful propositions these men represent, and, further, to bring them to the analysis of crime and social deviance, are important contributions to the several fields. An author who can cause us to organize thought around a topic—in this case, stigma—by pulling into the orbit such apparently disparate items as Renaissance Florence, Kendall's Tau, the Torah and Genet, deserves our attention and appreciation.

CONTENTS

INTRODUCTION

Men do not become what by nature they are meant to be, but what society makes them. The generous feelings and high propensities of the soul are, as it were, shrunk up, seared, violently wrenched, and amputated, to fit us for our intercourse with the world, something in the manner that beggars maim and mutilate their children, to make them fit for their future situation in life.*

THE CONCEPTS

The original Greek stigmatias were runaway slaves with a mark burned into their skins as a sign of disgrace. The biblical Mark of Cain as well as similar signs branded on murderers in primitive tribes were signs of pollution and divine wrath.[1] The stigmata of St. Francis of Assisi and the physical afflictions of certain other Catholic saints were regarded as signs of holiness, as reproductions of the wounds of Jesus Christ.

In contemporary disciplines the use of the concept "stigma" is far from consistent. It is applied in a large variety of situations in which individuals or groups are disqualified from full social acceptance, ranging from facial deformity[2] to mental disease.[3] A recent study on stigma includes in its analysis cripples, the blind, the deaf, Jews, Negroes, drug addicts, prostitutes and homosexuals.[4] We shall exclude from our analysis the physically deformed or afflicted, as these individuals and the groups are manifestly different. Their apartness is inherent in their physical attributes. We are concerned with the derogatory tags applied to social roles and statuses. Racial discrimination and ethnocentrism, especially if not originating from colour, would seemingly be included in our analysis, but we prefer to exclude these; first,

---

* William Hazlitt, *The Life of Thomas Holroft*

1

because their genesis and manifestations transcend our present domain of normative deviation and control; second, it would be presumptuous to introduce the vast and complex body of knowledge on social relations as a special case of a theory on crime and social deviation.

We shall therefore use the concept stigma as a derogatory attribute imputed to the social image of an individual or a group.

By social image we mean the sum total of an individual's social roles and statuses as perceived at a given time by his membership or reference groups. This definition implies the hypothetical perception by a group of an individual as "the distal object"[5]; that is, it imputes to the group qualities of perception and takes the individual as the raw material "out-there" of the group's perception. This, admittedly, is naive epistemology, but nonetheless is an adequate working definition for our present purpose.

Our study of social stigma is related to its effect on the aetiology of crime and deviation and its use by the various agencies of social control to curb the infringement of norms. In stressing social control we are limiting our analysis to social stigmata that are used as sanctions against those who have allegedly infringed some social norms, or stigmata that are incidental or are attached to other sanctions. Being branded as a "trouble-maker" is an example of the former and the stigma of being an "ex-con" is an example of the latter. We shall devote an entire chapter to the functions of stigma in social control, but the concepts of crime and social deviation, as used in this work, are defined here as follows:

Crime: In its legal sense crime is an act or an omission proscribed and punishable by law. A major impediment to the theoretical analysis of the concept of crime is the widely heterogeneous nature of human acts that are labelled criminal but which have no common behavioural denominator. This heterogeneity is largely explained by the fact that crime is related to two phenomena that are not organically linked: human behaviour and the criminal law.

In order to reach meaningful generalizations about human

2

behaviour, the scientist has to analyse types of behaviour that possess one or more characteristics in common; however, it is obvious that the mere fact that a large variety of different types of behaviour have as their only common denominator their being forbidden by criminal law is of little value to the study of crime.[6] On the other hand, the study of criminal law was for a long time detached from the analysis of the personality of its violators.[7]

Efforts to resolve this dilemma marked the beginning of scientific criminology. To free the study of criminal behaviour from its rigid legalistic boundaries Garofalo coined the concept of "Le délit naturel" to denote offences against the humanitarian sentiments of pity and probity.[8] Subsequent theories can be arranged between two extremes: at one end are those like Michael and Adler[9] who argue that the only possible basis for the definition and classification of crime is the legal one, because man is endowed with freedom of will and behavioural generalizations are therefore meaningless.[10] At the other extreme there are those like Clinard[11] who regard crime as a particular instance of socially deviant behaviour and deal with it together with mental disorders, divorce, racial discrimination and prejudice. Our approach is that crime is indeed a manifestation of social deviation, but is a special one; its characteristics make it a separate genre of social deviation even in the behavioural sense.

The social norms that govern the relation of an individual to his group differ intrinsically from the criminal law norms laid down by the legislator.

The criminal law norm is a social reality which can be studied and classified as a behavioural entity; it differs in kind from other social norms in the method in which it is enforced and in the consequences of its enforcement. The ritualistic elements in the criminal procedure, the special setting of a courtroom, the necessity to plead guilty or not guilty, the formal conviction and the subsequent publicity, make the criminal norm unique. The court of law is one of the most important social institutions in every society. The reactions to a summons to appear in court range from morbid fear to mild excitement. The criminal trial, in

3

which violators of legal norms must participate (if caught) is a unique social occasion. The ritual, the stigma of conviction[12] and the special types of sanctions (imprisonment, fines, etc.) place the legal norms on a behavioural level, that is, entirely different from that occupied by norms sanctioned by ridicule and ostracism, for example. The criminal procedure is not only an operation that links the legal and the behavioural levels of the norm but it is also a feature that differentiates it from all the social norms.[13]

Social Deviation: This is the general phenomenon of which crime is a special case; it is a rejection of society's values and norms and/or behaviour contrary to these values and norms. The manifestations of social deviation can be arranged along a continuum having at one end ideal-type conformism and at the other ideal-type deviation. This continuum, which is in fact multidimensional, and a suggested typology of relationships between deviation and social stigma, will be discussed at greater length in Chapter four. Social deviation as a function (in the mathematical sense) of social stigma can manifest itself in actual deviant behaviour. However, a stigmatized person can be a conformist in his overt behaviour but a deviant in his beliefs and values, and vice versa. The two variables relevant to social stigma as far as the stigmatized are concerned are thus behaviour conformity (or deviation) and value conformity (or deviation). We shall analyse at length the relationships between value deviation, deviant behaviour and social stigma.

THE PLAN OF THE BOOK

The first two chapters deal with the role of stigma within the various mechanisms of normative control. The chapter dealing with the function of stigma as a tool of social control is more of an extended descriptive definition paving the way for the study of stigma as a component of crime and deviation. The second chapter illustrates the case of psychopathy—presented as a stigmatic tool of normative control. Chapter three deals with the predisposing factors raising the probability of indivuals and groups being branded by stigma. Chapter four deals with the paradigm resulting from the relationship between value deviation, deviant behaviour and social stigma. The fifth chapter describes the dynamic process of stigmatization. The sixth chapter is an empirical study of Israeli prostitutes from North African authoritarian families, partly proving the applicability of the stigma premises to prostitution which combines elements of both crime and social deviation. Chapters 7 and 8 analyse the effects of stigma, both formal and informal, on the future behaviour of the stigmatized. Chapter nine relates stigma to criminal and deviant subculture formation. The last chapter is a case study of Jean Genet, the French *poete maudit,* who epitomizes to almost grotesque extremities the role of stigma in the making of a criminal, a pervert and an outcast. The style of the present work might seem quite unusual. Learned tomes are customarily written in parched language, which is supposed to lend them an aura of exact logic. We have tried to combine logic and intuition. In language, at least, we may deviate from the scholarly tradition.

CHAPTER I

THE ROLE OF STIGMA IN NORM-SENDING AND NORM-RECEIVING

In the village, without bragging, I have a bad reputation,
I do not harm anybody, going along my simple way,
                              but the good people don't like to see
One follow another road than theirs.
Everyone slanders me, save the mutes, of course.*

THE MODEL

The study of social stigmatization belongs in the general frame of reference of social psychology. A model of the processes effecting conformity to social norms must therefore analyse both norm-sending—transmission and enforcement of norms by the group—and the degree to which the norms have been received and internalized by the individual.[1]

A prior condition for norm-sending is a statement by the group of the behaviour that is desired and the consequences to the individual if he does not comply. The group must then maintain surveillance in order to determine the degree of compliance; and, lastly, the group has to apply sanctions to non-complying individuals.

Conformity to the norm ranges from mere compliance, where the individual is induced to conform by constant surveillance and the threat of punitive sanctions, through identification where inducement is by rewards, to the most complete conformity, which is the internalization of the norm by the individual; at this point surveillance and sanction are redundant because the norm is incorporated by the individual as an element of his personality.

---

* From a ballad by George Brassens

A. *The function of stigma in the statement of the rule phase of norm-sending is to contrast, visually or symbolically, the non-normative and the normative.* Historically, the function of a rule was to contrast, to distinguish the non-normative from the normative, a differentiation between good and evil. If law is to be a discriminating agent, it must use effective tagging tools: social stigma is a branding tool *par excellence.* The imputation of the non-normative attributes to an individual, object or group, not only focuses attention on the infringement, but also helps to delineate, by contrast, the rule itself. In polytheistic religions and in primitive cultures the wicked, the offending, and the evil were frequently invested with distinct deities. Ahriman, the Dark One, is equal in power to Ormazd, the God of Light, and he embodies everything which is in contrast to Ormazd. Ahi, the dragon, the adversary, was symbol of evil in the ancient religions of India. Even in monotheism in its most developed forms, there is the Antichrist, who provides the contrasting antithesis to Jesus, and the Sitra-Achara (the Evil One) always lurks on the fringes of Yahwa's domain. Manichaeism was long a companion of Christianity. The Koran contrasts the Sura of God and the believers with the Sura of the devil and the apostates. In the Middle Ages penitent sinners had to distinguish themselves from the rest of the community. "The head was kept shaven, the vestments were of sackcloth sprinkled with ashes, and baths were forbidden..." (the penitent) was cut off from all association with the faithful and was segregated with such strictness that everyone eating with him was deprived of communion. Whenever the faithful were gathered together in church the penitents were grouped apart in their hideous squalor... Their humiliation was utilized to the utmost as a spectacle and a warning for the benefit of the congregation."[2] In Nazi Germany, an authoritarian state where ambiguity could not be tolerated, the Jew was portrayed as the antithesis of the Teutonic superman. The Jew, as stereotyped, was more than a mere contrasting antecedent to the Nazi superman, he was an essential part of the Nazi ideology. The thesis and the antithesis, the ideal and its negation, were generally voiced togeth-

7

er. In a typical speech Hitler ranted: "Everything beautiful we see around us today is only the creation of the Aryan, his spirit and industry; only the bad things are the heritage of the Jew."[3] This is the basis of the declaration of Von Schönerer, the founder of modern political anti-semitism, some decades before Hitler: "We Pan-Germans regard anti-semitism as the mainstay of our national ideology."[4] The concept "Enemy of the people" seems to be a branding image not only of the dictatorship of the proletariat; political institutions and parties in every society from time immemorial have employed stigma to depict, tag and define images, ideas and behaviour which are to be contrasted with the normative.

Evil and sin have always been personalized and contrasted with the good and virtuous. Evil and corrupt men and women (especially witches) have been stereotyped in folklore as being conspicuously ugly. At one time the motion-picture industry almost sanctified the stereotypes of the "good guy" and the "bad guy". This use of stereotypes to denote the evil and non-normative and to contrast it with the good and normative can account partly for the various attempts to link certain biophysiological features to crime and deviation. Shakespeare's Julius Caesar says:

> Let me have men about me that are fat;
> Sleek-headed men, and such as sleep o'night;
> Yond' Cassius has a lean and hungry look;
> Such men are dangerous.

In everyday life, we tend to take stereotypes literally and we impute certain behavioural characteristics to individuals, relying on physiognomy and external appearance. Pseudo-scientific disciplines have been elaborated on this basis; some of them enjoyed great vogues, notably those of the phrenologist, Lombroso, with his criminal types, and the more sophisticated somatotypes of Kretschmer[5] and William James[6], Sheldon[7] and the Gluecks[8].

B. *In the surveillance phase of norm-sending the function of stigma is to deter; it relates to future conformity to the norm. For potential*

8

offenders or deviants, the stigma frequently has a greater deterrent effect than the sanction itself. The deterrent effect of punishment has two aspects: "individual prevention", which is deterring the convicted offender from committing further offences in the future, and "general prevention", which is deterring potential offenders. "Individual prevention" is not relevant in the present context because the convicted offender has already been stigmatized; the stigmata of additional convictions will matter less to him.

Physical branding, the pillory, the branks and the ducking stool were stigma penalties designed not only to degrade the offender but also to deter potential ones. As late as the 18th century we find statutes in Europe and England prescribing the branding of cheeks and foreheads of convicted felons. However, the social stigma of conviction is probably the most potent deterrent to potential offenders. A person who is not a professional or habitual criminal or a lawyer is rarely aware of the exact or even the approximate penalty he is likely to suffer for the offence he is about to commit, though he is, of course, aware of the possibility of detection and punishment. The fear of stigma is probably much stronger than the fear of punishment for the average law-abiding citizen. He is afraid of losing his job, of being ostracized by his business associates and friends, of the possible alienation of members of his family, of having to leave his neighbourhood or even his town. In the realm of social deviation, fear of stigma is actually the sole method of active surveillance exercised by society to ensure conformity. Fear of stigmatization as a "bore", a "troublemaker", an "impossible character", a "sex maniac" and a myriad of other tags is dreadful enough for the majority of people to try their best not to be so branded.

C. *Stigmata can be the sanctions themselves or they can be attached to sanctions. The stigma reflects the group's reaction to the infringement of the norm and can therefore serve as an index to measure the strength of the norm. The strength of the norm and the stigma are positively correlated: the graver the stigma, the harsher is the group's reaction to the breach of the norm (irrespective of the nature and severity of the formal sanction) and the greater is the inherent power of the norm.* Historically, the most ancient sanction for the infringement of norms, religious, legal or social, was the stigma of pollution attached to the offender.[9]

The bearer of the original Mark of Cain was not only damned as a fratricide, but the land that he cultivated was cursed: "When thou tillest the ground, it shall not henceforth yield unto thee her strength; a fugitive and vagabond shalt thou be in the earth."[10]

The pollution presumably stems from the identity in ancient times of social and legal norms with religious norms: the offender aroused by his act the wrath of the divine or other supernatural powers and was therefore cursed by pollution and stigmatized. Ranulf cites a 17th century English Puritan sermon: "Sinne leaves a kind of blemish and stains upon the soule, after the commission of it... The Scripture calls it the excrement of naughtiness, though the act of sinne is gone, yet there is a blemish on the soule.... So a man after sinne shall finde himself dull to any good, and prone to any evil... This is the staine of sinne."[11] This is a perfect illustration of a symbolic derogatory tag, social stigma. This pollution was deemed to be contagious; the stigmatized offender was very often segregated and ostracized. Frazer[12] cites instances of this stigmatized pollution. In ancient Attica murderers were ostracized and outlawed, and anyone could injure or kill them with impunity. If another trial was pending against a murderer he could return to defend himself, but he had to do so on board a boat and the judges conducted the trial on the seashore. The murderer was not allowed to touch the shore lest he pollute the land and the people by contagion.

Thucydides tells us the story of Alcmeon who was wandering over the earth after the murder of his mother; he had been told by the Oracle of Appollo that he would never find peace until he discovered some place which had not yet been in existence nor seen by the sun at the time he slew his mother; there he might settle: the rest of the earth was accursed to him.[13] Thus stigma and its social consequences historically preceded the formalization of sanction. Sanction was originally an expiatory act that was

10

supposed to cleanse and purge the pollution and stigma incurred by the violation. Philological support for this premise may be found in the source of the word punishment (*peine* in French, *poena* in Latin and ποινω in˙Greek) which is derived from the Sanskrit root *PU,* meaning to cleanse and purify. The crime offends the gods and causes pollution. The formal punishment cleanses the offender of his pollution and also appeases the gods. The phenomena of stigma and pollution as a consequence of violation of norms were almost universal, and there are numerous examples in mythology, drama and history. The Oracle of Apollo instructed Orestes to avenge the blood of his father Agamemnon, because the murderer had been cursed by the wrath of the gods and were the sin not expiated by punishment, the whole community might suffer diseases and disasters.[14] The Manteans of Ancient Greece purified themselves after they met the murderers of Arcadia.[15] The Trobriand Islanders stigmatized with pollution the perpetrators of incest;[16] this pollution was believed to be contagious and if not expiated by punishment, the whole tribe would die from terrible diseases. The Kikuyu tribesmen in Kenya used to purify themselves after a chance meeting with a murderer: every chattel or object which had come in contact with the murderer had also to be destroyed.[17] The Chama Indians forbade the murderer to wave his hands, comb his hair, or dine with his fellow tribesmen, and in the hunting period he had to camp far away from the tents of the rest of the tribe.[18] Another instance of stigmatized pollution has been described in a study of Amazon Indians. This is of special importance because these tribes were until recently isolated from foreign patterns of culture and they possess a whole system of purification rites, the sole purpose of which is to cleanse the tribesmen from the polluting presence of a murderer or other offender against tribal taboos.[19]

These examples, and many others which abound in both ancient civilizations and contemporary primitive cultures, illustrate the historical precedence of stigmatized pollution as the group's reaction to norm violation. The offence was generally related to transcendental powers and aroused the wrath of the gods;

11

this wrath was manifested in the stigma and pollution emanating from the offender. The formal sanction, which was usually accompanied by religious rites, expiated the pollution and stigma and appeased the gods. Expiatory rites eventually crystallized into our modern legal sanctions.[20]

Stigma as a formal legal sanction has been incorporated in some of the earliest legal codes in human history. We find in the code of Hammurabi the branding of the forehead as a punishment for slandering a votary or a married woman.[21] In the Manu laws of ancient India stigmata were used as formal sanctions and ostracism was the social consequence of this stigmatization.[22]

Branding as a formal sanction was also widely used in Persia of the Zend-Avesta.[23] Roman religious law *(fas)* prescribed as a sanction the stigma of ignominious to its violators to be followed by abrogation of certain civil and religious rights by the Pontifex.[24] The Roman *infamia* was in most cases a stigma attached to other legal sanctions. The *infamia* was formalized by a mark put by the Censor in the census list beside the man's name; this status involved the loss of certain legal rights, especially in matters of litigation.[25]

A narrower type of formal legal stigmatization was that of the *intestabiles,* persons who were disabled from giving legal evidence or being witnesses in any formal transaction. This stigma was employed in Rome as early as the XII Tables.[26] The Germanic laws of the early Middle Ages declared all serious offenders as "wolf". This meant being outlawed and liable to be killed on sight.[27] Lucas de Penna, in his treatise on mediaeval law, describes the *Bannitus* as a person who has been outlawed and stigmatized as a consequence of a crime or for some other reason deemed appropriate by the authorities. He was excluded from civil society and it was legally permissible to kill him.[28] Wolfgang describes the *gonga,* one of the lesser penalties of Renaissance Florence. The offender had to stand for an hour, bare-headed, his hat at his feet, his hands bound behind him to one of the iron rings in the wall; on his chest was a placard describing the nature of his crime. During this time the old bell of the prison was rung to announce the display to the public.[29]

12

Sanctions accompanied by public degradation and stigma were employed in many variations throughout Europe. Stigmatic sanctions were also inherent in the so-called "Poetic punishment"—a baker having to walk in the public square with the underweight loaves hung round his neck,[30] or a person who had stolen a cabbage from his neighbour's garden in 17th century New York being ordered to stand in the pillory with the cabbage on his head in addition to being banished from the colony for five years.[31]

In modern legislation these stigmata have been formalized in the loss of some or all of a person's civil rights following conviction: the rights to hold public office, to vote, to testify, to marry, to make contracts, etc. These formalized stigmata are distinct from the informal social and economic effects that follow the stigma of conviction. The various forms of total or partial "civil death"— legally imposed on an offender in addition to other sanctions—are modern counterparts of the Roman *ignominiosus*, the Germanic "wolf" and the mediaeval *Bannitus*.

Sanctions against social deviation are invariably accompanied by stigmata and have various social and economic consequences. Stigma as sanction is one of the most common components of socialization of children in the formative years; "bad boy", "naughty girl", "difficult child" are the most common tags used by the family, school, and other socializing agencies against nonconforming children. Adult society has a greater variety of stigmatizing sanctions ranging from blunt ostracism to subtle satire, derision or sophisticated caricature.

In primitive society stigma in the form of taboo is the most prevalent sanction for non-normative behaviour. Frazer cites many instances where the usurpers of the chief's authority, the unauthorized users of his property and clothes, the uninvited participants in his meals, became taboo. Being declared taboo[32] in primitive society is the strongest sanction imaginable and in some instances it amounts to a death sentence. A New Zealand native died of painful convulsions after becoming taboo for eating the Chief's food. A Maori Chief's tinder-box actually

13

killed several persons who lit their pipes from it: they died of fright on learning to whom it had belonged.[33] Death from taboo, although induced by shock from imaginary fear, is a potent reinforcement to the norm. For the savage, taboo is not a spiritual or intangible entity; for him it is, to quote Frazer,"as real as gravity and may kill him as certainly as a dose of prussic acid".

Taboos were the most widely used sanctions of primitive societies, and were applied to enforce dietary, familial and sexual norms and to sanction rules of property, war, ghosts, religion, and group solidarity.[34]

Among the Azande, being declared a witch is a sanction for social deviation and non-conformity to tribal norms. Evans-Pritchard states: "When Azande say that an action or feeling is bad they mean that it is socially deplorable and condemned by public opinion. It is bad because it may lead to witchcraft and because it brings the offending person into greater or less disrepute. .. It is in the idiom of witchcraft that Azande express moral rules which mostly lie outside criminal and civil law. The stigmatized person is outside the realm of the normative system of the tribe; he is a dog-like being, whose huts may be burned and whose women and children may be destroyed with impunity."[35]

The Roman declaration of *infamia* was used not only for legal infractions, but was quite frequently applied as a sanction for behaviour; the Censor had the authority, which he used freely, to inscribe the *notatus* of *infamia* beside the names in the census list of persons who had presumably misbehaved themselves or who were deemed to be discreditable or undesirable, but who had not necessarily been condemned by any formal legal action.[36] In other words, the stigma of *infamia* could be branded on any person who seemed to be deviating from the social norms as these were interpreted by the Censor.

In certain periods in the Middle Ages the tag of heresy was a sanction applied to diverse and heterogeneous modes of beliefs and behaviour. The common denominator of heretics seemed to be their deviation not from the prevalent religious dogma, but from the norms of society relating to everyday life. The heretic was a person who deviated from accepted norms in the use of language, dress, manners, sexual mores, or one who was conspicuous or different in his external appearance and behaviour.[37]

Stigmatization as a heretic was an extremely fierce sanction: it could be incurred for diverse and undefined reasons and sometimes for no apparent reason whatsoever. The results of being branded as heretic were, however, far from vague. Heretics could consider themselves fortunate if they were merely ordered to wear a yellow cross on their garments[38] because they frequently suffered far worse indignities at the hands of the Inquisition.

In modern society the sanction of stigma differs in kind and consequences from the mediaeval stigma of heresy and the primitive taboo, but its inherent nature is unchanged. An individual who differs in his personality or behaviour, or is considered different in a way that infringes the group's normative system, is liable to be stigmatized as being deviant; the social and economic consequences of this stigma are dependent on the severity of the infringement of the norm and are determined by the inner strength of the norm. The latter is positively correlated with the force of the stigma. It has been suggested that the inner strength of a norm can be measured by the "group's attitude" towards the violation of the norm. Sellin says: "A conduct norm becomes a rule which governs a specific type of life situation and is authoritative to the extent of the group's resistance to violation. The inherent energy of power of the norm, as just described, may be called its 'resistance potential'."[39] This resistance potential can be determined, according to Sellin, by means of one of the various techniques utilized to measure group attitudes, so that each norm is allotted a numerical value on a predetermined scale.

On the informal level, the group's attitude to the violation of a norm is apparent only from the stigma branded on the violators. The stigma, therefore, is the best instrument for measuring the inner strength of a social norm.

D. *The stigma as a means of social control is less effective with norm-orientated and inner-directed individuals and more effective*

15

with sanction-orientated and other-directed ones. We have noted the gradation of internalization of norms. If internalization is shallow, the individual complies for fear of sanction; stigma is most effective as a sanction at this stage of internalization because the individual is "sanction orientated". He complies not because an inner control has been formed by an internalized norm, but because he is afraid of sanctions or social disapproval—stigma. Chwast says: "The relationship between inner control and outer control is inverse. The more inner control the individual possesses, the fewer are the outer sanctions called for; the less the inner, the more the need for outer control[40]."

When internalization of the norm is complete and when it becomes a personality element, external controls in the form of sanction and stigma are superfluous. The individual becomes norm-orientated in the sense that his personality possesses a deeply internalized norm that serves as an inner control against deviant behaviour.

The sanction-orientated person, being "other-directed", that is, striving to comply with others' expectations of him, is pressed towards conformity by the fear of being branded guilty by "the others", whereas the norm-orientated person, being inner-directed, is prevented from infringing the deeply internalized norm by feelings of guilt, the pangs of conscience that would inevitably follow infringement or even the intention to infringe.

It is obvious that we are dealing here with the two extremes of a continuum; the middle range includes an indefinite number of possibilities where the degree of norm-internalization interreacts with the variables of time, place and social pressure to produce actual sanction- or norm-orientation. This phenomenon can be illustrated by a current theory of the aetiology of delinquency on the personality level, which states that "insulation against delinquency on the part of these boys may be viewed as an ongoing process reflecting an internalization of non-delinquent values and conformity to the expectations of significant others. Whether the subjects, now largely unreceptive to delinquent norms of conduct, will continue to remain 'good' in the future remains problematic. The answer, it is felt, will depend on their ability to maintain their present self-image in the face of mounting situational pressures."[41]

Another instance is the "identification", the intermediate stage of norm-internalization; this is linked with positive reward.

Socialization among the Dakota Indians, for example, was mainly on the identification level; fathers educating their sons would say: "thus will the tribe think well of you" or "you must be pure and honourable so that people will respect you".[42]

This reward-orientated socialization implies a negative sanction of being stigmatized by disrepute and disrespect. In addition to the two variables which we have considered as linked with stigma as a means of social control, we propose finally to relate the social control power of stigma to "solidarity" and "subjectivity".

Solidarity, ultimately, is the complete attachment of the individual to the goals and values of the group and his full internalization of its norms. Hegel regarded this state as: "the moral whole, which is that form of reality in which the individual has and enjoys his freedom." The solidarist would presumably agree wholeheartedly with Durkheim's conception of the normative structure of society and the axiomatic functionality of social solidarity. For Durkheim, ethics and even metaphysics stem from social solidarity: "Everything which is a source of solidarity is moral, everything which forces man to take account of other men is moral... and morality is as solid as these ties are numerous and strong. We can see how inexact it is to define it as is often done, through liberty. It rather consists in a state of dependence."[43]

Durkheim regards non-conformity to group values as not only deviating behaviour but also bad behaviour. The Durkheimian system of analysing conformity and deviation excludes the possibility that a society, although cohesive and replete with solidarity, could be anti-social. G. Nettler states: "The possibility that a society may be 'organized' on anti-social or unethical principles has been voiced by novelists—a possibility which Durkheim would have regarded as a contradiction in terms."[44]

The *subjectivist,* at the end of the continuum, regards group solidarity as oppressing and suppressing. A modern manifestation of this view of human society, or any human group, is expounded by Sartre in his play *No Exit:* "Hell is other people". To Sartre the only human reality in existence is the subjective consciousness and conception of the self *(pour soi)*. It is the only basis of values.[45] I can never be subjectively conscious of others. I am a mere object *(en soi)* in their subjective consciousness. My presence limits and obstructs their freedom and self-consciousness and vice versa. The result is that most of the interaction and inter-relations among human beings is initiated and terminated by fear, shame, pride and vanity. The only existing entity is the individual. Others are at best nauseating, and social solidarity (if it exists at all) is based on amorphous, vague and negative (from the individual's point of view) values. It should be stressed that apart from the simple arithmetic that a group is more than one individual, the distinction between solidarity and subjectivity is pure value judgement.

The analysis of the processes leading to deviation in the tradition of Durkheim and his followers is ultimately based on the value judgment that group cohesion, solidarity and conformity to the normative system are social (as opposed to anti-social) and good. "Outsiders" are detrimental to the interests of the group and their faulty solidarity inevitably injures the group itself. As to the basic value judgment underlying Parsons' exposition of deviation, we have Coser's assertion: "A persistent theme runs through almost all of the writing of Talcott Parsons; concern with these elements in social structures that assure their maintenance.. It may be said that all of Parsons' work, beginning with *The Structure of Social Action,* is an extended commentary on the Hobbesian question: How is social order possible? ...Parsons was led to view conflict as dissociating and disfunctional. . . as primarily a 'disease'."[46]

Implicit here is the assertion that conflict, deviation, rejection of solidarity, and non-attachment to the group are disfunctional and bad.

18

The "solidarity" exposition of deviation has as its source the axiomatic value judgment of deploring the secession of the lesser entity (the individual) from the larger entity (the group); however, another value judgment disputes the supremacy of mere quantity. "The majority is always wrong" brand of existential philosophy imputes falsehood, negativity and meaninglessness to the solidarity group.

Kierkegaard regards society (the public) as "an all-embracing something which is nothing... consisting of unreal individuals who never can be united in an actual situation".[47] For Kierkegaard, the individual is the only reality capable of knowledge, creativity and commitment. Society can have only a levelling, defacing effect on individuals and thus whatever comes from society is dehumanizing and bad. Heidegger regards society, the generalized other (*Das Man*), as the embodiment of impersonality, indirectness and tyranny.[48] Jaspers sees in society (especially modern mass society) an entity devoid of existence and therefore not authentic. Society is a "phantom...supposed to exist in a vast number of persons who have no effective inter-relations."[49]

The existentialists never bothered to construct a reasonable model of their premises and the sociologists ignored them almost completely*, thus most sociological literature on social deviation and anomie is "adjustment-centred", that is, it investigates the "deplorable" phenomenon of individuals who reject the benevolent and balancing embrace of the group and community. The positive goal is conformity to the normative system of society and the negative phenomenon is the deviation.

The individual is presumed to be maladjusted and wrong if his interests clash with the interests of the group. The "adjustment-centred" sociological exponents are thus reluctant to locate the causal processes of deviation and alienation in the social and normative structures/themselves.

On the other hand the existentialists' disdainful disregard

---

* One exception is Edward A. Tiryakians' exploratory effort, *Sociologism and Existentialism*. Prentice Hall. 1962

19

of social processes places the individual subjectivist on the "right side" of the continuum—and sets the group as the non-real, the arch-villain.

Our contention is that individual social stigma is the pressure moving an individual between solidarity and subjectivity, tagging him as conforming (good) or deviant (bad). This exposition of the concepts is, of course, confined to the two extremes of the continuum; the middle range as well as other pressures that lead to solidarity or subjectivity will be discussed in detail below.

Self and Social Image

The concept of "social image" has already been defined and analysed in the Introduction. "Self-image" in the present context relates to the individual's self-conception as a member of groups and the evaluation of his actual position and roles in these groups, as demonstrated mainly by Hyman's studies.[50] An individual's self-image is linked to his aspirations and expectations as to the positions and roles he wishes or deems himself entitled to play in these groups.

It should be pointed out that, for our purposes, the relevant relationship is the social image as perceived, not by the alters in the membership and reference groups but as conveyed to and perceived by ego himself.

E. *Stigma as a means of social control is more effective with solidarist individuals; the gap between their self-image and social image is narrower. It is less effective with subjectivist individuals with a wide gap between their self and social images.* A model of the effectiveness of stigma, utilizing Louis Guttman's Facet Analysis, can be represented thus:

The effectivness of stigma as social control would be related to:

$$\begin{Bmatrix} \textit{sanction-orientation} \\ \textit{moral orientation} \end{Bmatrix} \begin{Bmatrix} \textit{other directedness} \\ \textit{inner directedness} \end{Bmatrix} \begin{Bmatrix} \textit{solidarist} \\ \textit{subjectivist} \end{Bmatrix}$$

$$\begin{Bmatrix} \textit{Social image} \\ \textit{gap} \\ \textit{self image} \end{Bmatrix} \begin{Bmatrix} \textit{high} \\ \\ \textit{low} \end{Bmatrix}$$

20

The high-effectiveness profile is:
  sanction-orientation, other directedness, solidarist with a wide gap between self and social image;
whereas the low-effectiveness profile is:
  moral-orientation, inner-directedness, subjectivist with a narrow gap between self and social image.

To illustrate the application of these profiles, we shall start with that of high effectiveness, deliberately taking extreme cases for didactic purposes. Whyte, in his classic study of an Italian slum,[51] tells us of Alec: "The Nortons" were a clique whose favourite sport was bowling. Alec was a low-status member of the Nortons. He was also an excellent bowler, but his skill was apparent in individual matches only. When he bowled with the whole group, his performance was poor. Because of his low status within the group, he was expected to do poorly and he complied with this expectation and did poorly. This occurred every time he played with the group; he always had an "off" night. Alec was a solidarist: for him the group was supreme. He willingly sacrificed his aptitude for what seemed to him, cognitively or subconsciously, the supreme welfare of the group, that is, its hierarchy and rank structure. A far grimmer example, although not less adequate, would be Koestler's Rubashov, who was willing to degrade himself as a final service to the Party. In the first case, the group was less abstract and so was the cause, but the similarity is that both regarded themselves as nonentities when confronted with the "welfare" of the group.

Alec was definitely other-directed: he behaved in accordance with what his peers expected of him. He was an empty shell, a receptacle for the expectations of others. There was presumably very little difference between Alec's self-image and his social image as conveyed to him by his reference group. He imputed legitimacy to the norms set out by the clique; otherwise he would have revolted.

Alec was trapped by his label. He had to comply with the stigma. He had neither the option nor the ability to behave otherwise; the stigma of a bad bowler was part of the image of Alec manufactured by the Nortons. Furthermore, the Nortons' image of Alec *was* Alec, and if this image postulates that Alec is a bad bowler, although he isn't one, a bad bowler he should be.

An illustration of the low-effectiveness profile of stigma can be Allan Sillitoe's portrayal of a Borstal boy in *The Loneliness of the Long Distance Runner*. The boy could easily have won the race against the public school boy, but a few yards before the finish line, he is brought to defiance by an awareness of the absurdity of the set-up; the ambitious Borstal governor who wants him to win the race for his own egoistical ends, his father who died having slaved all his life for miserable pennies, the smooth and sleek politicians radiating hypocrisy from the television sets, the misery of his life in a slum and the meaninglessness of all his affiliations with society. With a mock-chivalrous wave of his hand, he lets the clean-looking public school boy overtake him and win the race. The lad seems to be the direct opposite of a solidarist, not only in his own contemporary group, i.e., the Borstal lads and authorities, but in society at large. He is not sanction-orientated, because he exposed himself to penalties and rebukes. He knew he was sure to suffer instead of obtaining the laurels he was sure to get had he won the race.

We may presume that he is norm-orientated, although we may only guess as to the system of norms to which he is orientated. He is not "other-directed", or he would have succumbed to the pressures of the group to conform to their expectations of him — in this case, to win the race. His social image is the "Long Distance Runner", the lower-class boy who went wrong but who will bring glory to the institution (and to the governor). For the Borstal lads, he is "our boy", to beat "them sissies" of the public school. His self-image is evidently quite different. He does not impute legitimacy to the social system to which he belongs: his self-image is conflict-ridden—his aspirations and expectations are worlds apart from his immediate social positions and roles. The social stigma which he knew would certainly follow his non-conforming behaviour was of no avail. The stigma, or the fear of stigmatization, was ineffective, for it did not prevent the behaviour it was deemed

22

to control. Alec and the Borstal lad represent near extremes in the continuum relating to the effectiveness of stigma as a means of social control. The ideal type extremes and stereotypes on various points along the continuum will be discussed in subsequent chapters.

CHAPTER II

PSYCHOPATHY AS SOCIAL STIGMA: A MYTH REVISITED

> *A lunatic is a man who preferred to become what is socially understood as mad rather than forfeit a certain superior idea of human honour. A vicious society has invented psychiatry to defend itself from the investigations of certain superior lucid minds whose intuitive powers were disturbing to it.**

STRUCTURAL PERSONALITY DEFECTS AND MALADJUSTMENT TO NORMS

In ancient times, certain forms of insanity were considered to be a divine affliction; epilepsy was for many centuries "the sacred disease". Frequently, however, the insane were included in the vast category of criminals, vagabonds, pariahs, and outlaws, whose deviation from society's normative systems was seen as conclusive proof of their communion with the devil.[1] This was inevitable because, as we have already mentioned, the mediaeval idea of heresy engulfed all those who were conspicuously different, and the insane are manifestly different in their behaviour and their conception of reality. Zilboorg says: "Every mental patient either aggressively rejects life as we like it—and he was therefore thought of as a heretic, witch or sorcerer, or passively succumbs to his inability to accept life as we see it—and he was therefore called bewitched."[2]

Eventually, the Inquisition lost its power and the public lost its interest in heresy and witchcraft. The insane were consequently either neglected or locked up together with criminals, drunks and vagabonds. Only at the end of the last century was some progress made towards the understanding of the phenomenology

* Antonin Artaud in an Essay on Van Gogh, *Les Temps Modernes*

24

of mental diseases, in the pioneering efforts of Charcot, Kraeplin, Breuer and Freud.

It is no longer a matter for controversy that mental diseases can be classified as organic or functional. In the former, the mental derangement is linked with an organic disorder, whereas in the latter there is no discernible material basis. The organically based mental diseases are excluded from our analysis because the diagnostic criteria are physical defects or injuries to the brain, and not social maladjustment. Mental retardation is also excluded on similar grounds.

However, there is considerable dissent among psychiatrists as to the definition and symptoms of functional mental aberrations; even the difference between sanity and insanity is a topic of endless debate. The interpretation of symptoms is often determined by cultural definitions and the subjective position of the diagnostician.[3]

The cultural approach to the aetiology of functional personality defects involves a wide range of relativity and tows it very closely to a tangential course with deviation from the modal norms in a given society. No one claims that the latter are readily measurable; however, the diagnoses of "mental illness" or, for that matter, "mental health" are then very much dependent on our ability to measure conformity and deviation. Exponents of the sociocultural approach to the genesis of mental illness have taken varied stances. The middle-of-the-road approach is characterized by K. Menninger[4] whose *The Vital Balance* is mainly an attempt to unify and redefine the symptoms and syndromes of mental disease in social terms of adaption and maladaption; whereas an extreme exposition is that of Szasz who regards functional personality defects primarily as deviations from the accepted model behaviour in a given society so that the psychogenic approach to "mental illness" is a convenient myth which has outlived whatever usefulness it might have had.[5] The implications for the general theory of psychopathology of this approach might, of course, be far-fetched and it would be presumptuous on our part to elaborate on them in the present context. However, some implications could be pointed out: If we exclude any somatic and psychogenic priority to the genesis of mental illness, e.g., psychosis and some types of neurosis, we could trace the transmission of these personality defects to social learning processes. This would bring the whole sphere of psychopathology into the sociopsychological area of the relationship of an individual to the normative system of the group or groups with which he interacts. This would be very much like the development in criminological theory in the last decades after the pioneering efforts of Shaw, McKay and Sutherland. Prior to this, the somatic and psychogenic theories reigned supreme in criminological theory. Lombroso, Lange, Hooton, and Kretschmer have postulated the aetiological primacy of bio-physiological factors to the genesis of crime. Burt, Healey and Bronner, the psychoanalysts, the Gluecks, Abrahamsen and many others have postulated the causal link between psychogenic personality defects and crime. Sutherland and his followers rejected these two approaches and brought forward their contention that crime is "normal" (i.e., to exclude any abnormalities of personality behaviour) and learned (to exclude any inherited crimogenic traits) behaviour. In other words, crime is by definition a social interactive phenomenon culturally transmitted by learning processes. The comparison of psychopathology and criminology might be untenable to some; however, both of these disciplines deal with statistically extreme human behaviour; and the sociocultural approach to the genesis of mental illness might eventually be a theoretical breakthrough not unlike Sutherland's innovating work in criminology. It might be worthwhile to note that even in such seemingly psychogenic phenomena as opiate addiction there is no organic predisposition. Without learned conditioning no addiction takes place.[6] As in criminological theory no psychological correlate has been found at the basis of the functional psychosis. However, now and again a novel attempt to link functional personality defects with some bio-physiological factors is being essayed, only to be either refuted by subsequent research or its methodological design discredited. The least we can say is that if there is any aetiological link between biophysical factors and the functional psychosis and neurosis, it has not as yet been proved to exist. We may be amply justified, therefore, in pursuing the sociocultural approach to the genesis of mental illnesses. Moreover, we may regard the stigma theory as a possible additional causal link to the explanation of mental illnesses in the sociocultural tradition. This is warranted by certain research findings. Fisher and Mendel[7] pointed out the transmission of functional personality defects through various generations of some families. These defects, which took the form of specific functional aberrations, were being transmitted as a part of the parents' socialization. Giffin and his associates[8] found a transmission of functional personality defects from parent to child as part of a transmission-through-socialization process of super-ego defects. The crucial point is that the child internalizes the neurotic behaviour of his parents more readily because he is seemingly exposed to the greater affective significance of these specific neuroses to his parents. Ackerman's role complementarity presupposes a reciprocity between parent and child insofar as the role expectancies of one tend to be observed and complied with by the other. In other words, psychotic or neurotic patterns of behaviour by the parent tend to create similar responses by the child. This is a partial result of the latter's interpretation of the personality defect of the parent as an expectancy for him to behave in a similar manner. These fragmentary, and to be sure, not exhaustive, empirical referents indicate the vast possibilities inherent in the sociocultural approach to the aetiology of functional personality defects. The concepts in a culturally based diagnosis of mental disease are very similar and even merge with the definitions of nonconformity to norms. Social stigma would then be a very frequent choice as far as sanctions are concerned. This theory, of course, is quite far-fetched and hypothetical. It is more proper to assume that on the practical therapeutic level there are discernible symptoms which could be described as new phenomena or processes taking place *de novo* in a certain individual's personality or behaviour. In relation to the neuroses and psychoses, this seems more feasible in light of the many recent attempts to unify and redefine the symptoms and syndromes of mental diseases.[9]

The main difficulty lies with the socially maladjusted or the so-called psychopaths. For a long time, this category has served for psychiatrists as a residuary criterion of diagnosis, a kind of psychiatric wastebasket to receive all the amorphic cases which did not seem to display any discernible symptoms of neurosis, psychosis or other recognizable mental disease.[10] The term psychopathy was coined by Pritchard to describe the "morally insane", i.e., those who are incapable of "conducting themselves with decency and propriety in the business of life".[11]

Indeed, no better stigmatizing tool could have been devised to brand with amorphic and vague excellence all the "indecent", "improper" and "undesirable characters" as psychopaths.

We could, therefore, identify from the outset the term psychopath as conceived by Pritchard as the ideal stigmatizing sanction for social deviants. However, our task becomes complicated by further developments in interpretation and analysis of psychopathy. Cason, for instance, made a thorough survey of the literature on psychopathy and gleaned 202 different terms by which the psychopath has been described, fifty-five different "traits" or "characteristics" of psychopaths and thirty "forms of psychopathic behaviour."[12]

A popular survey of psychiatry by a leading psychiatrist tries to define the psychopath by describing him, inter alia, in the following way: impulsive, fickle, unwilling to accept the results of experience and unable to profit by them, prodigal of effort but utterly lacking in persistence, plausible but insincere, demanding but indifferent to appeals, dependable only in his unreliability, faithful only to infidelity, rootless, unstable, rebellious and unhappy.[13] This array of "exact" diagnostic terms raises feelings of sympathy towards the psychiatrists who have to use them, and profound pity for the patients who may be branded for life as psychopaths because they seem to be "impulsive", "insincere", "unstable" and "unhappy". It is indeed no wonder that in 1952 the American Psychiatrists' Association removed

28

from its diagnostic armory the term "psychopathy".[14] The late Robert Lindner, a sensitive and theoretically profound psychoanalyst, expressed himself in the following manner in relation to the term psychopath: "Among those categories by which man describes his fellow-man is one that has served as a miscellany for many decades. It is only half-understood and less than half-appreciated. It is a Pandora's box, brimful with the makings for malignant social and political scourge. The name of this category is Psychopathic Personality. Its half-understood nature, evidenced by the multitude of terms by which it has been and is called—constitutional psychopathic inferiority, moral imbecility, semantic dementia, moral insanity, sociopathy, anethopathy, moral mania, egopathy, tropopathy, etc.—is further attested to by the contradictory multiplicity of its signs and symptoms. All those characteristics which, by any count, may be considered the negative of qualities suitable for current civilized communal living, have at one time or another been assigned to the individual called 'psychopath'."[15]

In other words, the terms synonymous with "psychopathy" have been perennially used to tag and brand the deviants from the prevailing normative systems in human societies; in Lindner's words: "Those searchers of the soul—psychiatrists and psychologists—have wasted much fine paper in vain attempts to attach a single group of signs to the disorder, unfortunately neglecting to extend their scientific objectivity to the proposition that *psychopathic behaviour is relative to the culture in which it flourishes and can be measured by no other rule than that of the prevailing ethic and morality.* So in a society where total abstinence is mandatory—as among the Brahmins of India— a sign of psychopathy would be inebriation; and among the prostitute priestesses of Astarte, the persistent continence of a beauteous devotee consecrated to the distribution of erotic favours would indicate a psychopathic trend. In short, psychopathy is a disorder of behaviour which affects the relationship of an individual to the social setting."[16]

However, some syndromes have crystallized lately for clinical use in the diagnosis of psychopathy or sociopathy. The following is a summarized formulation of these syndromes:

1. A lacking or a faulty conscience, causing amorality or moral ambivalence[17]. This lack of or faulty super-ego is quite similar to Pritchards' "moral insanity" or "moral imbecility".
2. The psychopath has no clear or consistent life plan[18].
3. The psychopath has no capacity for love or deep attachment to his fellow human beings; he has no friends, only acquaintances whom he wishes to exploit for his own egotistical ends.
4. The psychopath is "present-orientated" insofar as he is interested in fulfilling his present drives, wishes and sensuous pleasures immediately; he is unable to postpone his "cult of immediacy" in order to strive toward long-range accepted cultural goals.
5. The last trait of the psychopath, which is more of a result, an outcome of the previous syndromes, is his constant frustration because his personality traits, especially his "present orientation", lead him to clash with the normative structure of society and this, in turn, by a positive feed-back cycle, leads him to rebellion and aggression.[19]

It is stressed that the validity of these syndromes in the diagnosis of psychopathy is a matter of degree. Only when they reach a certain intensity will the person displaying them be diagnosed as a psychopath.

In the present context, however, we have to decide whether these syndromes do indeed define a specific clinical entity or if they are present in a varying degree within the whole population. To be more specific: if the distribution of psychopathic traits among the presumable psychopaths does not necessarily differ from the distribution of these traits among the whole population, we might be justified in hypothesizing that the term "psychopath" (and other related descriptions) are not so much a diagnostic tool of psychiatry as a stigmatizing sanction for social deviation.

There are as yet no clear-cut empirical findings to help us

decide one way or the other. We shall therefore have to confine our analysis to the hypothetical and theoretical levels. We have specified that the diagnostic significance of the syndromes of psychopathy is a question of their degree and intensity. The problem boils down, therefore, to the determination of the boundaries beyond which the syndromes will cease to be "normal" and signify an abnormality or pathology.

The problem of normality and abnormality in human behaviour is too complicated to be within the scope of the present work. It also lies mostly in the no-man's land between the behavioural sciences and philosophy. However, two aspects of normality should be considered in the present context, and these are whether the psychopathy syndromes are abnormal statistically and whether they are necessarily non-normative as far as the normative structure of society is concerned.

The statistical aspect of normality refers to quantity, meaning that in order to decide whether certain behaviour is normal, we must see the quantity of people behaving in a certain way, which distributes them in a normal curve (or any other parametric or non-parametric distribution), whether the particular behaviour in question deviates or not, and by how many standard deviations, from the modal values as measured by the mean, median or mode.

The socio-normative aspects of normality require that we determine first of all whether a social norm indeed exists and then whether the examined trait conforms to or deviates from this norm. The statistical and socio-normative aspects of normality are, of course, linked together; normality is therefore a function not only of the quality of conformity, but also of its quantity.

We propose, therefore, to examine the psychopathy syndromes and to formulate hypotheses as to whether they do indeed deviate from the statistical and social norm, in an attempt to justify their diagnostic value.

1. *The faulty conscience and amorality syndrome* could be evaluated in relation to the existing normative (moral) structure

31

of modern society. Not many would sincerely refute the fact that modern society is plagued by a chaotic (and sometimes almost non-existent) normative system. It represents a value vacuum where honesty in business, altruism, selfless devotion to a cause and even common decency are very often regarded as archaic relics to which people may pay lip service but very rarely adhere.

The prevailing norms in business and everyday life are, inter-alia, "every man for himself", "never do a favour because you'll get into trouble", "push to the top, never mind the others", "crime is not doing something illegal but getting caught". It is a matter of conjecture what would happen if abridged versions of Sutherland's *White Collar Crime*, Clinard's *Black Market* and the late Senator Kefauver's report on the link between politics and organized crime were to be incorporated in the primers of the first grades of school. The late President Kennedy's revelation that his father told him that "all businessmen are S.O.B's" might provide a clue for his fierce realism in solving labour disputes; but not everyone can be as fortunate in his early socialization. One possible result of this "experiment in realistic education" would be a reluctance to brand people as psychopaths because they are immoral, egotistical and dishonest. The fallacy of imputing a pathological trait to some people because they seem to be amoral and lack a super-ego, guilt feelings or a conscience, stems from an illusion. The latter results from the discrepancy between the professed and actual extent of the internalization of a normative system by the members of a given group. We could discount as hypothetical instances of socialization where the social situation is depicted as close to reality as possible, complete with "cut-throat" business competition, graft in politics, partiality in the administration of justice, and that "honesty is the worst policy" as far as upper vertical mobility is concerned.

Today it does take, however, some years, agonies and "learning the hard way" for someone who has absorbed an image of a society in which "honesty is the best policy" to be aware of the social reality, to use one of Lind's ambivalences, that "business is business and a businessman would be a fool if he did not cover his hand." [20]

The Greeks were quite near to this kind of realistic education with the many instances of punishment without crime in their mythology and tragedy. Sisyphus and Polycrates were punished for no other reason than being too successful in many trades and possessions also coveted by the Olympians. They raised the envy and jealousy of the gods (the Greek brand of human deities) and man, and were given to feel the wages of *hubris*. Prometheus was punished for performing what seemed to be a morally commendable deed, whereas Oedipus was first seduced by the gods to commit a crime (sin) so that they would be justified in punishing him.

Calhoun [21] points out that this is typical of the Greek's realistic attitude towards life, not burdened by such illusory abstract constructs as justice and morals. The Greeks presumably wished to point out that life is tough, rough and hazardous, and those who are seeking divine justice, rewards for "good" deeds and deserts for "bad" ones might as well chase a minotaur. *Dike,* judgment, is a late invention; the ancient Greeks' advice to mortals is to bear their *moira* not as a cross but as a defiant torch. As for Tantalus, Polycrates, Sisyphus and others who cannot understand the point of their plights, we have the advice of Camus who, in the tradition of the authentic Olympians, tells us:

"Sisyphus' fate belongs to him. His rock is his thing... Convinced of the wholly human origin of all that is human, a blind man eager to see who knows that the night has no end, he is still on the go. The rock is still rolling... Sisyphus teaches the higher fidelity that negates the gods and raises rocks. The Universe without a master seems to him neither sterile nor futile... The struggle itself toward the heights is enough to fill a man's heart. One must imagine Sisyphus happy." [22]

Though it is, of course, questionable whether socialization in ancient Greece was conducted along these lines, we know that it is definitely not so in modern society. The bad wolf is always caught in the end and killed. The wicked queen is punished and Snow White lives happily ever after. You should "love thy neighbour as thyself". No primers evaluate the proposition that this is impossible or even undesirable. It is better to give than to receive—is it really?

There are, therefore, two levels of quantitative analysis: the extent to which a proclaimed normative system is actually adhered to; and the amount of mere lip service paid to it.

Many factors have lowered the status of conventional religious morality in modern society. One is associated with the constant attacks by some schools of thought on "decadent bourgeois morality", "the tyranny of the weak against the strong", the "unconscious lust" and "sour grapes" attitude that, it is claimed, underlie moral and righteous indignation. Nietzsche, that great foe of Christian morality, led the attack by announcing:

"Weakness is to be falsified into desert... And impotence which requiteth not is to be falsified into 'goodness', timorous meanness into 'humility'; submission to those whom one hates into 'obedience' (namely to one who they say commands this obedience; they call him God). The inoffensiveness of the 'weak one', cowardice itself, in which he is rich, his standing at the door, his unavoidable necessity of waiting comes here by good names, such as 'patience', they even call it the Cardinal Virtue. Not-to-be-able-to-take-revenge is called not-to-will-revenge, perhaps even forgiveness ('For they know not what they do'; we alone know what THEY do). They also talk of 'love for their enemies'— and sweat in doing so."[23]

Anyone who has read the *Genealogy of Morals* (or who has been influenced by its ideas) will be reluctant to profess adherence to virtue, forgiveness and selfless idealism without feeling at least an aftertaste of hypocrisy.

The psychoanalysts carried on from this point, and declared that morality is derived from inner conflicts and from the instability of emotional pressures. Our desire to commit immoral acts is clothed and muffled in righteous indignation. The moral indignation helps us to overcome our tendencies toward immorality.

No one, say the psychoanalysts, is more bitter in condemning the "loose" woman than the "good" woman who has on occasion guiltily enjoyed forbidden fantasies herself. "Why dost thou lash that whore? Strip thine own back; thou hotly lust'st to use her in that kind for which thou whipp'st her,"[24]

Totalitarian ideologists, from the Jesuits to Fascists and Communists, eliminated the individual as the focus or the judge of right and wrong. The end justifies the means; the individual, his likes and his dislikes, his needs, his rights and his very person should be sacrificed on behalf of the future flourishing and glory of the order, the movement, the party or the masses. The individual is wrong if his interests clash with the interests of the group. There is no subjective evaluation of deeds, the only legitimate criterion being the objective good of the common cause. Pity, love, personal conscience and honour are at best tolerated, but God (or the Führer, or the Party) forbid should they interfere with the common cause. "Fair play" and mistakes committed in good faith have no place in the totalitarian normative system. Only results count; there can never be a morally wrong success or a morally right failure.

The justification of the sacrifice of the individual for the common good is a better, more just society. But the history of the twentieth century has shown the dishonesty, the implicit mendacity, and the downright inhuman cruelty of totalitarian governments.

The Judeo-Christian concept of morality now belongs to fairy tales and nurseries (where it is not taken seriously any more). As an active force in modern society, it is as real as Unicorns or Atlantis.

Religions (or, at least, the monotheistic faiths) have been a source and a basis of morality because they believe that the divine entity is just and good. The basic religious conviction is that the power of God is not arbitrary and that His nature is characterized by morality and justice[25]. We do assume, of course, that religious belief is sincere, and we do not deal with the hordes of religious hypocrites who feign piety for social or for material ends. The difficulties here for our purposes are quite obvious. Religious belief is closely connected with religious indoctrination and training from a very early age. The dogmas of Catholicism and the daily rituals of Judaism are ingrained into the personality of the child by a conditioning process that cannot possibly be repeated at an advanced age, but today this education rarely builds a religious belief that is strong enough to support an internalized moral system. God's justice is more likely to be doubted (a sin in itself) and Job's bitter accusation that the "earth is given into the hands of the wicked; He covereth the faces of the Judges thereof; If not them, who is it?" [26] is likely to be hurled in the face of the priest, minister or rabbi.

A common secular substitute of morality in modern society is the awareness that playing according to the "rules of the game" is simply prudent, that the most important thing is to keep out of trouble. This is actually a completely amoral solution, a sort of a maxim for survival in an absurd social system. This "rules of the game" approach finds a corollary of the "adjustment" craze in the western (particularly in the U.S.) image of a balanced personality. This cynical solution has a wide range of action: at one end, behaviour is modified by the fear of harsh sanctions, and at the other, even by mild social pressures.

The "rules of the game" advocate adjustment to harsh and cruel standards of competition; the other alternative entails social ostracism, economic hardship, or "rotting half your life in prison".

Some people want to play the game according to their own "illegitimate" rules which can be more risky but are sometimes worthwhile. They point out that even in the "legitimate racket" there is no security. The "rules of the game" are based on convenience and not on normative moral convictions.

This brief outline of the status of morality in modern society makes us reluctant to apply "amorality" or "faulty morality" as significant criteria in the diagnosis of psychopathy. The next question is whether society is capable of sustaining an effective moral system. The first difficulty is to identify the norm of the type of morality to which we refer. On an abstract level we have

36

the teleological utilitarian conception of morality, which is the most common system of ethics; moral behaviour is not an end in itself but a means to achieve reward.[27] This system of ethics has a built-in, self-defeating mechanism because a man who anticipates any sort of gain can be disappointed and eventually become embittered and cynical. A more durable system of ethics is the deontological one that sees righteousness as its own reward and the idea of justice as based on a categorical imperative, on a duty to do right and to punish the wrongdoer.

Another conception of morality, which we have already mentioned, is the one that regards the individual as a component of society: the premise of any system of ethics is the existence of society and the necessity for its continuation. The regulation of the interrelations of individuals as particles of a greater whole is the basic "good". Durkheim, the chief exponent of this view, says: "Law and morality are the totality which bind each of us to society, which make a unitary coherence of the mass of individuals. This conception of morality does not need a metaphysical basis because it stems from the fact of the existence of the individual and the existence of society.[28]

A modern existentialist conception of morality is voiced by Camus, in *The Plague*, where a solution to the absurdity, the meaninglessness of life and its value vacuum, is presented with brilliant simplicity: "Why do you show such devotion," asked Tarrou, "considering you don't believe in God?" "I have no idea what's awaiting me," answered Rieux. "For the moment I know this: there are sick people and they need curing. Later on perhaps they'll think things over and so shall I, but what's wanted now is to make them well. I defend them as best as I can, that's all. One thing I must tell you: there's no question of heroism in all this. It's a matter of common decency. That's an idea which may make some people smile, but the only means of fighting a plague is common decency."[29]

The question we must ask is: what prevailing system of ethics should constitute the norm, the teleological utilitarian, the religious, the deontological categorical imperative, the Durkheimian social harmony and solidarity or the Camusian common decency? From this multitude of systems that are not necessarily cumulative and are perhaps even contradictory, it is not possible to constitute a single clear-cut normative system. If we combine this observation with our earlier hypothesis that modern society is largely amoral, we can see that ethical systems are detached from human society, although lip service is paid to them. Thus, lack of morals or faulty morality is too wide a trait to constitute a clinical diagnostic tool. There is an analogy with feeble-mindedness: when Goddard found that more than thirty percent of the U.S. Army in the First World War were mentally defective, he was sensible enough to realize that the defect lay more with his diagnostic criteria than with the U.S. Army.[30]

2. Our second syndrome relates to the *psychopath's confused goals and his lack of a life plan.* Here again we should examine the diagnostic value of this syndrome in view of the fact that modern society in the second half of the twentieth century is characterized by ruthless, suicidal and insane power struggles, by ambiguity of aims, confused motives and insecurity. On the state or community level it is plagued by anomie, a state of norm-lessness where religion, tradition, "the American Way of Life", communism in the U.S.S.R., and other ideologies are not strong enough to support a solid value system.

A glimpse at the main themes of contemporary literature and art reveals the overwhelming preoccupation with despair and helplessness. The atomized urban individual is not a master of his "life plan"; he is a helpless cog in the vast machinery of modern industry, commerce, and the colossal bureaucratic structures. It would be superfluous to describe the subjugation of the twentieth century individual to the needs for specialization in modern technological society. This atomization process inherent in modern mass culture frightened Ortega y Gasset into a hysterical lament: "The characteristic of the hour is that the commonplace mind knowing itself to be commonplace, has the assurance to proclaim the rights of the commonplace and to impose them wherever it will. The mass crushes beneath it everything that is different, everything that is excellent, individual, qualified and select."[31]

A less value-laden analysis of the attributes of the deperson-alized and meaningless mass has been made by Heidegger. He coined the concept *Das Man* to denote the generalized other,[32] the impersonal man in the street. *Das Man* is a watered-down ambiguity that suits everyone's purposes. *Das Man* is always optimistic—thus typical of artificial togetherness; in public, one "always feels better and fine", *Das Man* is a levelling force vulgarizing strangeness and originality into familiarity; it abhors insight and expresses itself in banalities and small-talk, loaded with common clichés. Sartre develops Heidegger's views with a Gallic lucidity that is certainly more readable than the latter's dry Teutonic technicalities. A major theme in *Etre et Néant* that is relative to our context is an extension of Heidegger's concep-tualization of *"Das Man"*. The subjective being-for-itself *être pour soi,* which is the manifestation of consciousness and authentic existence, is objectified into non-authentic existence by the presence of the collectivity of thirds—"the They"—who are utterly distinct from humanity and in whose eyes hu-manity is wholly objectified. This unreal Third is the victim of the limiting concept of otherness. . . The "us-object" is offered to each individual consciousness as an ideal impossible to attain, although everyone keeps the illusion of being able to reach it, progressively enlarging the circle of communities to which he does belong.[33] The "They", the generalized others, produce the stereotyped "us-object" as a collective unreal and unattainable ideal. According to Sartre, the individual's recognition of the meaninglessness of these life-goals manufactured by the "us-objects" is in fact profound insight and intelligence and not a syndrome of psychopathy. Fiedler epitomizes goallessness: "There is a weariness in the West, a weariness with humanism itself which underlies all the movements of our world, a weariness with the striving to be men."[34]

From the goalless and anomic society we turn to the goalless and anomic individual. The latter is not a specifically modern

39

phenomenon. Toynbee tells us: "The way of life that we have called detachment has been given a variety of names by various schools of adepts. From a disintegrating Hellenic World the Stoics withdrew into an 'invulnerability' and the Epicurians into an 'imperturbability' as illustrated by the somewhat self-conscious epicurean declaration of the poet Horace, when he tells us that 'Fragments of a ruined world strike me unperturbed'."

From a disintegrating Indic world, the Buddhists withdrew into an unruffledness (Nirvana). It is a way that leads out of This World; its goal is asylum... The impulse that carries the traveller along is a push of aversion and not a pull of desire.[35] Goallessness and drifting as a norm were preached by the Taoists: "Great Tao is like a boat that drifts; it can go this way, it can go that."[36]

In the Middle Ages, aimlessness and withdrawal from this world were denoted by the generic name of accedia. Wordsworth expresses his longing to withdraw from "the heavy and weary weight of all this unintelligible world".[37] The modern goalless individual is the outsider as portrayed by Dostoyevsky's *Notes From the Underground,* Sartre's *Nausea* and the avalanche of drugs, sex and hair literature and drama with Burroughs as God and Ginsberg and Hoffman his prophets.

The sociological analysis of the goalless individual has been carried out by Merton[38]. He described the retreatist who rejects the culturally accepted goals and the social norms; he exists only physically in society, but culturally he is outside it. These are not only the *clochards* under the bridges of the Seine and the Bowery bums but a wide array of individuals in modern society who regard life as a meaningless burden. More numerous are the goalless individuals whom Merton named ritualists. These have rejected social goals and confine themselves to their daily tasks as petty officials or their automatic and mechanistic tasks in factories and services. Our analysis reveals, therefore, that *prima-facie* goallessness is too widespread a phenomenon in modern society to serve as a diagnostic syndrome or a *sui generis* pathology, i.e., psychopathy.

40

3. The psychopath is also characterized by *his inability to love and his incapacity for deep emotional attachment.* Marcel Pagnol says: "Life is an auction; men put up their muscles or their brains, women their bodies, it's all the same." [39] The prevalence of love in society can be examined both on the social and individual levels.

War as a social phenomenon is, of course, the epitome of hate, death and destruction, but many other social institutions are also saturated with aggression and hatred. The Phoenicians threw their sons into the white-hot furnace of their Moloch; the Egyptians, Jews, Assyrians and Babylonians slaughtered slaves, their fellow-men or offspring to appease the wrath of their deities; the Inquisition, with its torture-wheels and auto-da-fé, at one time almost personified torture, agony and hate; favourite pastimes of *Homo Sapiens* from time immemorial have been Roman gladiators, knights' tournaments, corridas, cock fights, public hangings, boxing, detective stories, the *Daily Mirror*, and the *News of the World*; modern war novels are full of hatred, blood, violence, pain, torture, destruction and death.

The actual situation, however, as described by Eric Fromm, is as follows: "If we speak about love in contemporary Western culture, we mean to ask whether the social structure of Western civilization and the spirit resulting from it are conducive to the development of love. To raise the question is to answer it in the negative. No objective observer of our Western life can doubt that love—brotherly love, motherly love and erotic love—is a relatively rare phenomenon, and that its place is taken by a number of forms of pseudo-love which are in reality so many forms of the disintegration of love." [40]

The overspecialization of modern society, the standardization of life, have made love and strong emotional attachment superfluous, hindrances to the norm of the smoothly flowing impersonality of bureaucracy and automation. One of the hypnotic-sleep indoctrinations in Huxley's *Brave New World* is: "When the individual feels the community reels".

Modern marriage, according to Fromm, is an *"égoisme à deux,*

41

a well-oiled relationship between two persons who remain strangers all their life". Sex is the all-important, modern pastime, creed, art and industry.

Sex is the modern equivalent for "to be in love". Detachment, emotional independence and apathetic aloofness are some of the major norms of the modern middle classes.[41] Indeed, Freud stressed his basic premise that man is by nature aggressive, competitive and hostile to his fellow-men. Depth and sincerity of emotions are not considered *bon-ton* in a society dedicated to pseudo-love, pseudo-friendship and shallow secondary relationships.

In the cut-throat, competitive and manipulative structure of commerce, industry and universities, strong and sincere emotional attachments are bound to hinder upward vertical mobility.

On the individual level, we have the existentialists, especially Sartre's assertion that love is an ontological impossibility. Alter is always an object (*en soi*) for ego and can never be a subjective entity *(pour-soi)* for ego; the result is that not only is emotional attachment bound to be faulty[42] but also that love can be interpreted as a subjugation of ego to alter which inevitably results in conflict; the Hobbesian *homo homini lupus* and his own "hell is other people" hold good according to Sartre not only for human interaction in general but also for the illusion of love.

A recent sociological treatment of love as "the polar case of intrinsic attraction" is largely in the Sarterian style. Blau regards love as a power struggle where each opponent offers his affection for a bargain. He offers it as a bait and withholds it to gain ascendency. "Even a mother's devotion to her children is rarely entirely devoid of the desire to maintain their attachment to her."[43]

The syndrome of lack of or faulty emotional attachment is obviously too widespread in modern society to serve as a criterion for diagnosis of the *sui-generis* type of person, in our case the psychopath.

4. *The present-orientation syndrome* of psychopathy should be examined vis-a-vis our affluent society. Conspicuous consumption has been described and documented in many works.

We can add a little to the detailed scrutinization of modern affluent society by a long list of writers from Veblen to Galbraith. The emergent picture is a society the main values of which are linked to monetary gain, entertainment and sensuous pleasures. Nothing is more important than money and "the good life". The smart man is one who gets more pleasures and services for less money and effort.

There is a constant pressure on the individual to spend more and consume more goods and services. Many status symbols are linked with conspicuous consumption. People do not regard the future as an altogether different dimension from the present: their orientation is on the present and its lucrative gains and hedonistic pleasures; this is called by Reisman "the cult of immediacy",[44] i.e., constant sensual indulgence and other material pleasures, living the life of the moment, and *après moi le déluge*.

Here again, we may avail ourselves of Fromm's aptly phrased statement: "Man's happiness today consists in 'having fun'. 'Having fun' lies in the satisfaction of consuming and 'taking in' commodities, sights, food, drinks, cigarettes, people, lectures, books, movies; all are consumed, swallowed. The world is one great object for our appetite, a big apple, a big bottle, a big breast; we are the sucklers."[45]

The "cult of immediacy" deepens and widens with increasing urbanization and standardization of production, consumption and the mass media. The cult of mediocrity is linked to the needs of mass production and standardized tastes in goods and services. The mode, the mean and the median are the idols of modern society and its dreads and anxieties are measured by the number of standard deviations from the modal values. This levelling process creates an image of the social situation the edges of which have been blurred and focal points unduly accentuated. The mass is intolerant of ambiguity. It wants a clear-cut image. It is insensitive to finesse; in order to be effective, a stimulus should hit it bluntly on the head. Sophisticated computers are fed by their high priests the relevant data of the prevailing tastes for the colour of egg yolks, colour of cars and the circumference

43

of the bust of the latest bedroom goddess. Occasionally, the prophecies of the electronic brains do not coincide with the interests of the high priests and their sponsors; enter the image makers. Pohl and Kornbluth, a team of science-fiction writers, described a society run by Madison Avenue. Society today is buffetted by image makers towards conspicuous consumption. Presidential candidates and *Encyclopaedia Britannica,* whatever their merits, owe their popularity to the same techniques that sell Kelloggs Corn Flakes and Carnation Milk.

In this "present-orientated" society of ours, the psychopath cannot indeed be unique.

5. If we wish to identify *aggression as one of the symptoms of psychopathy,* it would be pertinent to quote from one of Freud's later and more mature works: "The truth behind all this—one so eagerly denied—is that men are not gentle . . . a powerful measure of desire for aggression has to be reckoned as part of their instinctual endowment. This aggressive cruelty usually lies in wait for some provocation, or else it steps into the service of some other purpose; it also manifests itself spontaneously and reveals men as savage beasts to whom the thought of sparing their own kind is alien . . . . Culture has to call up every possible reinforcement in order to erect barriers against the aggressive instincts of men and hold their manifestations in check by reaction-formation in men's minds; with all its striving, this endeavour of cultures has so far not achieved much. The time comes when everyone of us has to abandon the illusory anticipations with which in our youth we regarded our fellow-men, and we realize how much hardship and suffering we have been caused in life through their ill-will."[46]

The innate aggressivity of human beings has found many institutionalized outlets: domestic quarrels, tribal skirmishes, national battles and world wars. The aggressivity of individuals has been diverted from in-group members to out-groups, and the definition of friendship or alliances is frequently individuals or groups who have common enemies. Human aggression has also been channelled into various kinds of entertainment and

44

sports from the German duelling fraternities to the Japanese judo. In many societies, aggressivity is considered manly behaviour, and if a person does not want his virility to be questioned, he should respond by physical violence to the slightest provocation. In Western society open physical violence is mostly shunned, but there aggressivity has been channelled into the normative system; only its form has been changed, not its nature. The attitude towards aggression is laden with value judgment. We evaluate differently an aggressive businessman and an aggressive robber, but aggression per se cannot be regarded as a diagnostic symptom.

We are now in a position to conclude our somewhat lengthy analysis of the syndromes of psychopathy and to relate it to the stigma theory.

The analysis of syndromes reveals, at least hypothetically, that their statistical prevalence is far too wide to justify their diagnostic use for clinical purposes. The behaviour represented by these syndromes does not necessarily infringe real norms, as distinguished from the ideal ones to which lip service is paid. It can be claimed that these syndromes are an asset to individuals in their aspirations to climb the social and economic status pyramids of society. Indeed in the modern bureaucratic and power structures, lack of these syndromes is a hindrance to the upward vertical mobility of the aspirant "organization man" or future member of the "power-elite".

Thus, the so-called psychopath does not necessarily differ from the rest of the population in his personality structure. If the same character traits are attributed in a derogatory sense to the psychopath and in a neutral or commendable sense to a bureaucrat, an executive, a lawyer or a politician, the key to this differential treatment must lie in the social context of the syndromes and in the differential response or reaction of society towards a given behaviour. The derogatory branding of individuals with the tag of psychopathy could prove, therefore, to be a sanction for poorly or non-managed conformity; the latter will not necessarily be linked to the professed syndromes of

45

psychopathy but to any deviation or conspicuity in the regular relationship of an individual to his group.

Psychopathy is therefore more appropriately regarded as a stigmatizing sanction for non-conformity than a personality defect or a pathological syndrome.

CHAPTER III

DEVIANT BEHAVIOUR AND VALUE DEVIATION AS A PREDISPOSITION TO SOCIAL STIGMA

*When a prominent citizen gets jammed up with the rules, there are always a lot of folks, ready to turn on the brine for him. But when some bezerk that no one ever heard of gets found out, they rush him off to the sneezer or jail, with never a sob gulped out on his behalf.**

THE AETIOLOGY OF STIGMA

An aetiological theory of social stigmata must operate on two different theoretical levels. The first level will identify factors that are linked with social stigma and will assess the strength or significance of this link. These factors can be called the *configuration of predisposition*. They raise the probability that a certain individual or group of individuals will be branded with social stigma. The second level of analysis will deal with the dynamic process by which society or its relevant organs perform the actual stigmatization. This level will not employ probability concepts, but will analyse causal relationships. Two groups of predisposing factors will be studied: The first includes those related to deviant behaviour, and the second, to value deviation.

Deviant Behaviour as a Predisposition to Social Stigma

When the actor himself is the actual object of his deviant behaviour, the deviation is inwardly directed. However, if the behaviour is directed, and generally it is, toward the group and its social institutions, it is outwardly directed. We shall plot this dimension against the apparent motivation of the deviant behaviour as it is manifested in the deviant acts themselves.

* Damon Runyon

		Apparent motivation				
Inwardly directed ←						→ Outwardly directed
autistic	self-destruc-tive	escapist	bohemian	accidental	acquisitive occasional, semi-professional, professional	rebel chaotic ideational

This scheme does not imply any static typology of deviations. Types may be mixed, and a person can pass from one type to another in rapid succession or at long intervals. The following is not an exhaustive typology, but it does illustrate some basic types of deviant behaviour that can be related to social stigma.

A. Autism: Autistic behaviour can be described as a predisposing factor raising the probability, in a specific cultural context, of a man being stigmatized as a social deviant. The aetiology of stigmatization depends on the cultural definition of autistic behaviour and a specific cultural reaction to it in a given place and time. An extreme manifestation of inwardly directed deviation can be seen in the *autistically alienated person.* Some of the advanced stages of schizophrenia are characterized by a complete breakdown of the individual's ties with reality; he can crouch in a corner and vegetate or be gripped by hallucinations. Although the hallucinations are possibly associated with the individual's motor activity, their link with reality is slight or non-existent.

The most apparent characteristic of schizophrenia is a person's withdrawal from reality "in which thinking, feeling and action are no longer dominated by contact with other people or outside events, but are given over entirely to a world of fantasy whose only counterpart in the experience of normal people is the world of dreams."[1]

According to White, the common form of schizophrenia is characterized by lack of ambition for personal advancement,

48

apathy, withdrawal and idleness, whereas the severe catatonic state is marked by a prolonged stupor, immobility, complete disregard for surroundings and the patient is apparently totally absorbed in a "silent inner dream."[2]

However, we are dealing here with the overt manifestation of autistic behaviour; it will be fruitful to examine identical or similar autistic modes of behaviour in different cultural settings. We shall disregard, for the purposes of our present analysis, the different aetiological processes which doubtless vary from one culture to another. We are concerned here with the attitudes, the responses, the reactions of the ego's reference groups or membership groups to his exceptional mode of behaviour. The fact that a person behaves in an extraordinary manner will presumably evoke an extreme reaction from the group. Our concern, however, is whether the group's reaction to ego's autistic behaviour is one of acclaim or sanction.

An essential aspect of the Hindu Yoga is complete detachment from the realities of life, achieved by certain hypnotic techniques. Indians used the "Japas" or the technique of ascetism, "in order to become yoked with the absolute."[3] Outwardly and behaviourally, the state achieved by the Yoga technique resembles catatonic schizophrenia. A contemporary Yogi saint describes the mystic's trance as follows: "The state of hallucination is a temporary one. A person should learn to control his mind. What comes after such mental discipline is mystic experience, what appears in the uncontrolled state of mind are hallucinations . . . The mystic's mind is blank, his experience is chainless and without object."[4]

In Western society, the Yogi would have a fair chance of being institutionalized as a catatonic.

The Bhagavad-Gita sings the praise of Yoga as follows:

> In a fair still spot,
> Having fixed his abode—not too much raised,
> Nor yet too low—let him abide his goods.
> A cloth, a deerskin and a Kusha-grass.

There, setting hard his mind upon the One,
Restraining heart and senses, silent, calm,
Let him accomplish Yoga, and achieve
Bareness of soul, holding immovable
Body and neck and head, his gaze absorbed
Upon his nose-end, rapt from all around
Tranquil in spirit, free of fear, intent,
Upon his Brahmacharya vow, devout,
Musing on Me, lost in the thought of Me.[5]

Taken out of its cultural context, this could be seen as an ode to the combined autistic manifestations of schizophrenia.

According to Jainism, there are fourteen steps by which the soul emancipates itself from Karma. The most important of these is the complete detachment from the enjoyment of the senses. Emancipation from Karma requires limited eating, abuse of the body (such as pulling out the hair by the roots), and also the practice of developing indifference to the body, even to the point of standing motionless in some sacred place until death comes.[6]

The word Nirvana is derived from the Sanskrit and means "annihilation". Nirvana, as taught by Gotama Buddha to his disciples, is complete autistic abnegation of the self: "Now this, O Monks, is the noble truth of the cessation of pain; the cessation, without a reminder, of that craving, abandonment, forsaking, release, non-attachment."[7] The manifestations of Nirvana experienced by the Master himself were the elimination of desire, the annihilation of individual consciousness, the passing away so that no passion remained, the giving up, the getting rid of craving and desire. This state of eternal bliss could have earned Gotama Buddha the additional title of schizophrenic if diagnosed by a modern Western psychiatrist. A similar fate would befall many other hermits, ascetics and mystics.

Autistic behaviour as such is indeed a predisposing factor to stigmatization in some cultures, but the ultimate causal process is the cultural definition of the behaviour. In one culture autistic behaviour is branded with the social stigma of schizophrenia by means of psychiatric diagnosis and incarceration in a mental hospital, while in another culture or period it is cherished as sainthood. Autistic behaviour does raise the probability that an individual will be branded with stigma, but in isolation it is not enough because the same or similar behaviour can be tagged differently in different cultural contexts. We shall deal later with the dynamic process which actually brings about stigmatization on those who are exposed to the predisposition configuration.

We can assume that for the autistic individual the efficacy of stigma as a means of social control is very low. He displays all the low-efficacy factors listed in the previous chapter. He is inner-directed. Sanctions—stigma inclusive—are cognitively remote. The fear of stigma is either "shut-out" from his inner world together with the rest of the "outer-world" as we see it, or is distorted beyond recognition and thus stripped of deterrent significance. For similar reasons the legally and the criminally insane are not amenable to sanction deterrence.

B. Self-destruction: Suicide is an extreme act and it raises the probability of extreme social reaction. Social stigma is then a function of the identification of the relevant others with ego's suicide. Stigma would presumably be branded on egotistic and anomic suicides and in cases where self-destruction is considered normative, on individuals who refrain from committing it. The aetiology of suicide has been extensively studied and documented. We are concerned, however, with the social aspects. The suicide in our model is less removed from reality than the autistic. He has contact with a world that to him is so absurd, meaningless or tormenting and unbearable and has enough initiative to desire to sever himself from it altogether.

Suicide, like autism, is an extreme behaviour, and the group's reaction is generally extreme; it is rarely apathetic or indifferent. Albert Camus in his *Rebel* and earlier essay on "The Myth of Sysiphus" postulates that the main ethical issue is whether a mans' taking his own life is justified or not in given circumstances. Humans by the thousands all over the world are throwing themselves from high buildings, jumping from bridges, cutting their veins or their throats, taking poisons, taking sleeping pills, shooting or burning themselves; soldiers sacrifice themselves for their country, Indian widows throw themselves on the funeral pyres of their husbands; the Japanese have their Kamikaze, and the South Vietnamese Buddhists occasionally immolate themselves. The relevant question in the present context is whether the group's attitude towards the suicide or attempted suicide is derogatory and socially stigmatizing, or is laudatory and attaches the laurels of a hero to the suicide's grave.

Durkheim noted that the real difference between what he called anomic and egoistic suicide on the one hand and altruistic suicide on the other is society's differential attitude towards these acts by which it stigmatizes the former and approves of the latter.[8] The anomic suicide could be stigmatized as a weakling who is broken by a sudden economic change and driven to take his life in the way so many did in the great economic depression of the early 'thirties. Egoistic suicide is the ultimate in retreatism of those who have completely renounced social goals and norms.

As far as the stigma theory is concerned, no distinction is necessary between the anomic and egoistic suicides. Both would be stigmatized for religious reasons; thus, Judas Iscariot's suicide was regarded as a graver sin than his betrayal of Christ.[9] According to Jewish religious law, a suicide is buried outside the boundaries of the cemetery. In totalitarian countries, he is likely to be condemned for depriving the state and party of his services. On moral grounds, the suicide may be labelled a coward and an irresponsible person who abandons his dependents without protection and security. The stigma will be less severe or will disappear altogether in cases where identification with the suicide's act would be more feasible, e.g., if he committed it because he suffered from an incurable disease; the attitude in these cases might be; "There but for the grace of God go I".

52

Normative suicides include those of old people in some cultures, *hara-kari,* suicide of the offended and humiliated, the ritual suicide of wives, servants and slaves of the deceased master.

Suicide as a punishment is also normative in the sense that the impeachers of Socrates and the colleagues of a Prussian officer accused of treason would regard the suicide as expiating to a certain extent the stigma of the alleged crime.

Hitler's unsuccessful attempt to induce his friend Ernst Rohm to shoot himself in his prison cell is an illuminating example of this, as is Rommel's suicide.

Finally, we have the other extreme of heroic and legendary suicides, the subjects of national epics, e.g. the Kamikazes, virgins who killed themselves in order not to be violated by the foe, and the defenders of Massada, who preferred mass suicide to being captured alive by the Romans. In this case, Josephus Flavius has been stigmatized in Jewish history because he preferred to live rather than die with his comrades.

As a means of social control, stigma has little effect on those who are affected with the urge for self-destruction. Moreover, some people do have a pathological urge for self-punishment and self-degradation. Masochists actually seek punishment, including stigma. Stigma obviously cannot deter exhibitionists who seek attention by being the centre of a criminal trial. This would also be the case with persons who would intentionally get involved in an unpleasant or humiliating situation in order to satisfy their inner craving for punishment and degradation. Cases of criminals returning to the scene of their crime, or "forgetting" some obvious clue to their identification, are counted not only by fiction writers, but are documented by many criminal investigators. These phenomena have induced some psychoanalysts like Theodor Reik to conclude that the whole range of crime and deviation is caused by the criminal's and deviant's craving for punishment and sanction due to inner guilt.[10] We may confine ourselves to those who have a self-destructive urge without trying to assess their numbers, and say that for them stigma is not an object of dread but of greed.

C. The escapist: Conflict situations within the family in the formative years, intolerance of ambiguity and achievement-orientation due to early insecurity are factors predisposing an individual to retreatism. The same or similar predisposing factors can initiate a process of retreatism that will eventually result in institutionalized escapist behaviour that is not stigmatized. Drug addicts and alcoholics, the *clochards* under the bridges of the Seine, the hoboes in New York's Bowery, and the vagabonds all over the world are the rejects of the crushing mills of society who escape to temporary euphoria by guzzling heavy sweet wine, smoking hashish or "mainlining" heroin.

The aetiology of retreatism has been studied intensively in the last decade since the classical exposition of personal anomie by Merton. His main premises were that retreatism occurs when some individuals fail to achieve social success goals by legitimate means, and they have internalized some normative prohibitions against using illegitimate means to achieve these goals. The result is that they renounce both goals and means and become completely asocialized.[11] Ohlin and Cloward added some other theoretical premises to the process leading to retreatism by hypothesizing that the total rejection of social goals and the means of achieving them might also be caused by socially structured barriers, like racial prejudice, to achieving these goals. An alternative process is the "double-failure" where an individual who failed to achieve some goal by legitimate means, and then tried to resort to illegitimate means but failed there too.[12]

The retreatists have therefore been rejected by and in turn rejected the legitimate achievement pyramid. They either had normative inner barriers against joining the illegitimate structure or had been rejected by them too. Their solution became a collective fringe existence, where the main interests in life are "kicks" and euphoria.

We might add some other factors which would predispose a person to retreatism. These are based on one of the findings of Dynes, Clarke and Dinitz. The latter uphold empirically the psychoanalytic contention that burning ambition and high

54

aspiration are an anxious quest for security in people who had an unhappy childhood and experienced unsatisfactory inter-personal relationships in the family; on the other hand, those whose early family relationships were satisfactory looked for security in personal happiness and inner satisfaction rather than in ambition and personal achievement.[13]

The other factors which might well be at the basis of the anxiety ridden socialization are what we in another instance have referred to as conflict situations within the family unit during an indi-vidual's formative years.

A tentative list of "conflict situations" could include: marital maladjustment, discord of parents regarding main values and norms: attitude towards authority, private property, education, and resort to violence, which might be relevant to forming chil-dren's attitude towards delinquent or nondelinquent behaviour, value and norm discord between parents and children, degree of consistency of parents in disciplining their children, value and norm discord between the parents and other socializing agencies, i.e., school, church, youth club, etc.

Another factor which is linked to the adequate, conflict- and tension-laden socialization in the formative years is intol-erance of ambiquity, an inclination to see things in "black and white". "Greys" and ambiguity are very similar to the feared value confusion and insecurity of the formative years.

There is a tendency to generalize negativity and blame the whole of society for certain particular failure experiences, pre-paring the ground for the *ressentiment* rejection of social goals.

We shall describe a hypothetical case to illustrate the process of retreatism. An individual who grew up in an anxiety-laden family unit plagued by conflict situations and tension experiences traumatic insecurity and anxiety which in turn motivate him to desire frantically to achieve security or what deems to be acceptance by the socioeconomic elites. Power, social status and money for him equal security and lack of anxiety.

These pressures predispose the individual to intolerance of ambiguity and ruthlessness as far as achieving the success goals is concerned, because the alternative to achieving this power is to regress back into the traumatic anxiety and insecurity of his formative years. However, he is subject to the stifling effects of a self-defeating mechanism. On the one hand, he is driven by an achievement urge to overcome the inner insecurity of a conflict-ridden childhood; on the other hand, the same tension-ridden early socialization creates an intolerance of ambiguity and a tendency to generalize negativity which makes him ill-equipped to achieve success goals. Reality is very rarely black or white; consistency and perseverance in goal achievement are very often tedious. With recurring failure experiences, frustration, self-pity, generalization of hatred and *ressentiment* creep in and pave the way for the process of retreatism. A partial empirical proof of this process has recently been provided by a study of a group of vagabonds in Israel.[14] The presumably higher instance of retreatism in modern society is due to the fewer institutionalized avenues to retreat that are not stigmatized by society. Individuals in modern society are more and more under the influence of what Ortega y Gasset termed *alteracion,* and Riesman called "other-directedness", a "radar-like sensitivity to how one is navigating in the social world, and the tendency to make that navigation into an end of life as well as a means."[15] The "inner-directed" individuals are therefore more likely to be labelled "marginal" because they do not conform to the prevailing trend of "joyful" adjustment to the expectations of others. The label "marginality" alone is a social stigma because: "All these people who do not fit, who do not hang together in the way that they are supposed to feel, are unorganized. They have nobody to define them."[16]

In ages or cultures where the subjects of transcendence, salvation, damnation, purity of soul and pollution were more imminent, "inner-directedness" would be more the norm, and the culture would provide ample institutionalized means for individuals to introspect, to brood alone, and marginality or retreatism would be imbued with a culturally accepted meaning; it would be normal or even laudable behaviour.

56

In Mediaeval Europe all retreatists could lose themselves in the innumerable monasteries (in France alone, there were in the year 1100 some 540 monasteries): they could choose a Carthusian monastery usually situated in a secluded place where each monk worked, ate and slept in his own separate cell and practised almost perpetual silence. They could join a Cistercian monastery where even literacy was unnecessary. The modern *clochard* would not be the object of social stigma or an instance of retreatism; he could join one of the holy orders of mendicants, drift and carry on his tramping not only with impunity but with the halo of a saint. Here again retreatism might have been caused by a process similar to that which we have noted in the Bowery tramps, the "fringe men" and the vagabonds of Eilath, but the social stigma on the latter and the institutionalized retreat of the former determine not only their social image but also their self-image.

Stigma as social control would presumably be quite effective at the initial stages of marginality where a person is still ambivalent toward the social goals he failed to achieve. But he drifts beyond the "sour grapes" *ressentiment* attitude towards society; he severs his links with its normative system. In the gutters he can make little use of social reward or censure, and is less vulnerable to stigma.

D. The Bohemian: The true bohemian is different from the pseudo-bohemian in that the latter is "other-orientated" and does not deviate in his behaviour from the expectations of others. Here again, social stigma might turn into social acceptance and esteem depending on the change of attitude of certain relevant others towards relatively few of the true bohemians. The intellectuals and artists whose *raison d'être* is the expression and formulation of feelings and ideals in words, plastic arts or other creative means of expression are very often detached from and indifferent to the prevailing norms and values of the society they live in. Their creativity and methods of operation do not permit them to get involved in the "rat race" for power, social status and wealth. For deeper insight and better observation, the bohemian divorces himself from actual social realities so that he may gain the necessary distance and perspective to observe and analyse these same realities.

Salomon says: "The bohemian situation, and the marginality of the bohemian himself, who frequently will remain forever a stranger . . . contains both a positive and a negative function: positive, in that it chooses social distance in order to construct true standards; negative, in that it withdraws from social responsibility for selfish reasons . . . If it is the occupation of the intellectual to present perpetually to the world the difference between perfection and reality, then the intellectual is forced outside reality itself."[17]

The essence of the bohemian deviation is the physical and moral detachment from the group: the different ways of looking at things, and a different grading of values. Paradoxically, these bohemians have always expressed aesthetically and expounded intellectually the existence, goals and ideals of the group, due to their spectator role and their deeper insight gained through perspective. The deviation of the bohemian is characteristically described from the group's side by Montesquieu who says: "that which shocked me most is that they (the bohemians) are quite useless to their country and amuse their talents with puerilities. For example, when I arrived at Paris, I found them warm at dispute over the most trifling matter imaginable. It was all about an old Greek poet."[18]

Bohemians may sometimes be the nucleus of a sub-culture, but very often this café-society degenerates into pseudo-bohemia. The hordes of bearded loafers and their blue-jeaned female companions in Greenwich Village, the "existentialists" on the Left Bank in Paris who drop the names of Sartre, Jaspers, Heidegger and Marcel without having read a word of their writings, cannot, in modern society, be regarded either as authentic bohemians nor even as deviants. These groups of a very few real artists and a multitude of self-styled artists, perpetual would-be artists

58

and camp-followers are an integral part of society—an institutionalized layer of the social stratification. The crucial point, however, is that they are accepted as such by the other strata of society. The pseudo-bohemia and self-styled "beat" and "hippy" sub-culture, are therefore integrated in the social structure. The perennial sign of true bohemia—disregard of all goals that are not aesthetic or artistic—is almost non-existent in the lucrative modern café-society. The latter includes the most ardent conformists in another sense, they follow exactly the middle-class concept and image of the bohemian and outsider. The trademarks of the pseudo-bohemian are the external and formal ones of dress, mannerism and demeanour. The bohemian essence is very rarely deeper than the dishevelled clothes, the unshaven face and the tortured look. It would seem that when a certain "beat" or "camp" movement becomes institutionalized, it may either crystallize into a sub-culture, or sweep a whole branch of art or entertainment. The Beatles, the Rolling Stones and their likes have conquered the teenage music market.

In other words, pseudo-bohemia as a group phenomenon is not really deviant behaviour and is therefore outside the scope of the present analysis—suffice that we have distinguished it from and contrasted it with deviant bohemia. However, even with the latter, the differential social attitude would ultimately decide on the label, whether to brand a Van Gogh or a Gauguin with the stigma of an outcast, or enthrone (for a while) a Voltaire as a royal poet laureate and Henry Miller as a favourite court-jester of the west-coast intellectuals. The "success" of a bohemian, measured mostly by the sale of canvas, music or verse, would elevate him by a swing of the social pendulum from the gutters and social stigma to acceptance and celebrity. This change in social attitude would presumably affect only a meagre few. The relevant point here is that his switch from stigma to acceptance would not necessarily be linked with or caused by a change in the bohemian's behaviour, although social acceptance might cause a subsequent "softening by prosperity".

The control of behaviour by stigma would be ineffective with a Van Gogh. He took it upon himself to raise a one-man revolution. He no doubt suffered from stigma and his burning zeal to innovate caused many clashes with his surroundings which eventually shattered his sanity. But he did not succumb to the stigmatizing pressures as far as his innovations were concerned. His life as a bohemian was determined by his inability to cope with the demands of relatives, fellow artists and critics in the realm of his art. This was precisely the reason for his deviance. He could not possibly have conformed to the norms of his contemporary academicians and preserved his *raison d'être*. For him, the points of least resistance were his social links and the reality of others. The synthetic bums, on the other hand, brandish their main stock-in-trade, powerful social antennae, at the relevant others to detect and predict what is "in" and what is "out", what shape of toilet basin is fit for the museum and which should be placed in municipal lavatories, what pornography is "camp" and what is plain old dirt. For these, stigma is not only the most powerful control; it actually shapes their whole "other-directed" existence.

E. The accidental deviant: The accidental deviant exhibits a statistically modal behaviour which becomes a labelled social deviation by its detection and ensuing stigma. The latter might be responsible for the further, habitual deviance of the stigmatized accidental deviant. A person may commit certain acts which are clearly deviant but not really intentional or persistent, e.g., short-lived escapades to places, hide-outs, alcohol or women. These are committed by most people a few times in their lives and for relatively short periods. A very important factor which links this type of deviation to our main dimension of the present analysis is whether the accidental deviation (especially on the short-lived escapade) has been detected, sanctioned and socially stigmatized or has passed unnoticed. This may well determine whether the accidental deviation develops into a more persistent pattern or remains a passing episode.

Many youngsters indulge in occasional acts of petty theft,

violence, forbidden pleasures and escapades. This may range from stealing a boat or a car for a joy-ride, through actual stealing of money from parents or relatives, to the escapades of adolescents as in *Catcher in the Rye*. Many studies reveal that the apprehension of youths and their trial before a juvenile court with the ensuing stigma of juvenile delinquency and its social and economic consequences can in fact be responsible for further deviation and delinquency. The very successful principal of a high school reminisced with the author about his childhood days, recalling how he used to steal apples from the market daily. Once when he was caught, the vendor wanted to drag the boy to the police station but the mother reasoned with him and he agreed, for a consideration, to drop the matter. The mother punished the boy afterwards but he was sure that his whole life would have been changed if he had been brought before a juvenile court judge, sentenced, and stigmatized as a juvenile delinquent. A study on middle- and upper-class delinquency in Israel revealed that the rate of recidivism of these boys was significantly lower than in the control group of lower-class delinquents.[19] This was partially attributable to the tendency of the middle-class family to "straighten things out" with the complainant, not to resort at all to the law-enforcement agencies and to cushion the effects of the boy's encounter with the police, juvenile-court judge or probation officer.

The conforming bourgeois might find himself from time to time on a binge, involved in an escapade with a woman or in an illicit transaction, or temporarily embrace some "radical" ideas. If not caught and stigmatized, a "Babbit" would invariably be re-embraced by the ever-loving citizenry of Zenith or Middle-town to be elected president of the local Rotary Club or to office in the Freemasons Lodge.

F. Acquisitive deviant and criminal: Criminal justice stigmatizes a small proportion of the offenders because only a part of the offences committed are brought to the knowledge of the police and their perpetrators brought to justice. Many offenders, even if detected

61

and apprehended, are not stigmatized due to their socioeconomic status. This category includes all the property offenders, racketeers, white-collar criminals and "sharp" businessmen who are motivated by rarely more than one maxim: "to make as much money as possible in the shortest possible time". Being caught breaking the law is considered "bad for business" but, if necessary, is taken to be an occupational risk. This acquisitive type of deviance should be sub-classified into "occasional" and "professional", the latter being perpetrated by a distinct type of offender who looks upon crime as his trade. This type is often highly skilled and the training for his profession is relatively lengthy and arduous. The semi-professional type stands halfway between the two. This type, although frequently engaged in crime, is not yet a full-time professional.

Our main concern here is whether criminal behaviour as such is sufficient to brand a person as a criminal and deviant or if criminal behaviour is only a predisposing factor, social stigma being the *causa causans.* The idea of justice has undergone only small metamorphoses from the codes of Hammurabi, Leviticus, Numbers, and the talionic Roman Tables. Justice is done if the wrongdoer suffers (i.e., is punished) in proportion to the objective severity of his crime. The pragmatical application of justice has no doubt evolved immensely during the ages; we no longer kill or maim so many people. We also adhere more to the deterrent, preventive and reformative aspects of punishment than to the original retributive justice. However, the idea of justice has remained basically the same, i.e., that criminals should be punished (or "treated" and "corrected") and some restrictive measure be imposed on them as their just dessert, irrespective of the utilitarian objectives of punishment. The latter are, strictly speaking, foreign to the pure idea of justice. Kant illustrated this point by stating that "even if civil society should dissolve with the consent of its members . . . The last murderer found in prison must first have been executed, so that each may receive what his debts are worth."[20] This is the postulate of the categorical imperative of justice. It is elementary that justice is done in only a fraction of crimes because only some of the offences are known to the police and only some of the perpetrators of these are detected and sentenced.

Justice, as actually applied by the so-called machinery of justice, is feasible only in relation to offences known to the police and these are not necessarily the majority of offences actually committed. A realistic hypothesis might be that crimes known to the police are the minority of offences actually committed in any given society. There are various reasons for this:

In many cases the victims of crime do not wish to notify the police lest they are charged as accomplices. Prostitutes very rarely inform on their pimps, and victims of violence who belong to a criminal subculture will not report the offences committed against them for fear of sanction from their own gang.

Many victims of confidence tricks are reluctant to report the offences to the police because they would not want other people to know how foolishly they have been taken in. This happened not infrequently in Israel during the strict foreign currency regulations: crooks operating in couples sold their victims a wad of green pieces of paper covered at each end by a one dollar bill.

Other instances are linked to sexual offences; the victims of offences very often refrain from notifying the police in order to escape the unpleasant publicity and the gruesome details of the interrogations and trial. This is particularly true with minors whose parents might prefer not to perpetuate the child's traumatic experience by repeated reconstructions of the sexual assault during interrogations and trial.

There are many cases of tightly-knit groups, such as labour unions, cooperatives and the Israel *kibbutzim,* which do not inform the police of offences committed by their members, because they prefer to "arrange matters within the family".

Certain supermarkets in Chicago notified the police of only 9% of thefts committed on their premises during a period of six months, because they wished to prevent what they regarded as undesirable publicity.[21] "White-collar crime", i.e., the offences

63

committed by businessmen and politicians, are not adequately represented in the criminal statistics. White-collar criminals do not regard themselves as offenders or deviants and the public generally regards them as respectable citizens. Sutherland claims that many families who belong to the social elite of the U.S.A. are the descendants of the "robber-barons" and others who amassed their fortunes by illegal transactions. Of special interest is the fact that a certain Leonor Lorry, a railway executive, after having been convicted of embezzling a quarter of a million dollars, was elected Chairman of the New York Chamber of Commerce.[22] The public does not hasten to brand the stigma of crime to the white-collar strata of society, because it is almost taken for granted that people who are in business, in politics and in some of the professions do infringe, to a varying extent, some of the laws they come across in the course of their trade or profession. There is a harsh social stigma on murderers, burglars and rapists, but a businessman who files his income-tax returns punctually and honestly is regarded by many as a strange creature.

Managers and executives have relatively easy access to the "right contacts" in the higher echelons of the administration and political pressure groups. This is relevant particularly in the U.S., where the prosecutors and judiciary are politically elected. There is also a similarity of social background and status among the executives and businessmen of large companies and the elite of government administration. The latter are appointed to high positions in the large companies, and vice-versa. This might result in the "soft treatment" of many businessmen and enterprises in cases where they have been careless enough to get entangled in criminal "inconveniences." This should be evaluated while bearing in mind the well-known statement that "what is good for General Motors is good for U.S.A.".

The unduly small representation of "white-collar criminals" in the criminal statistics can also be attributed to the tendency of companies to "arrange matters" with the embezzling employee in order to save part of the money or to avoid publicity.

64

Another important fact is that only some of the offenders, who commit a fraction of the sum total of offences known to the police, are detected and apprehended.

The figures from some years ago for major cities in the U.S. revealed that only 25% of the perpetrators of serious offences were detected by the police. The rate of detection of offences in 2,000 cities in the U.S. in the year 1958 was 94% of murders, 73% of rapes, 79% of assaults, 20% of thefts.[23] In this context, the most recent data for the U.S. are provided by the report of the President's Commission of Law Enforcement and Administration of Justice. This report indicates that aggravated assault and larceny involving sums of over $50 occur twice as often as they are reported and there are 50% more robberies than are reported. In some areas, only one-tenth of the total number of crimes are reported to the police. Of the neighborhood commercial establishments surveyed 74% do not report to police thefts committed by their employees.

The average percentage of arrests ranges from 91% for homicide to 20% for larceny.[24] The data from England show an average detection of 25% of the serious offences with a marked dispersion of the type of offence.[25] In Israel, the rates of detection for the year 1961 were 91% of offences against the person and sexual offences and 28% of property offences. For the year 1962, the rates of detection were 92% of offences against the person and sexual offences and 30% of property offences.[26] More relevant to the present context is the fact that criminal justice is quite partial, that is, it is unjust. The notorious "fix" in the U.S. and similar arrangements in other countries provide relative immunity from criminal prosecution for certain groups and classes, whereas other groups, especially ethnic minorities (e.g., Negroes in southern U.S., Turks in Cyprus, Jews in some countries), have an initial disadvantage in conducting their defence against the criminal charge. Many studies have recorded the partiality of the administration of criminal justice at its various stages.

Release-on-bail procedures in two major cities of the U.S.

65

were found to be highly detrimental to defendants of low economic status.[27] The most conspicuous findings of this study were that many defendants were unable to furnish bail even when the amount set was nominal, and that these detainees were more likely to be convicted and were much more severely sentenced than defendants charged with similar crimes who were free on bail pending trial.

Studies on the sentencing policies of criminal courts revealed that the nature and severity of sanction were very often determined not by factors related to the offence and personality of the offender, but by factors foreign to correctional needs (or to justice): these include the personality of the judge, his personal views on social values, his political convictions and the defendant's class and socioeconomic status.[28] These differential policies are particularly apparent with juvenile delinquents. The rates of delinquency known to the police (or to the probation service) are unfavourably biased against the lower-class youth. The Porterfield study revealed that 100% of the research population (437 college men and women) had admittedly committed, in their pre-college years, acts for which other children (mostly lower class) of the same town were brought before the courts and branded as delinquents.[29] Nye[30] and Andry[31] report that many police officers, when catching a boy from a "good", that is, middle-class, home committing an offence, send him home with a kick in the pants, whereas a lower-class boy is taken to the police station and criminal proceedings are initiated. Students in England are often "drunk and disorderly", but very rarely spend nights in gaol, whereas working class boys often enjoy the hospitality of Her Majesty's prisons for identical behaviour.

A recent study on the socioeconomic effects of criminal conviction[32] revealed that unskilled workers charged with assault suffered a severe narrowing of employment facilities, even if *they were subsequently acquitted.* On the other hand, the practice of a doctor found guilty of malpractice increases after conviction, because of the powerful support of fellow physicians who, out

66

of sympathy, referred more clients to their delinquent comrade. This again not only proves that "law is like a cobweb; it's made for flies and the smaller kind of insects, but lets the big bumblebees break through",[33] but also upholds our thesis that justice is not the ideal measuring rod to define crime and to divide the criminal from the honest. The stigmatizing tools of society are not necessarily wielded by justice.

G. The chaotic rebels: The chaotic rebellion of youth as a pre-disposing factor to stigmatization as a social deviant is a statistically modal behaviour of adolescents and post-adolescents. Stigmatization of such behaviour would depend on the relevant adult's identification or non-identification with a given type of youth activity. The chaotic rebels are the increasing number of "rebels without a cause", the herds of aggressive teenagers and young adults who, throughout the world, vent in rage negativism and aggression triggered by *ressentiment.* Here the group, its values and norms are rejected and attacked, but the aims and motivations of the rejection are either confused or non-existent. These violent teenagers are very often organized into gangs; they have their own norms and ways of acting, e.g., special clothes and mannerisms, but the latter are mainly concerned with form and are apparently not at all goal-directed.

Many studies have noted the negativistic aggression, the seemingly purposeless vandalism of much delinquent behaviour. Some of the current explanations of this "rebellion without a cause" are focused on the insecurity of youths who only half-heartedly infringe upon the middle-class norms and who, in order to overcome the guilt feelings thus created, express their reaction in exaggerated bravado and aggression against the subconsciously cherished middle-class norms.[34]

However, this overt aggression may be not so much a reaction formation as a direct and positive rebellious act, a battle-cry against "double thinking", "double talking" and the clearly contradictory and confused value system of socializing agencies, families, schools, church and other social institutions. If certain

67

current theories on the process of adolescence are correct, maturity is the ability to reconcile the contradictory postulates of culture, to develop a selective attitude towards various groups, a selective memory that determines whether the injuries have been inflicted by one's group or suffered by it.

Adolescence is characterized by a yearning for absolute values and a desire for sharply defined roles. Youth is described by countless works of literature not only as a seething cauldron of idealism and *Weltschmerz,* but is also as passionately in favour of consistent statements of facts and rules which are otherwise known (in unscientific jargon) as plain honesty.

Gobseque, that stingy old scoundrel created by Balzac, sits before the fireplace with his teenage friend and promises him a loan without guarantees, because up to twenty, a person's best guarantee is his age, and because "you, my young friend, are idealistic; you visualize great ideas, basic truths and beautiful Utopias while staring at the dancing flames. At my age, however, we see in the fireplace plain burning coal." A youth whose socialization is plagued with conflict situations is more liable to reject the idea of adjustment to contradictory, hypocritical and confused sets of norms. If this is adulthood, he prefers the more direct behaviour and clearly defined normative system of the delinquent or "street-corner" subculture; because of his inability to internalize contradictory norms and adopt inconsistent and selective attitudes, he can be branded as "infantile", "rigid", "a permanent adolescent", a "trouble-marker", thereby being pushed further to the delinquent gang where the "hypocrites" who manage the "legitimate" rackets are rarely described in ambivalent terms.

The chaotic rebellion of adolescents, which is a universal phenomenon, will be defined and labelled as delinquency, hooliganism, or bad behaviour, depending on the generalized adult disposition: to stigmatize it, to be indifferent towards it, or approve of it. The chaotic rebellion of adolescence is so widespread (the Mods, the Rockers, the Blouson-noirs, the Halbstarke, the Hooligans, the Stilyagi, Hell's Angels, Teddy boys, etc.)

68

that it cannot be regarded as the specific, localized or limited behaviour of disturbed or maladjusted youths. This seemingly normal behaviour (depending on the angle from which we look at it) becomes branded as conspicuously deviant by the stigma attached to it by the world of adults. The aetiology of the chaotic rebellion can perhaps be traced to faulty socialization processes in the formative years, but the defiant attitude is much more concerned with the cultural mandates as a whole.

The self-defeating conflicts, contradictions and ambiguity inherent in the normative systems of groups have been widely studied. In a primitive society, for example, an extreme form of self-defeating and contradictory cultural norms can be found among the Ojibwa Indians. The Ojibwa boy is trained for the role of successful hunter and warrior, yet goal-attainment is psychologically penalized, because he becomes more vulnerable instead of more secure. The boy is trained not to rely upon the "weak and competing humans about him" but to seek the aid of supernatural beings. Attainment of this power purchases the respect of others, but they fear him, leave him alone, and other hunters jealous of his power direct their power against him. The constant pressure to attain a goal which is self-defeating leads to melancholia, violence and obsessive cannibalism, all subsumed under the Ojibwa term "Windigo".[35]

The ability to come to terms with cultural contradictions is considered to be a manifestation of "maturity", but the chaotic rebel can be unable or unwilling to accept the basic hypocrisies of our society or to use double standards or a selective approach. It is thus almost inevitable, that such behaviour begets for the rebellious youth the stigma of "childish", "immature", "infantile", "rigid" or "an impossible person".

Our modern educators and socializing agencies see to it, therefore, that those manifestations of spontaneity and individuality are suppressed very early in order to prevent the catastrophe of "immaturity", "rigidity", and "maladjustment". This suppression of spontaneity increases, as Fromm pointed out, the necessity and chances of conformity; the deterioration

69

or even loss of "the self" produces a profound doubt of one's identity that is solved by joining the herd, the group. Many feeble "I's" find their sense of direction and security in a tough "We". Society has always found stigmatizing explanations for the negativistic attitude of the chaotic rebel. Max Scheler sees in him Aesop's fox, full of a "sour grapes" *ressentiment* of the cultural success goals that are beyond his reach. The Freudian and other psychoanalytic schools see the chaotic rebel as a personification of the primaeval and basic death-wish whose subconscious aim and reason for his rebellion are to be stigmatized as deviant and ostracized: a symbolic death.

The rebel does not, of course, enjoy his stigma and he wishes, if he is not a masochist, to be rid of its social and economic consequences; he wants to be accepted as a non-conforming rebel, and his really tragic plight begins if he is unable to realize that he is asking for the impossible.

Membership in rebellious youth gangs raises the probability that a youth will be identified as a delinquent or deviant, but here again the causal process itself is supplied by social stigma. The case of the Beatles in Britain is an outstanding example of this. The Beatle phenomenon reduced the juvenile delinquency rate in Liverpool to an unprecedented rate. This is because many juvenile gangs formed themselves into Beatle-groups. The British public did not choose this time, for reasons which we shall analyze later, to stigmatize the Beatles. The Prime Minister posed for a photograph with them and the Queen gave them the O.B.E. This identified their apparently chaotic and rebellious behaviour as normatively permitted and approved by the adult world.

H. The ideational rebellion: Ideational rebellion is the most outwardly directed deviation and is therefore more predisposed to extreme social reaction, both positive and negative. The power-backed stigma against ideational rebels is the most extreme because the very existence of the power-elite in society is endangered by it. The rebel with an ideology wishes to overthrow governments,

70

change social, economic and religious institutions. He is motivated by his faith that when his ideologies or goals govern the fate of the group, the road will be paved towards equality, justice, power, revolution, peace, utopia, etc. The aetiology of ideational rebellion on the social level is beyond the scope of the present work, but we can attempt to delineate some causal pressures toward ideational rebellion on the individual level.

Ideational rebellion should have been preceded by internalization and acceptance of group goals or norms. A youth who has received a relatively defined and stable normative system from his socializing agencies expects the groups with which he is associated to adhere to a clear, non-ambiguous normative system, a system which, if not monolithic, at least has many absolute values at its base; he is bound to project his inner image of absolute values on to society at large or at least on to his reference groups. Only a society which displays an orderly and consistent normative system similar to his own gives him a sense of security and belonging. In other words, the potential rebel takes the first steps on his Via Dolorosa equipped with a tightly normative system relatively immune to pressures to conform exerted by groups, and expects the culture of these groups to be loaded with absolutes as meaningful as his own.

This naturally pushes him into a conflict with society and its institutions for which he is ill-prepared. He is confronted with a normative system which functions (or misfunctions) according to criteria widely divergent from his own and which do not tally with any rules comprehensible to him. He soon discovers that social acceptance and sometimes survival itself call for adjustment to rules which have nothing to do with absolute or transcendental values but are geared to relative and shifting power structures of social and political organizations and institutions. This is what is meant when he is urged "to grow up", "to learn the facts of life", "not to be childish", to be "smart, realistic and flexible".

The prospective rebel proceeds further and refuses "to grow up", or to "play the rules of the game", because his inner normative

71

structure rejects the ambiguous cultural mandates and confused values of the society to which he is supposed to adjust. At this stage he is ready to follow any revolutionary movements, political innovators, utopians, or any "ism", because these are based on meaningful values. However, utopia is an unattainable vision and on the endless road most rebels, social reformers, political innovators, founders of religions and so forth succumb either intentionally or owing to an inevitable occupational hazard of leaders, to the pursuit of power; political and bureaucratic control becomes the only feasible and realistic goal; social control may or may not be instrumental in achieving the cause, but it is certainly instrumental in preserving the position of the power elite.

As far as ideational rebellion is concerned, the power-backed social stigma is all-important. Here, more than in any other instance of pre-disposition to deviance, the social stigma is the crucial factor in the definition of the behaviour. When Batista is in power, Castro is the rebel, traitor and criminal.

Value Deviation as a Breakdown of Involvement

Albert Camus sees the absurd as the confrontation of the irrational world and "the wild longing for clarity whose call echoes in the human heart."[36]

In crude epistemology this would mean that the absurd is a disjunction between one's own ideal image of what things should be and what they are now.

We propose a conceptual revival of "Accidie", "Acedy" or "Accidia" to denote an individual's breakdown of involvement in the realm of value in the way that "Anomy", "Anomie" or "Anomia" was resurrected from the 16th century usage to denote normative disintegration in society.

The need for a specific concept for value deviation stems from the fact that most, if not all, exponents of disorganization, anomie and alienation from Durkheim through Merton and Parsons to Seeman and others, deal with value deviation and deviant behaviour as a single entity. At most they regard value deviation as a predisposing factor to deviant behaviour.

Accidie, however, pertains to value deviation alone, and it may not and need not have any overt behavioural manifestations. The fourth cardinal sin, Acedy, was not caring: "The fourth heed of the beast of hell is slouth (sloth), whyche is callyd of clerkys accidye".[37] This is the state of mind of heedlessness associated with depressive detachment, passivity and sadness. Accidie is a state of mind of an individual; anomie, even as expounded by Merton in relation to individual modes of adaptation, is an attribute of the group. Merton says: "Anomie refers to a property of a social system, not to the state of mind of this or that individual within the system . . . Anomie, then is a condition of the social surroundings, not a condition of particular people . . . to prevent conceptual confusion different terms are required to distinguish between the anomie state of individuals and the anomie state of the social system."[38]

Our conceptualization of accidie to denote value deviation as distinct from anomie and from other modes of deviant behaviour would probably be approved by Merton. The latter's exposition of anomie and deviation and also that of Parsons and Seeman are more of a static description or typology, while we see accidie as a dynamic process: "The church appeared as old because your spirit was aged and already faded, and powerless from your ailings and doubts. For as the aged, having no hope any more to renew their youth, expect nothing but their last sleep; so ye, being weakened by wordly affairs, yield yourself up to accidies and cast not your cares upon the Lord, but your spirit was broken, and you were worn out with your griefs." The dynamism of our conception of accidie rests in its being the final link in a trichotomous chain—first the initial normative gap between the ideal image and perceived reality, second the congruity-motivated involvement to bridge this gap, and finally in case of failure, a breakdown, a stultification of involvement.

In a sense, our conception of accidie is despair in the realm of values, whereas anomie can be described as the faulty coordination of goals and means (by Merton) or the disjuncture between the congruity motive and the activity-passivity continuum (by Parsons). This, to be sure, is the initial normative gap only, and is prior to ego's involvement to bridge it. Moreover, Merton's and Parsons' modes of anomic or alienative "adaptations" may be regarded, paradoxically, as "success-stories". Ritualism, for instance, is one of the "adaptations" or "adjustments" most coveted by employers the world over. The ritualist employee at the assembly line or at a desk in an impersonal bureaucracy is an asset. His ability to raise means to the level of ends makes him an "ideal worker", a "perfectly adjusted individual" and "an integrated team-worker", to use the jargon of the industrial psychologist. Value deviation can be a predisposition for stigmatization insofar as it is a precursor of deviant behaviour. It can precede or accompany deviant behaviour. This is so in most cases of self-destructive, escapist, criminal and rebellious behaviour. Most of the cases of value deviations, even it not accompanied by deviant behaviour, would be predisposed to social stigmatization if they were to become known to the stigmatizing agencies of normative control.

CHAPTER IV

DEVIANT BEHAVIOUR, VALUE DEVIATION AND SOCIAL STIGMA

I *am daring*
you *are reckless*
he *is delinquent**.

THE THREE DIMENSIONS OF SOCIAL DEVIATION

In Chapter 3 we analysed some modes of deviant behaviour and discussed the probabilities of their being predisposing factors for branding individuals or groups with social stigma.

As value deviation is presumably linked with deviant behaviour, these variables are multiply correlated with social stigma, which becomes the dependant variable; these three are multiply correlated with the total syndrome of social deviation as defined in Chapter 1.

This chapter examines the inter-relationship between value deviation, deviant behaviour, social stigma and the entire syndrome of social deviation.

1. *The "true" solidarists:* In every society there is a core of respectable, law-abiding, god-fearing citizens. These presumably belong to the middle class or its equivalent in Communist countries. They are the masses who find security in quantitative means, medians and modes because "everybody else" or his neighbour is also doing it. Their conformity is proverbial. The French wine-grower and British shopkeeper do not, as a rule, have the time or the inclination to question the current prevailing norms.

This cult of mediocrity can be traced back to ancient Greece.

* Robert K. Merton

Apart from the basic *Meden Agan,* "nothing in excess" (which is equivalent to "follow the mean"), a "dominant passion" in the Greek national character was for harmony, sobriety, moderation, and a sense of balance.[1] Those who did not comply with these basic norms met the righteous indignation of Nemesis and the wrath of *Dike.* The savage Furies, servants of *Dike* would punish even the sun if it dared to swerve from its path.

This is *Hubris*—the infringement of one's lot in existence; "hubris should be extinguished with greater zeal than a fire."[2] It is difficult to dispute the premise that this Hellenic normative trend has its legitimate or illegitimate descendents in the Protestant Ethic and the European burgher. The model of the latter "should be industrious and active. He should lead a regular life. God hates all disorder in money matters and in household affairs, as well as *unordentliche Liebe* and disordinate passion; a man should be parsimonious and take care of his property."[3]

Reckless found the curve of crime and deviation in the U.S. to have two modal values, one of the lower socioeconomic levels,[4] the other of the higher classes with the middle class constituting the low valley between the two peaks.

There is almost a consensus of opinion that the more a society becomes urbanized, industrialized, specialized and bureaucratized, the fiercer are the pressures to conformity. Nietzsche in his *Will to Power* deplores what he describes as a natural and inevitable levelling process of individuals into mass-produced mediocre entities. His value-laden rage against the cult of mediocrity and the hatred of excellence is sad because he refused to come to terms with an inevitable process, a process which began when Prometheus showed an ape-man how to make fire. Perhaps chained Prometheus struck his chest in atonement on realizing that his good intentions paved the road to hell, but it was too late, and a chain-reaction had started; industrialization breeds specialization, bureaucracy and anonymous "team enterprises"; smooth bureaucracy levels down and smothers any innovation. Ortega y Gasset laments the disappearance of protagonists and the flourishing of the chorus, the fact that to be different is to be indecent.

76

The mass crushes beneath it everything that is different, everything that is excellent, individual, qualified and select; nowadays, "everybody" is the mass alone.[5] Even those who subscribe to the Spenserian idea of progress deplore this dictatorship of the masses over the minority of individualists. Many of us would join the authors of the *Lonely Crowd* and *The Organization Man* in a league attacking discrimination against individualistic innovators, were such a league formed. There is no difference between the discrimination of a person because his skin is too dark or because his thoughts are too bright.

However, we must avoid value-laden analysis and shall describe pressures to conformity as a conflict between the degree of specialization of society and the degree of specialization of the individuals who comprise it. We shall liken society to a living organism.[6] but only for limited methodological purposes, as we do not subscribe to the organistic fallacy in sociological thought. The human individual is highly specialized in his biological functions, the cells serviced by the bloodstream and the organs coordinated by the central nervous system. Society, by comparison, is a crude living organism; individuals (its body cells) have to move from one place to the other, to work, to be fed, to be entertained, to rest. Its coordinating nerve system is primitive, crude, and harsh, like a shark's diminutive brain. The highly specialized human individual is much too sophisticated for the crude superstructure which uses him as one of its cells. The road to conformity (and its synonyms in the educational and mental health jargons, socialization and adjustment) is a continuous process of amputation and lobotomizing. The main problem in this context is that the conformity of individuals is geared not so much to the existing normative system but to the image of the latter as created by the various image makers through the mass media.

The gap between the social norms and their image, as conveyed to individuals, can be infinitesimal or infinite. The image industry must enlarge, gloss over and glaze the objects it has to "build up" or "promote". The means of communication used by the

77

image makers cannot be of the multiple-nuance brand. The advertising copy, the "box-office" movie, the "king-makers", and the celebrity manufacturers employ endless repetitions, booming echo-chamber, dazzling Klieg lights, masking make-up.

Complicated hues, subtlety, undertones, and the rough edges of reality are suppressed or simply ignored. The language of the image makers is the Orwellian Newspeak which "was designed not to extend but to diminish the range of thought. . . All ambiguities and shades of meaning had been purged out of them so far as could be achieved; Newspeak was simply a staccato sound expressing one clearly understood concept. One called upon to make a political or ethical judgement should be able to spray forth the correct opinions as automatically as a machine-gun spraying forth bullets. . .its vocabulary grew smaller instead of larger. Each reduction was a gain since the smaller the area of choice, the smaller the temptation to take thought."[7] The image makers in society are not concerned with building bridges between actual social norms and their images: on the contrary, they regard their task as purging the images of any traces of reality. The image, not the thing, becomes the reference point and the focus of interest. This preeminence of the image over reality is the essence of Boorstins' analysis of the value system of modern society, illustrated by the following dialogue:

> *Admiring friend: My, that's a beautiful baby you have there.*
> *Mother: Oh, that's nothing—you should see his photograph.*[8]

Heidegger points out that individuals invariably taint reality with their moods; Jaspers assures us that all individual knowledge is achieved by interpretation of the social institutions and organs. The latter, in order to achieve a feasible degree of communication, must standardize and homogenize their images in order to create a common denominator of comprehension. This patently artificial levelling makes the images, not the social situations, the bases for beliefs and normative systems. Consequently, ideologies, cultural goals, expectations and aspirations are bound to be modelled on and orientated toward the social images, and not their counterparts. Conformity, or true "solidarity", therefore, involves the adherence to norms *as conveyed to individuals* by the communication media. These are of necessity based on streamlined essentials like the criminal investigator's "identi-kit", which draws only the major features of a face. The blur, the smear, the curve, the streamlined shadow, the gag, the gimmick, the catch-phrase, the hit, the bang are the image-maker's tools.

The third levelling force pressing towards conformity is related to our affluent society's norms of consumption. The "true soli-darist" will have to undergo a treble chipping-down and honing process, the first by the mass culture itself, the second by the image makers who manufacture images of social norms that have little or no resemblance to the norms themselves, and the third by mass production and standardized consumption. This process of the levelling of individuals is largely enforced by social stigma as a tool of social control.

2. *The victims:* The value and behaviour conformists who are branded as criminals and deviants are more numerous than one might want to believe. Social stigma of crime and deviation, being an act of power practiced by the ruling elite, has been used extensively for many purposes, irrespective of whether the stigmatized person is guilty or innocent, a conformist or a deviant. In politics, the stigma of deviation has been a favourite weapon. Ostracism in ancient Greece was invariably preceded by branding the would-be outcast as anything from a polluter of youth to a poisoner of wells. This smear technique has not really changed in modern politics. Stigmatizing techniques have merely become more subtle, more sophisticated and more effective.

Religious and political witch-hunters are rarely interested in the deeds or even the identity of their victim; they want a witch to burn.

Leaders of groups know very well that nothing strengthens the morale and solidarity of the group more than focusing its hate on an inner enemy who "betrays" the people. It helps if there are some conspicuous targets such as Armenians in Turkey,

Turks in Cyprus and Jews in many countries, but if there is none, one can be invented. Innocent persons are convicted and punished in judicial processes, some maliciously, like Dreyfus, others mistakenly, like Timothy Evans. Social stigma is also branded very effectively by the vast channels of gossip and rumour; these very often affect people irrespective of whether their values or behaviour are conformist or deviant. In other words, in "true" victimization, the constitutive factor is pure social stigma, and not any value deviation or deviant behaviour on the part of the victim. Of course, the victims are not chosen at random; there are reasons for choosing them and not others, as we have seen in Chapter II, but these reasons rarely have anything to do with the overt justification. The reasons are related to the image of the victim, his social roles and status. The hypothesis here is, therefore, that the conspicuity of the victim in the overall existential sense is much greater and more socially visible than in other instances of stigmatization. Statistically, he will be far removed from the modal value of the normal curve: very wealthy or poor, a genius or a moron, a celebrity or a Jean Valjean; even physically he will tend to look like an Olympian or a Quasimodo. Another premise is that the victim and the stigmatizing agency are likely to interact socially, or to be linked in a way which will make the stigmatization objectively more feasible. This factor is well illustrated by analogy to the criminal-victim relationship in criminology. The so-called "victimology" branch of criminology investigates the relationship between criminal and victim as far as social proximity, family or business connections are concerned. We know, for instance, that in crimes of violence the victims and the criminals tend to be of similar social groups, who live not far apart and have some kind of mutual business or dealings.[9] In cases of homicide, murderers and victims tend to be linked in a relationship of husband and wife, lover and mistress, prostitute and pimp, or criminal and (shady) business associate. Victims of sexual offences are mostly known or are even closely linked to the perpetrator of the offence; in many cases she (or he) would be more of an enticer or even a seducer or an actual (or moral) blackmailer. In property offences, especially in confidence tricks, gambling or obtaining money by false pretences, the victim is generally lured and trapped because of his desire to make easy money, and he is not concerned with the legality of the transaction. If we try to relate these findings to our context, the analogy is that the stigmatizer and victim are very rarely strangers, and in most cases familial, social or business proximities exist.

The mythical figures of Prometheus, Sysiphus and Tantalus belong to the society of Olympians. Oedipus and Polycrates were kings, and Socrates and Trotsky belonged to the social and power elite of their societies. Politicians and social climbers rarely direct their arrows against individuals outside their social or political strata. Gossiping matrons aim their poisonous tongues and menacing stares at members of their own membership or reference groups.

A third factor in the genesis of victimization by stigma, and perhaps the most important for us, is that the victim is linked in a symbolical or a subconscious way to a deficiency or want of the stigmatizer. The free-loving woman is stigmatized as "loose" or "promiscuous" mainly by those whose sex lives are too restrained or unsatisfactory in other ways. The hearty and immediate relationships of the lower (or working) classes are labelled "vulgar" and "common" by those who practice cold and polite detachment. The intellectual is tagged as a "radical egg-head" by the ignorant. The creative genius is branded as a "lunatic crackpot" by the masses of mediocrities. The well-to-do Jew is called "the thieving Jew" by the achievement-frustrated lower middle classes. A brilliant illustration is Andersen's baby swan who was forced to accept the majority opinion that he was an ugly duckling.

3. *Inner conflict:* This heading includes many whose behaviour has been described by us previously as escapist and self-destructive. These individuals have internalized the main norms and values of society. However, the latter are very often contradictory or ambiguous. A person who is intolerant of ambiguity can find

81

it very difficult or even impossible to come to terms with a patently contradictory, ambiguous and confused system of values. The inevitable result is inner conflict, and in extreme cases, escapism and even self-destruction. Here a person sincerely accepts the values of the group to which he belongs, but because he tries to absorb them without being prepared to make compromises, he will be defeated. He cannot cope with the norms and values of society at their face value. Honesty, decency and devotion were for him at some stage not mere words, but meaningful mandates. He was conditioned to look for the real event and not the pseudo-event, to strive for authentic achievement and not only for the reputation of achievement, but he realizes that these and many other norms and values are paid only lip service by the group, and that conformity to the group actually requires an almost boundless elasticity toward these values. On the other hand, his socialization (and also, perhaps constitutional factors) makes it impossible for him to "adjust". His quest for these perfect, and therefore unreal and non-existent values, and his insistence that others do the same, make him a Don Quixote, a naive person, an "infantile adolescent" or "rigid perfectionist". This contrast between the institutionalized values and the subjectively perceived image of these same values has driven many to rebellion, to Zen Buddhism or one of dozens of cults, either religious or political; but those who were disenchanted or for some reason could not find solace or refuge in the quest for absolutes started whirling on the positive feed-back vicious circle of being regarded as Don Quixotes, infantiles, "confused", "unrealistic" and finally acting the part. This, of course, is a favourable background for escape to a "devil-may-care" attitude: alcohol, drugs, fits of depression and even suicide

Another factor associated with the present type of deviation is a low frustration level; a person with a thick hide "adjusts" better. It is difficult for an oversensitive personality to integrate smoothly into the play of master and servant, employer and employee, organization-man and party member. At the first failure, the first injury to previously internalized norms and values, he may back out and retreat to a road which leads to behaviour deviation and stigma, without being necessarily deviant as far as the group values are concerned. He can profess adherence to the values, but claim that the group has falsified them. This suits Sartre's Garcin's state of mind when he says: "So, this is hell, I'd never have believed it, if you remember all we were told about the torture-chambers, the fire and brimstone. Old wives' tales. There is no need for red-hot pokers. Hell is other people." [10]

Kleist's Michael Kohlhaas is a good example of extreme value conformity which results in deviant behaviour and stigmatization. Some individuals internalize deeply some of the values and norms of their culture and cling to them even at a very late stage of their lives. Which particular personality components induce an individual to cling tenaciously to these values and norms are not known, but such an individual perceives and absorbs literally such values as justice, morality, friendship, honesty, patriotism, equality, etc., which are postulated by family, school and other socializing agencies. The agencies do not in fact portray a realistic image of the values and norms which actually prevail in society, but of those with which society is supposed to comply. The relevant point is that personality theories regard maturity and even sanity as a result of an individual's ability to take the values and norms postulated by the socializing agencies "with large chunks of salt".

Freud's "ego" and Erikson's "ego-identity" are defined, inter alia, by the extent to which an individual has internalized the norms and values of society in their flexible, relative, and very often contradictory essence as they actually prevail in society. There should always be a no-man's land between the normative and the non-normative where most people roam from time to time. *"Meden Agan"*, "the middle way", "adjustment", "to realize the facts of life", "see things as they are", are synonyms for the mandate that one should erode the norms and values of society so that they fit the fallibility and vulnerability of human nature.

However, in the present context we are concerned with the individuals who accept certain norms and values in their abstract, absolute form, people who refuse or are unable to compromise. They impute reality to stated values and find that the actual application is but a sorry reflection. These individuals are not satisfied with the patch of light in the cave, they are after the glittering rays of the sun. The process which differentiates these individuals from the majority who manage "to grow up" is beyond the scope of the present work, which is concerned with the phenomenon and its consequences. The individuals who cherish their own values will eventually find that their realities clash with those of others. This can, of course, lead to rebellion, such as the attempt to impose one's image of norms and goals on others, to the crimes of a Michael Kolhaas, who tries to assert his image of justice by force, or to the tragicomic exploits of Don Quixote, whose ideals engulf him completely, dominating his behaviour while the reality of others is neutralized in an hallucinatory image. If an individual remains at the stage of value deviation without necessarily proceeding to deviant behaviour, he can still be recognized as a value deviant and be stigmatized as such.

4. *The privileged:* Auguste Comte, that cornerstone of positivism who initiated an intellectual revolution in 19th century Europe, was living for quite a long time on the earnings of his prostitute wife. This did not harm his eminent status among philosophers, statesmen, theologians and businessmen.

As a sweeping generalization, we can state that those nearer to the law-makers and rule-setters feel freer to infringe upon these laws and rules without being stigmatized or regarding themselves as deviant. "What the Rabbi permits himself to do, should be forbidden to an ordinary Jew." Ranulf and Aristophanes inform us that the Athenian aristocrats revered the traditional morality in public but never took it seriously in private. In "Ion" Euripides eulogizes the rape of Kreusa as a young girl by the God Apollo who apparently had a taste for minors. Kreusa laments and accuses: "You, son of Leto, who

84

dispense your oracles to all without distinction, you, the lawgiver, you allow yourself at the same time to ravish maidens and desert them to beget children and not care if they die." The Greek deities with the human frailties not unlike the mortal elites felt themselves free to infringe upon laws that they themselves had made. The proximity of the lawgivers to the law seems to make them lax in compliance. Agostino Chiqi had one mistress buried in the chapel of St. Gregorio, and had his son by another mistress baptized in the presence of the Pope and fourteen cardinals.[12] Simony, the perennial device for filling the purses of the higher echelons of the church, was formally punishable as heresy with perpetual seclusion. But the Inquisition was far from eager to prosecute simoniacs; in fact it appears never to have prosecuted them.[13] The benefit to clergy of both *ratione persona* and *ratione materiale* amounted to relative, and in some cases, complete immunity of the theocratic elite of the Middle Ages from criminal prosecution.

One explanation for the lack of social stigma in these cases is that "the privileged" usually belong to the power and social elite of society, and that stigma on the social level is an act of power perpetrated by those who are in possession of this power: the privileged are usually the stigmatizers.

It would seem, therefore, that those who wield the power to stigmatize will be reluctant to apply it to themselves. C. Wright Mills' analysis of the political, social and business power-elite of the U.S.[14] revealed an image of this elite which is not necessarily characteristic of the U.S. only. The ruling elite of the U.S.S.R., the British Establishment and the power castes in countries which have had enough time to breed them, will reflect *mutatis mutandis,* a similar image. There is a social similarity and affinity between the members of these castes. A business executive is appointed as a government executive. A lawyer representing big business or a politician is appointed to the judiciary. A Nixon and a Dewey can represent big business. Top executives of General Motors and Ford Motors can be appointed as Secretaries of Defense. A Pompidou, chairman of the Rothschild Bank, can become President of France. In the U.S.S.R. the political, economic and army elites are even more socially monolithic because they passed together through the mills of the Communist Party.

Conflicts in these castes are, of course, rife, but cohesion is much more fundamental and it is held in a balance of checks and counter-checks. Mills says: "The major vested interests (of business, labour and government) often compete less with one another in their effort to promote their several interests than they coincide on many points of interest and, indeed, come together under the umbrella of government. The units of economic and political power not only become larger and more centralized; they come to coincide in interest and to make explicit as well as tacit alliances."[15]

Indeed, the non-stigmatization of elite cliques and caste members is often the result of tacit, covert or subterranean affinity of explicit "give and take" arrangements. The tacit subterranean attitude stems from an identification with reference, membership and other "We" group members: "No harm, if old Charley lets off some steam"; "This is the way it always was with Jones, even in his school days"; "I remember once it happened to me also"; "We always do these things, don't we?"

Another attitude is that "we (the elite) have our extra responsibilities so we must also have our extra privileges". This takes many forms, ranging from pre-paid fishing trips and call-girls as part of one's pay-roll or expense accounts, to the practice of leaders of hard-of-hearing associations who allow themselves to shun and snub socially the individuals with deafness (or other handicaps) who actually raised them to prominence. To this Goffman comments stoically: "It is known that a confirmed high position in some small close-knit groups can be associated with a license to deviate and hence to be a deviator. The relation of such a deviator to the group and the conception members have of him are such as to withstand restructuring by virtue of the deviation."[16]

The overt arrangements for a relative immunity from stigma

86

and sanction are various "fund-raising" procedures of political parties which range from mild blackmail to straightforward extortion and embezzlement. The "fix" arrangements among the law enforcement agencies and the politico-economic elites, the symbiosis between the gambling, narcotics, and procuring syndicates and some of the show business and entertainment professions and the mutual favoritism among the various power elites are other examples of this. These arrangements are held together and perpetuated by the realization of the various elite factions that "we are all in the same boat" and "each one of us has a skeleton in his cupboard". If one is stigmatized, the others are bound to follow. Disclosure, divulging information to "unauthorized bodies" or worse, or exposing oneself to stigma, is the ultimate sin. This is the main reason why anti-graft or anti-corruption campaigns are not Herculean tasks, but are, in fact, quite harmless, because the campaigners wish to reverse roles, and wish to stigmatize the stigmatizers—an almost impossible task. Short of successful revolution these reformers generally end up by being stigmatized themselves as "radicals", "troublemakers", "unsound of mind", "Don Quixotes" or "enemies of the people". They underrated the potency of social stigma; they are weak and are therefore the recipients and not the wielders of stigma.

The extent and volume of norm violation, legal or otherwise, of the power elites have been recently studied widely. The pioneering studies of Sutherland on white collar crime are notable.[17] A remark of his on the conflict theory of the social system substantiates, to a certain extent, our observations as to the unstigmatized deviation of the privileged power elite. "When an interest group secures the enactment of a law (or, for that matter, upholds or promulgates another social norm), it secures the assistance of the state in a conflict with a rival interest group; the opposition of the rival group thus becomes criminal . . . wrongful acts are characteristic of all classes in present-day society; the upper classes are subtle in their wrongdoing, the underprivileged classes are politically important and they prohibit the wrongful acts of underprivileged classes, but the laws are defined and implemented in such manner that many of the wrongful acts of the upper classes do not come within their scope."[18].

Short[19] and Porterfield[20] showed the relative immunity of men and youth of the upper classes from arrest and stigma for their crimes or social deviations. The Kefauver hearings on organized crime[21] and other sources cited by Mills[22] examine the exposed tenth of the iceberg of crime and deviation of "the privileged". We can only guess about the submerged parts of this iceberg, which are not only unstigmatized but also not detected. The deviation of "the privileged" is not stigmatized because it is institutionalized.

The elite's preoccupation with aggression stems from time immemorial. Wars and leadership in wars were their natural and most important tasks. From the Roman Centurion through the mediaeval Chevalier to the German duelling fraternity, aggression was considered manly. The modern power elites do not resort to the now unfashionable physical aggression, but an aggressive executive, a "tough" administrator, an "iron-fisted" chairman, are some of the coveted titles of "the privileged".

This elite's aversion to menial labour is proverbial; a gentleman was once defined as one whose hands were white and soft. The working or lower classes should work and not be lazy; this is the norm, but the aim of the elite is elegant leisure. The sanctity of private property is the norm, so long as it applies to their own property or interests and the attitude of others to this property, but not when it is applied to the interests of rivals or outgroups. "The privileged" do not regard themselves as value deviants nor are they stigmatized by others because of this selective morality. This moral schizophrenia has been called by Mills "the higher immorality". His following observations make an excellent epilogue to our present analysis. "The absence of any firm moral order of belief makes men in the mass all the more open to the manipulation and distraction of the world celebrities . . . to a sort of Machiavellianism-for-the-little-man. There they vicariously enjoy the prerogatives of the corporate rich, the nocturnal antics of the celebrity and the sad-happy life of the very rich."[23] Is this the reason why the masses are reluctant to stigmatize "the privileged"? How can they mar the idols of their dreams and fantasies?

5. *The Levantine:* The extreme manifestation of the levantine is behaviour according to the external forms and attributes of a culture while being ignorant or disregarding its contents and intrinsic values. It is manifest with members of oriental and eastern cultures who are exposed to European culture, and also in other cultural contexts. The Middle Eastern levantine adopts occidental languages, dress, mannerisms, and takes care to furnish his house according to the latest ads in glossy journals. He is not acquainted with nor did he have the opportunity to become interested in European literature, art, history or in internalizing the values of European culture.

In many instances, levantinism results from a failure or partial failure of imitation or rebellion. Individuals or groups in a society regard the adoption and absorption of a more "advanced" and "progressive" culture as a panacea for all miseries and social ills; eventually the task proves to be too formidable or the internal admixture of the cultures is seen to be impossible, and the innovation or rebellious zeal to integrate with the "enlightened" culture deteriorates into a superficial and shallow imitation of its external manifestations. On the group level, this can take the form of an Atatürk or a Zaglul Pasha burning with the fervour of making Turkey and Egypt "Modern Occidental" nations, ending in the pitiful image of levantine bourgoisie in Alexandria and Constantinople whose original oriental values and culture are still patent below the surface. The group's reaction towards this behaviour is far from derogatory, because usually those who display the external trademarks of the "advanced" and "modern" culture belong to the social elite and are idolized by the ignorant multitudes. European culture followed Spengler's design. It towered in its technical achievement to space flight and nuclear energy and declined in spirit to the abysmal nausea of Sartre, the hopeless men of Becket, the monstrosities of Ionesco, the agonies of Durrenmatt and the obscenities of Genet. This is a tired spirit, desiccated, inanimate, hovering pointlessly like last year's cobwebs in the high arches of a Gothic cathedral, deserted by its spiders long ago. But in the not distant past the spirit of Europe was a carnivore, devouring, swallowing, destroying, incorporating and changing less predatory cultures than itself. On its way it left many victims who have been afflicted in various ways and manners; one of the hangovers of this carnivorous European gluttony is levantinism. The levantine is essentially a shallow absorber of culture because levantinism was mainly associated with members of oriental and mid-eastern cultures who have been exposed to European culture. However this may happen and must have happened with other predatory cultures like the Hellenic, the Islamic and the Hindu, the Egyptian, the Mayan and other carnivores who swept on their way, clashed with and devoured herbivores or less aggressive cultures.

Historically, a levantine, in the sociological connotation of the term, was a European who had "gone native" in the Middle-East. Only lately has levantinism been used (but not studied) in the sense of the present context.

A blending of cultures, in this sense, can produce a new organic entity whereas the levantine melange is bound to remain a barren admixture. Kroeber says: "Cultures can blend to almost any degree and not only thrive but perpetuate themselves. The classic Greek civilization was a mixture of primitive Greek, Minoan, Egyptian and Asiatic elements; Japanese civilization is partly indigenous, partly Chinese, partly Indian and Western in its technology. . . the greater part of the context of every culture is probably of foreign origin, although assimilated into a whole that works more or less coherently and is felt as a unit."[24] However most encounters, or to be more exact, clashes of Western culture with other cultures have resulted in various degrees and shades of levantinism.

Toynbee says: "In the struggle for existence the West has driven its contemporaries to the wall and entangled them in the meshes of its economic and political ascendency but it has not

90

yet disarmed them of their distinctive cultures. Hard pressed though they are, they can still call their souls their own."[25]

This would be the case if the subjugated cultures managed to preserve the core of their indigenous cultures, which is hardly likely in the modern era of rapid social change. More often their cultural soul, to use Toynbee's simile, has withered away and in its place they have adopted the watered-down version of Western culture.

One of the most appropriate expositions of levantinism in the sense of our present context, although somewhat extreme, has been stated by Ben-Dov as follows: 'European culture' is indeed a formal value-system which has been abstracted from the various European national cultures. 'European Culture' as such has, therefore, no specific contents or concrete entity." He proceeds to describe the encounter between the Eastern Europeans who formed the elite of the Jewish community in British Mandatory Palestine, and this 'Western-culture', an encounter which resulted, according to Ben-Dov, in a superficial levantine absorption. He says: 'There have been, of course, Jews who did almost achieve an inner cultural identity and absorbed the contents of such national European cultures as the French, English, Polish or Czech cultures, but these Jews are irrelevant to our present discussion. The culture which has been established in Palestine was fostered by trustees of European culture who did not achieve inner identity, contentwise, with this European culture. Their inner cultural affinity remained Jewish. However, there is no such thing as a Jewish-European culture as far as the content of culture is concerned, because Europe has not been abstracted from Judaism, no intrinsic content of national Judaism has been incorporated in "Europeanism"—Jewish-European culture can therefore exist as a form devoid of contents."[26] This shell of European culture super-imposed on a content-less Judaism is nothing but levantinism as conceived in our context. Levantinism is the offspring of a clash, a conflict which has been solved in a unique way. This holds true both on the social and on the personal levels.

We have already mentioned that levantinism of groups can be the result of culture conflict due to sudden and abrupt social change. This, of course, is one of the basic premises of Durkheim as to the genesis of anomie, but we are confining our analysis to culture as experienced by groups or individuals in the process of internal or external migration. Rapid industrialization or urbanization or other factors linked to internal migration cause groups and individuals to move from rural to urban areas whereupon the tribal, familial or communal structures which supported their normative system suddenly looses its binding power: the "wetbacks" who cross over the Mexican border to the U.S., the South American Indian villagers who flock into big cities, the African near-areas labour force which migrates to the big towns as household help or menial labourers, the migrant lads from the Arab villages in the Galilee who flow into Tel Aviv as construction workers or dishwashers. This sudden transition leaves a wide open gap, which is filled by the least resistant and most conspicuous aspects of city culture, such as neon lights, technical gadgets, movies, entertainment, flashy clothes and all the other externalized attributes of the street culture. The same process takes place with external immigration: the Puerto Ricans in New York, the West Indians in London and certain immigrant groups in Israel.

The levantinization generally occurs when the encounter of the migrant patterns of culture with the receiving ones is in the form of a clash: the migrant patterns usually give way and disintegrate, a value confusion ensues, and the absorption of the receiving culture, e.g., over-rapid "Americanization" or "Israelification", occurs in an externalized, shallow, levantine manner.

This process has been avoided by some of the Japanese and Jewish cultural enclaves in the U.S. and some of the Kurdish or Morrocan communities in Israel, which have kept relatively intact the social and cultural institutions of their countries of origin. This preservation exercised a degree of social control and helped to preserve the cohesion of the family unit.

The aetiology of levantinism can generally be traced to a failure of innovation: the Afro-Asian intellectual, the South American revolutionary, the idealistic communist. They bring from abroad or from books new ideas, new techniques, schemes for raising the standard of living, eliminating malaria, trachoma and syphilis, introducing more efficient and less corrupt bureaucracies and installing a postal service or a telephone system that really works. Reality, however, is rarely cooperative: there are no roads to carry heavy trucks to convey equipment. There is no money, no trained workers to construct the roads; very few people understand technical matters, the population is so entrenched in its traditional routine that few avail themselves of or are even interested in new services. The Western idea of hard work, the concepts of accuracy or time itself are foreign, undesirable or meaningless—what is the big hurry? And the great dream deteriorates into rusty, unused or broken equipment, the clerks continue their perennial slumber, with timetables and efficiency charts decorating their desks or walls. The ideas of progress or innovation are slowly covered by dust from the scorched desert plains or by entangled vines reaching from the humid jungle. The innovator is discouraged, deflated, disgusted and succumbs to his private hibernation retreat surrounded by the external remnants of his dream, a few gadgets, a few beverages, a few clothes and half-baked knowledge sent over to him from the faraway "progressive" culture. This is the main current of individual levantinism.

6. *Defiance:* This is the syndrome of value-deviation described in the introduction to this work as the subjectivist's detachment from group values. The defiant stands apart from the group in his beliefs and values, but in his behaviour he does not necessarily deviate from the accepted social norms. The defiant is the value-deviant for whom Orwell's Big Brother created the "thought police", but who to a lesser degree is stigmatized in most societies by the branding mechanism of the group, although behaviourally, he is conforming, or to be more exact, he does not display any overt signs of deviation. The defiant who is "inner-oriented"

feels that his quest for meaning or his struggles (if he has any) with problems of creativity would not be solved by anchoring himself on the *esprit de corps* of the herd. Outwardly, he may perform his daily task and infringe upon no more norms than his fellow citizens. However, he does not go out of his way to be "a good mixer", or "a right guy". His behaviour conformity consists of the dues he pays to society to be left alone in peace, but he is not—because his spectator role towards the group and its values is misunderstood and feared. The value-deviant does not cherish the role of an outsider, but his wish and efforts to be accepted as such by the group can prove to be futile. A positive feed-back cycle of rejection and counter-rejection ultimately leads him to be branded with the stigma of the outsider.

The sense of meaninglessness and the absurd have been documented by the existentialist philosophers. Camus says: "This world in itself is not reasonable, that is all that can be said. But what is absurd is the confrontation of this irrational world and the wild longing for clarity whose call echoes in the human heart." [27]

When group goals, causes and aspirations become non-feasible or seem to lead nowhere, the agonizing meaninglessness of everything becomes clear to a person who had previously acquired a personal normative system. True defiance begins from here; without it the negation of everything takes the form of the obscenity of a Norman Mailer or the self pity of a Henry Miller.

Senselessness, meaninglessness, absurdity or nausea acts mainly in the realm of social interaction, i.e., attempts at social solidarity. Kierkegaard calls the social group "an all-embracing something which is nothing. . . consisting of unreal individuals who never are and never can be united in an actual situation or organization". [28] For Sartre, society is the untruth. [29] The relationship of all alters to ego are, by definition, fragmentary, unreal, disturbing and nauseating.

The negative aspect of defiance leads to the rejection of society, of the group, as untrue existence, as meaningless interaction devoid of real value. This rejection is the condition precedent

94

to accepting the individual as the only true and meaningful entity. The much-abused existentialist statement that "If God is dead, Man is God" is imbued for our purposes with a new meaning; when all the utopian deities become mirages, the group "isms" nothing but words and the solidarity apostles prove to be false prophets, the individual human being becomes the centre of creation.

Karl Jaspers voices this revelation when he says: "This limitation (the impossibility of subjectively knowing alter) leads me to myself, where I can no longer withdraw behind an objective point of view that I am merely representing, where neither I myself nor the existence of others can any longer become an object for me."[30]

The extreme manifestation of defiance negated the value of all solidarity and group control, irrespective of its ideational basis—the metaphysical, categorical imperative, the social ethics of Durkheim, the social religion of Saint Simon or the "historical necessity" of Marx.

On the behavioural level Camus' "judge-penitent"[31] portrays the defiant's rejection of group goals, social values and norms, not a "sour-grapes" rejection or a retreat fired by resentment. The "judge-penitent" achieved success and social acceptance, but rejected them wilfully and consciously because the social system and its norms seemed to him absurd, i.e., meaningless in the logical, teleological and ontological sense, a system that operated from nowhere toward nowhere, and seemed to serve or have served no purpose. He was, of course, stigmatized and rejected by society, but then in the water-front bistro in the Hague, social stigma does not count.

On the philosophical level the defiant is a Sisyphus. A Camusian Sisyphus, who conforms in his behaviour, performing "the chain of daily gestures. . .with a heavy yet measured step toward the torment of which he will never know the end."[32] He knows that the whole thing is meaningless, he rolls the rock uphill, licking stamps, paying bills, commuting to work, pounding the typewriter, selling stockings, while being fully aware of the absurdity of his perpetually self-repeating toil. He feels he is a guinea-pig in some incomprehensible experiment but he does not complain, having the professional pride of a guinea-pig. He wishes to be left alone but he is not. Society does not allow half-hearted external conformity, social stigma would push either toward value conformity—Orwell's Winston believing that $2+2$ makes 5 and liking the idea, or towards behaviour deviation like the "judge-penitent" spending his last days in a bare room, dying as an outcast and a pariah.

7. *Successful sanction-orientation:* For many people the barrier against crime and deviation is not the restraining power of an internalized norm, but the fear of painful sanction. If they regard themselves as immune from the sanction or the possibility of being detected as very remote, they would and do commit crimes and deviant acts and are not stigmatized. We have already noted that crimes known to the police represent only a part of the total number of offences committed. The rate of many deviations, from homosexuality, lesbianism, etc., to smoking "pot", is believed to be much higher than the "official" or "known" rates.[33]

These secret crimes and deviations would rock the foundations of the normative system of society were they to come to the public knowledge, but luckily enough "what people do not know does not hurt them" and the multitudes of secret criminals and deviants would join in the chorus (they more vociferously than others), righteously stigmatizing one of their crowd who happened to be detected and exposed.

8. *The "true" deviant:* Finally, we have the category of those who openly reject the group's values, break its norms and are subsequently stigmatized. These include most of society's "official" criminals, pariahs and outcasts.

In our model of social deviation, we analysed three independent variables: value deviation, deviant behaviour and social stigma, the independent variables being the total syndrome of social deviation of individuals. It is our hypothesis that the power of these three independent variables is far from equal, the most

96

forceful being social stigma; the second, deviant behaviour and the least powerful, value deviation.

The following is a paradigm of social deviation:

Value deviation	Deviant behaviour	Social stigma	
—	—	—	*"true" solidarist*
+	—	—	*the levantine*
—	+	—	*the privileged*
+	+	—	*successful sanction-orientation*
—	—	+	*victimized*
+	—	+	*defiant*
—	+	+	*inner-conflict*
+	+	+	*"true" deviant*

(+)   *signifies presence of the variable*
(—)   *signifies absence of the variable*

We thus have seven major types and grades of social deviation which could be sub-divided when actual testing and measurement is carried out. These types are ideal and therefore non-existent, but they could serve as interval marks on our continuum of conformity and deviation. The further grading of the types, their place on the continuum and the soundness of the model itself, will be determined by subsequent empirical testing.

CHAPTER V

THE PROCESS OF SOCIAL STIGMA

> *"Think of it please, I am different from others, yes different, but I am not an enemy. I am a soviet person and my art is not subversive—it is only different. In this tense atmosphere anything which is different would seem subversive—but why do you have to look for enemies, to create monsters where there are none?"**

THE MODEL

The predisposing factors mentioned in an earlier chapter can be quantified into a configuration of probabilities indicating that a certain individual or group will be socially stigmatized. In this chapter we shall try to delineate the causal process which leads the stigmatizers to brand a social Mark of Cain on individuals and groups. Our proposed model synchronizes two levels of causal analysis. The first is a configuration of predisposing factors, the second, a chain of dynamic pressures leading a given individual to associate with criminal groups and absorb their patterns of behaviour. The predisposition configuration is a set of factors which in a given culture raise the probability that an individual exposed to them will be more vulnerable to the second process. We stress the cultural element because the factors in the predisposition configuration vary from culture to culture. Our model obviously cannot enumerate all factors, but consists rather of those independent variables found to be significantly associated with the dependent variable: social stigma. Our method of analysis is to trace first the psychogenic causal pressures of stigma, then the sociopsychological factors of stigma which stem from the relationship of the individual to his group; finally

---

* *Andrei Siniavsky. In his trial before the People's Tribunal in Moscow,* 1966.

to examine the meaning and nature of stigma as a social act of power.

A CAUSAL MODEL OF SOCIAL STIGMA

Deviant Behaviour   *predisposing factors*   *Value Deviation*

The Dynamic Process of Stigmatization

Psychogenic Motives

1. Outlet for Aggression.
2. Projection of Guilt.
3. Displacement of Resentment.
4. The stigmatized as "scapegoat".

Socio-Psychological Pressures

5. The Stigmatized a symbolic source of danger.
6. Relative powerlessness.
7. Vulnerability to the source of stigma.
8. "Somebody to look down upon".
9. "Explaining away" alter's achievement.

Social Level

Social Stigma as an Act of Power.

Stigma as an Outlet for Aggression and Projection of Guilt: Inner aggression and the projection of guilt for the stigmatizer's own deviational tendencies are the subsconscious sources of social stigma. On the subconscious level the urge to stigmatize is presumably linked to the inner aggression of individuals and groups. Inner negativity and group tension find at least partial release in the derogatory branding of individuals and groups. Social stigma is an institutionalized safety valve and is thus similar in function to the fights of the Roman gladiators, bullfights, public hangings, wrestling and boxing matches. The mechanism of projection as a psychogenic source of stigma has been described by Flugel as follows: "[People] experience delight in gossip and scandal in which they gloat over the pecadillos and moral frailties of their neighbours and acquaintances. They are indulging their own guilty desires vicariously, preserving their own virtue intact (the implication is that they themselves would never partake in such scandalous proceedings as those under discussion) and expressing their disapproval through appropriate inflections of the voice and shakings of the head."[1]

Stigma feeds, therefore, on guilt feelings that are in turn nurtured by the suppressed antisocial or deviational tendencies of the stigmatizer. Society is riddled with innumerable normative mandates, proscriptions and prohibitions. Faulty or inchoate internalization generates conflicts and pressures to infringe upon these norms, resulting in guilt feelings which feed the urge to stigmatize others whose overt behaviour seems contrary to the same norms. The stigma is a subconscious substitute for the sanction that the stigmatizer wishes to inflict upon himself. In psychoanalytic terminology the hypothesis is that the righteous indignation inherent in social stigma helps the super-ego of the stigmatizer in its constant battle with his own aggressive and deviational tendencies.

The psychoanalysts see a certain necessary equilibrium between the inner destructiveness and aggression of a person and the controlling checks of the super-ego: the stronger the person's inner deviational tendencies, the stronger will be his urge to stigmatize others. If the urge to stigmatize is strong, the super-ego would seem to be the loser in this struggle.

The pressures to stigmatize are directed more inwards than outwards, in that the real object is ego's own aggression, and the stigmatized alter is only a symbolic receptacle. This mechanism of projection sheds some light on the stigma of pollution mentioned in Chapter 1, which was branded on criminals in ancient and primitive societies. The projection of guilt can well account for the retributive passion against wrongdoers.

Even the rationale of the aggressive stigmatization was presented vicariously; the criminal's acts had raised the wrath of the gods which endangered the community.

Displacement of Resentment and the Stigmatized as "Scapegoat": The release of frustrations and resentment provided by the subconscious mechanism of transference and scapegoating is also the catalyst for the psychic genesis of social stigma and allows it to crystallize against a specific individual or group. If projection is the directing outwards of ego's own subjective states—here, aggression and negativity—"displacement", another psychoanalytic concept, imputes these inner states to the wrong objects or sources. Displacement in our case is the direction of aggression and resentment toward an untrue, a "displaced" source of the stigmatizer's own frustration. Both projection and displacement are defence mechanisms vital to the preservation of equilibrium. An individual's sanity is preserved by diversion of his gaze outward from the inner snake-pit of aggression. Attributing frustrations and failures to their true source, i.e., the self, can be damaging and sometimes disastrous. People cannot bear to face the truth on a cognitive level, so they impute the same intolerable attributes to some convenient and symbolically relevant others. These apparently basic mechanisms of survival were bestowed on individuals in society by whoever gave the carnivore its fangs and the scorpion its sting. Projection, transference and scapegoating are basically defence mechanisms of individuals in interaction. But the individuals availing themselves and making constant use of these processes (most of humanity, to some degree) are on the side of the stigmatizer and not of the stigmatized. We shall later see that stigma is one of the most potent cohesive elements which strengthen the normative systems of in-groups. An individual who pushes himself toward neurosis, depression and melancholia by opening the sluice gates of his inner inadequacies, is ill-equipped to be an "adjusted" member of society. Stigma is therefore a tool of the group, the collective, to ensure the supply of well-functioning spare-parts—the individuals.

Stigma strengthens the group, pacifies its individuals, and takes the bugs out of their system by projecting and displacing their mental malformations and moral excrements. If certain individuals, to some of whose innovations the group owes its welfare and progress, get badly hurt in the process, that is just too bad; one should know, as we have all known, from the XII Tables to Durkheim, that *Salus populi* is *suprema lex*. This fact is as inevitable as it is unpalatable—especially to those who were brought up to believe that cruelty lies only in the domains of the Jaguar, the horned viper, and the Marquis de Sade.

Scapegoating as a step on the path to social stigma can be traced to the ancient rites of the displacement of evil to inanimate objects, other people and gods. Frazer gives many instances of the displacement of evil to a human scapegoat who thereby becomes a vehicle for the evil which is carried away from the individual or group (in our case the stigmatizers).[2]

The dying god as a scapegoat, practised in many ancient and primitive societies, reaches its peak in the expiation of humanity's sins by the dying Christ on the Cross. Stoning is another case of the displacement and transference of evil and guilt to a human scapegoat. Everyone in the stoning group transfers—symbolically, by throwing the stone—the evil from himself to the presumed, and now obvious source of the evil, the stoned individual.[3]

The following are typical illustrations of the displacement mechanisms of scapegoating as the basis of social stigma.

Steinbeck recounts his conversation with an American farmer: "You think then we might be using the Russians as an outlet for something else, for other things."

"I didn't think that at all, sir, but I bet I'm going to. Why, I remember when people took everything out on Mr. Roosevelt. Andy Larsen got red in the face about Roosevelt one time when his hens got the croup. Yes sir," he said with growing enthusiasm, "those Russians got quite a load to carry. Man has a fight with his wife, he belts the Russians."

"Maybe everybody needs Russians, I'll bet even in Russia they need Russians, maybe they call it Americans."[4]

Adolf Hitler taught his followers to vent all their inner frustrations and all of their failures on the perennial scapegoat—the Jew: "The Jew founded capitalism and invented the saying that 'business passes over corpses'. The Jew founded world communism and became the common demagogue so that the stock exchange Jew and the Jewish labour leader work hand in hand (to subjugate and destroy the world). While Moses Kohn sits in the directors' meeting advocating a policy of firmness—that is, hostility in the face of the workers' demands—his brother, Issac Kohn, stands in the factory yards, stirring up the masses (thus creating confusion and havoc). The Jews are, therefore, a people of exploiters and rascals. The Jew never founded a culture but has destroyed hundreds of cultures. The Jew has nothing of his own to which he can point. Everything he has is stolen. Aryans and anti-Semites of all nations, unite in the struggle against the Jewish race of exploiters and oppressors of all nations."[5]

Another instance is the first-hand impressions of a journalist who recently visited China: "The U.S. plays the role of the constant arch-enemy. I participated in some anti-American demonstrations. Indeed the faces of the demonstrators were twisted with hatred. In Canton the 'platoon leaders' examined the ranks of the demonstrators and rehearsed with them the anti-American slogans. My interpreter, a gentle and intelligent student, told me about the skeletons of small children which have been exhumed from their graves in an American mission. The interpreter was convinced that the children did not die from disease but were killed by the nuns."[6]

In these instances the value of the displacement mechanism of scapegoating toward a whole group is in their extreme and clearly illustrative nature. The variations are numerous. An enemy of the people can be an individual, like Leon Trotsky, or an individual may transfer and generalize his hatred to a whole group. What is important for our present purposes is that the displacement channels the reservoirs of hatred and resentment bred by frustrations and failures towards an individual or a group who thus becomes the object of social stigma.

103

The Choice of Objects: The choice of objects of social stigma is governed by conspicuity and differences which arouse fear and anxiety in the stigmatizer. The latter is less able to identify with the victims and therefore projects and transfers to them his inner aggression and guilt in the form of social stigma. The choice of the objects is also determined by their relative powerlessness and vulnerability to stigma.

The choice of the stigmatized is, of course, very often rational and formalized as in the cases of clearly illegal or deviant behaviour. In other cases, although the choice is irrational and subconscious, it is not random. A major factor determining the choice is the objects' being different in a symbolically relevant way and therefore disturbing or appearing dangerous.

One of the most ancient sources of ethnocentrism lay in the fact that the members of out-groups were not only different, but actually dangerous; not potential but real enemies. [7]

In ancient Greece, where policy-making was quite often realistic, stigmatization by ostracism was achieved by "chipping off the tallest ears of corn", [8] those which seemed to be more conspicuous than necessary and the question which was asked from the assembly in a manner quite relevant to our context was: "Is there any man among you who you think is dangerous to the state? If so, who?" In other words, we have here conspicuity and danger; difference equals or implies danger—this seems to be the most obvious criterion for the attributes and therefore choice of the stigmatized. The same theme recurs with apparent clarity in Greek mythology and drama. It seems that the real reason underlying the punishment of Prometheus was not the ethically commendable deed of bringing fire to humanity, but that his outstanding knowledge of architecture, astronomy, mathematics, medicine, navigation and metallurgy filled Zeus with jealousy and anger. [9] Prometheus was not only an innovator, but outstanding, different (and therefore dangerous) in many other ways. Tantalus was another innovator who was punished for proving that the sun is a mass of white-hot metal. [10]

Greek tragedy shows in many instances that stigma befalls

a person who is too conspicuous, too wealthy, too successful or too wise, thereby bringing upon himself the jealousy of the gods (and man).[11] Stigma as sanction is therefore not necessarily gained by deviation from moral standards or laws. Man is often sanctioned for no apparent reason. A person has his *moira* and if he exceeds it by being conspicuous in any way he commits *hubris* and arouses the jealousy of the strikingly anthropomorphic Greek gods.

Herodotus recounts the message of Artabanos to Xerxes: "You see that God hurls his bolt against those living beings that tower above the rest. He does not suffer them to exalt themselves. The small ones on the other hand do not bother him. You see that the lightning always strikes the tallest houses and trees. For God loves to set a limit to everything that rises too high. For God does not suffer anyone but himself to harbour proud thoughts."[11a]

The *hubris* of Agamemnon was his being awarded a hero's welcome by the Greeks as the "highest of all who walk on earth today."[12] We may note that though it was the crowd who committed the *hubris* Agamemnon was doomed, because: "The black furies wait, and when man has grown by luck, not justice, great, with overturn of chance; they wear him to a shade, and cast down to perdition, who shall save him?

In the excess of fame is danger: "With a jealous eye the lord Zeus in a flash shall smite him."[13]

Again we have a clue to the main criterion of social stigma: "In excess of fame is danger". But to whom? Apparently, it is to the jealous multitudes (the gods). Drachmann comments on the theme of punishment without offence in Greek tragedy: "Our first question, when the immediate effect of the magnificent drama has subsided, is this: But what has he done? Done? answers the Greek in astonishment, he has not done anything. That is just the point of it; it has all happened unknown to him.—Well but then it is all the most outrageous injustice.—I do not understand you, says the Greek; do you mean to deny that such things can happen to you, any day, nay at any moment? Or are you

105

even for an instant safe from the invasion of the most appalling horror that your mind can grasp? If you are, you had best realize what human life is. This is what Sophocles' drama should help you to do." [14] The epitome of this theme is reached with Polycrates, King of Samos, whose *hubris,* according to Herodotus, was his conspicuous success and outstanding prosperity.

It must be stressed that conspicuousness, as a criterion for the choice of the stigmatized, links up with our exposition in Chapter I of stigma as a means of social control. The innovator, the different and strange, apart from arousing fear, are also likely to be non-conformist and are therefore more prone to conformity by the pressures of social stigma. This is also tied up with the mechanism of taboos which we have already mentioned briefly. The most discernible criteria for pronouncing a thing, or a person, as taboo are that they are strange, incomprehensible and therefore dangerous. [15]

The Azande will proclaim as witches persons who are deformed, ill-tempered, glum and who behave in a bizzarre manner—all these signs show their potential danger, and they are therefore stigmatized and ostracized. [16] We mentioned earlier that the criteria for proclaiming a person a heretic in the Middle Ages were his different ways of life, peculiarities of conversation, strange language, dress, manners or unusual restraint in conduct. [17] If a Jew is bizarrely attired, a Negro black, if someone has a strange family life and different sexual mores, a foreigner acts queerly or an intellectual has strange and dangerous ideas, he is different, incomprehensible, and therefore arouses anxiety. The stigmatizer cannot identify with them, they are "not people like us" [18] and they are thus suitable to be the objects of the stigmatizer's projection and displacement mechanisms.

Another factor that helps the stigmatizer to choose his object is the latter's relative powerlessness. Although this seems to contradict our previous section where the stigmatized was described as a source of danger and anxiety, and therefore presumably powerful, it certainly is more than random coincidence that the subconscious of the stigmatizer imputes danger to individuals who in fact prove to be powerless. The witches could not quench with all their supernatural power the fires of the *auto-da-fé*.

Levy-Bruhl states that, in many societies, powerlessness, misery and misfortune alone are considered proof of guilt and the plight of the victims is considered to be justified even by themselves.[19] The powerless of low socioeconomic status are thus choice objects for stigma.

Trotsky, the fearsome Enemy of the People, was pitifully vulnerable to the assassin's ice-pick, and the omnipotent Elders of Zion were disastrously absent when they should have prevented the massacre of six million Jews.

These, of course, are extreme instances but our contention is that in the realms of crime and deviation the stigmatized is invariably in the weaker position. The offender, when arrested, tried and imprisoned, is confronted by the forceful machinery of police, judiciary and prison service. The press then puts the finishing touches to his social image.

The stigma of deviation is also attached to those who cannot fight back. The stigmatizing organs of society apparently choose the areas of least resistance—not unlike the bully who makes sure that his victims are unlikely to strike back. The village vicar, the local rabbi and the suburban priest are quicker to pour fire and brimstone on the village whore or on the public-house drunks than on the mayor who patronizes the whore or on the Scotch-soaked local magistrate.

The third factor determining the choice of object is the conscious or subconscious vulnerability. The "accident-prone" person has his counterpart in semi-scientific exposition of an individual who "attracts aggression" and antagonism. The psychoanalysts identify this factor with the inner guilt of a person continuously seeking punishment to expiate the guilt of an unresolved oedipal or other complex.

Religion can enhance this process, because, according to Theodore de Beze's *Confession of Sins*, beatitude consists in "recognizing our faults more and more" so that sanctification consists of a strengthening of our feeling of complicity in the vastness of evil committed in our world. This makes for the raw material of stigma. Here the quest for stigmatization is matched by the urge to stigmatize.

Somebody to Look Down Upon:
Social stigma in an achievement-obsessed culture serves as an illusory achievement technique where real achievement has failed or is insufficient (as defined by the stigmatizer). Because achievement is relative ego can "achieve" by derogatorily branding (stigmatizing) alter. An individual growing up in a conflict-ridden family or disorganized and tension-ridden community or society is inclined, in varying degrees, to anxiety and insecurity which lead him in turn to excessive ambition and thirst for power in order to overcome his inner anxiety and to achieve the security he lacks. In our achievement-obsessed culture this leads, as Karen Horney states, to a self-defeating vicious circle: achievement of social goals meets an objective barrier insofar as upper-vertical mobility is pyramid shaped and the "room at the top" becomes progressively limited; moreover, there are class, race and other non-merit barriers to achievement. The more one fails, the greater becomes one's frustration and insecurity, and the more one is compulsively driven towards achievement to quench the thirst for security.[20] This quest for the "jackpot" frequently ends in further failure. Here projection and transference techniques come in to provide an answer, an explanation of the failures in achievement by transferring responsibility to a scapegoat. When an achievement-obsessed individual or group craving for success in compensation for insecurity and anxiety does not achieve these goals, it will try to "achieve" status—not to achieve higher status itself, but to lower the status of the stigmatized. This is the actual function of stigma, and is recognizable in the gossiping matron belittling the looks of a special rival as well as in the perennial inclination of this socially insecure lower middle class to ethnocentrism, anti-semitism and racial discrimination.

Tenenbaum, writing one of the most penetrating analyses of Nazi racism says: "In general it seems that there could be no 'true Aryan' without a Jew somewhere in the background. This may sound like a paradox, yet it can be easily explained. German racists needed both an 'Aryan' and a 'Semite' race to balance each other off. As in a cable-car mechanism, the two pulleys are needed to compensate each other: down goes the Jew, up goes the Nordic. The superiority of the Aryan is predicated on the inferiority of the Semite."[21]

A recent study on the genesis of anti-semitism in Germany and Austria concludes, after a rigorous statistical analysis, that, in these countries, it drew very little strength from the working classes or the aristocracy, and grew largely from the lower middle classes, mainly the proliferating new class of white-collar workers. "Economically they were almost indistinguishable from the proletariat. In social status, however, they were distinct from the working classes and in a society as rigidly hierarchic as the German, they were strongly endowed with *Standesdunkel* or 'consciousness of class superiority'; they were therefore preoccupied with keeping the distance from those below."[22] The more they could stigmatize, degrade and oppress those below, in this case the Jews, the higher became their relative status. There is no objective point or level from which status and class can be measured. If one cannot climb the tower, one can deepen the abyss. One of the highest scores for anti-semitism in the 'Authoritarian Personality' study belonged to members of other minority groups who experienced severe status anxiety. The Mexican by birth and the Italian-American displayed the pattern of "shifting the onus" of defamation to other groups in order to put their own social status in a better light.[23] Indian castes just above the untouchable Sudras are the most ardent supporters of the caste system.

The need for someone to "look down upon" as a source of social stigma can be seen on both sides of the legal barricade. In order to achieve its objectives, the police, society's main organ of social control, must be the ardent protectors of society's norms and they are presumed to be adherents of its normative system. Compulsive over-conformity is the rule, being more middle-class than the middle classes, holier than the Pope. However, many policemen are far from the idealized image of the law-enforcer, and compulsive over-conformity can lead more to ritualism than to actual achievement within the ranks or outside it. Many police officers are arrivistes in the ranks of the middle class, the acknowledged reference group of most police forces. They may have originated from the lower classes, working classes and slums. They usually experience status anxiety and can be alienated within the authoritarian and bureaucratic machine of their force. This, as Chwast points out, can be transmitted lower down by "driving his knee into the groin of a sexual offender while imprecating 'You dirty degenerate', or rudely ignoring a Negro woman's hesitant request for directions, or referring to newly arrived, foreign-born residents of low-income areas as 'animals' ".[24] The criminals on the other side of the barricade are quite hierarchical in the structure of their groups and a professional burglar looks down with scorn on a mere pickpocket. In a study carried out recently in Israel as to the relationship between the prostitute and her pimp, it was found that the prostitute's necessity for her pimp, is mainly emotional; in most cases she recruits herself a pimp, a man she can call her own, even if she has to pay for it enormously—all her earnings and frequent beatings; this need is strongly linked to her social stigma and degradation. One of the prostitutes said to the interviewer: "I don't kid myself, I know I'm a whore, and I admit it to myself, I am also prepared to hear it from everybody else except from my man. We are partners in this mud together and he has no business snubbing me. I dare him to call me a whore and I'll throw him into the gutter. I need someone I can look straight in the eye, and who is in the same dirt as I am in. No!" she added emphatically, "he is even dirtier because he lives off my body—it is kind of good to have somebody around who is dirtier than a whore, dirtier than myself."[25] Let us conclude this section by referring to the scholastic work *On Defamation*

110

by Hafetz-Haim, one of the most renowned rabbinical moralists of 19th century Europe. He scorned the slanderers, the coarse-of-heart, who strive to heighten themselves by belittling others who, by ridiculing others, deem themselves wise and gentry of the land.

They are no doubt blind to their own afflictions; otherwise they would not have scorned their peers.[26]

"Explaining away" alter's achievement. Stigma attached to alter's person, related to his successful innovation or imputed to his achievement, can "explain away" his performance so as to narrow the gap of "relative-achievement" between ego and alter. Here again we may start from Rosenzweig's basic dichotomy of an individual's or group's reaction to failure and frustration:[27] they can blame themselves or blame society. In the case of self-blame the process of stigma does not, of course, pertain. In the so-called extro-punitive instance, where ego's defeat, loss of face or poor performance is attributed to alter, to a group or to a society at large, stigma can be invoked to "explain away" ego's defeat and alter's victory-

It should be pointed out that material explanation of alter's performance is impossible, because it implies ego's inferiority and constitutes self-blame. The relevant reaction is derogatory and stigmatizing, to explain away alter's superiority. This is another instance of "relative-achievement": if I cannot be as good as alter, I can at least neutralize his success by bringing it down to my level. The Nazi ideology, for instance, stressed that Germany did not actually lose the war, the war which should have been fought properly, as among knights of the Nibelungen. "It was not they, the celestial Teutons, who had lost the war, it was the Jews and the Marxists who slyly and surreptitiously had administered the fatal stab in the back which made them reel and falter."[28] It was not a fair fight. However, no logical or material link need be apparent between the stigma and the superiority of alter; usually the connection is superfluous or non-existent. Cause and effect seem to be irrelevant for "explaining

111

away" alter's success by means of stigma. This is most apparent in the stigma applied against creative innovators.

The following imaginary conversations could have taken place, and there is reason to believe that in some form variations of them did take place.

"Van Gogh a painter? Don't say that or Ingres will turn over in his grave. That fellow can't draw a straight line—besides he is an exceptionally thick-headed Dutchman."

"That fellow Gershwin takes old Chasidic melodies and makes jazz out of them—anyhow, what does a Jew know about Negro music?"

"I say, old boy, Allenby tells me that fellow Lawrence made the Arabs fight the Turks—he says it is a real uprising." "Yes, that pompous bantam, always the loner, no *esprit de corps;* he always acted kind of queer."

Another type of "explaining away" by stigma links the stigma to alter's achievement or better performance by a seemingly "logical" explanation—it "explains" alter's specific performance in a given case in terms of his presumed derogatory attributes or traits.

"Yes, Joe won yesterday at poker—it is the gypsy blood in him, they are always sharp at cards."

"Bill won the weight-lifting contest yesterday in the gym." "Yes, it runs in the family, his father was a porter and used to carry round pianos."

This instance of "explaining away" by stigma is masterfully portrayed by O'Henry; at the factory-workers' ball, two lads compete for one girl: one of them is more handsome and a better dancer; for some time he passes as Irish but when he turns out to be a "dago", the other loses all interest in the competition—he has already won by being Irish, and Guiseppe the "dago" has lost even before he starts to dance.

Social Stigma as an Act of Power:
The stigma of maladjustment is acquired in a way similar to that of a criminal. It is not necessarily linked with ethics, metaphysics

112

or justice but with an act of power directed against an individual or a group too conspicuously different, whose existence or behaviour is detrimental to the power-backed stigmatizing agencies. The essence of social stigma on the social level is embodied in Inez Cirano's statement to Garcin in Sartre's *No Exit:* "You are a coward, Garcin, because I want it to be so."

The Roman *infamia* is the most appropriate illustration of stigma as an act of power. The criteria for this declaration were so amorphic as to amount to a complete freedom for the Censor to brand any person he chose with the stigma of *infamia.*[29]

We might refer to Thrasymachus' assertion that justice is the interest of the stronger[30] and Machiavelli's formula that virtue = intellect + force.

Sumners' description of the normative basis of social mores fits the conception of stigma as a social act. "Nothing but might has ever made right. If a thing has been done and is established by force, it is right in the only sense we know, and rights will follow from it which are not vitiated at all by the force in it. We find men and parties protesting, declaiming, complaining of what is done and which they say is not 'right' but only force. They lose sight of the fact that disputes always end in force. Therefore, might has made all the right which ever has existed or exists now. The habit of using jural concepts, which is now so characteristic of our mores, leads us into vague and impossible dreams of social affairs, in which metaphysical concepts are supposed to realize themselves, or are assumed to be real."[31]

Pressure, coercion and stigma are applied by the group (or by individuals who possess enough power to do so) when some interest or value of the group (or of a powerful individual) has been infringed upon or injured. No other criterion has the same significance. Justice (natural or positive), ethics, piety and "positive" values are at best only formal and idealized criteria for differentiating between the delinquent and the good, the misfits and the "adjusted." Our hypothesis is that the criterion which actually triggers the process of dividing the criminal and non-conformist from the law-abiding and conforming population

113

is the power element of social stigmatizing. No other criteria would serve to define the Mythical crime of Prometheus and the anti-social behaviour of Socrates, Alcibiades, Savonarola and Jesus Christ; they acted against the interests of groups which had enough power to ostracize them and ultimately to exterminate them.

In the last analysis a criminal, a deviant or an anti-social person is one who is branded and treated as such by a group or an individual with the power to do so. The Mark of Cain, therefore, consists mainly in an exercise of power by the branders to put tags on individuals or groups who "don't fit in". The branding of a person as "deviant", "queer", troublemaker", "rigid" and "maladjusted" is inherent in the normative authority of the power elite in a group. In the case of crime there are certain legal barriers to the branding machinery of society, but not so with stigmatization of a person as deviant and maladjusted.

The term "adjustment" in itself is associated with the use of power and pressure. In fact, "adjustment" is a virtue prescribed by those whose interests it serves, who have the power to enforce it and apply sanctions to those who are maladjusted. It need not necessarily involve real conformity; and superficial compliance is sufficient. What you have to do is "not to be a troublemaker", "to do what you are told", and "not to rock the boat".

The criteria for stigmatizing a person as deviant are necessarily amorphous, and change with every shift in the power structure of government, bureaucracy, custom and other components of the normative system in a given society. The effects of social stigma are powerful. Once started, the segregating and stigmatizing pressure leads down, and the way back upwards to regain social status is blocked by many barriers.

Criminals, pariahs and outcasts are made, therefore, not so much by law, morals or God, as by man through social stigma.

Camus' judge-penitent assures us: "Believe me, religions are on the wrong track the moment they start to moralize and fulminate commandments. God is not needed to create guilt or to punish. Our fellow men suffice, aided by ourselves. You were

114

speaking of the Last Judgment. Allow me to laugh respectfully. I shall wait for it resolutely, for I have known what is worse, the judgment of men. For them there are no extenuating circumstances."

Mr. K. was not familiar with the nature of social stigma when he insisted on his innocence; the Mark of Cain alone was more than enough to establish his guilt.

In the following chapter we shall present an empirical application of the stigma theory to the aetiology of prostitution.

CHAPTER VI

AN EMPIRICAL REFERENT: SOCIAL STIGMA AND PROSTITUTION

> *. . . But I would like to know what kind of blood is in my boys. When they grow up– won't I be looking for something in them?" "Yes, you will. And I will warn you now that not their blood but your suspicion might build evil in them." "But their blood–" "I don't very much believe in blood", said Samuel. "I think when a man finds good or bad in his children he is seeing only what he planted in them after they cleared the womb".* *

In this chapter we shall attempt to apply the stigma theory of crime and deviation to the aetiology of prostitution in authoritarian oriental families. We propose to apply this theory in a form amenable to research on the genesis of prostitution as reflected in a proposed research population of prostitutes in Israel of North African origins. It should be pointed out, however, that the theoretical exposition of stigma goes beyond the topic of prostitution, which is here used as an empirical referent. If we regard prostitution as a specific type of deviant behaviour we do not exclude it from the generic pattern of social deviation. This chapter is thus an application of the stigma theory to one type of deviation as an illustrative case.

In our analysis we will first apply stigma premises to the aetiology of prostitution; and then examine some primary empirical findings, methodological suggestions and referents.

We shall present the model of the stigma theory as applied to prostitution and then examine each component separately.

STIGMA TRANSMISSION

The stigma is presumably transmitted by the parents, especially the father, and sometimes by the siblings or other individuals

* John Steinbeck, *East of Eden*

116

outside the nuclear family. The first factor predisposing a parent to transmit derogatory tags to his family is his change in social position and/or personal loss and deprivation. Such changes in the status or role of the parent can occur prior to or following his immigration to Israel; in the latter case it would be an instance of culture conflict—status and role conflict followed by social and economic hardships. This factor is evident among most of our research population, as the overwhelming majority of North African immigration to Israel has taken place since the establishment of the State in 1948, in the immigration waves of 1949–1952 and 1956–1957. Another predisposing factor, not necessarily linked to social change is the personal incapacitation of the parent: physically through accident, illness, etc., mentally or socially through loss of job, failure in business, etc.

Another factor is the tendency of the parent or other relevant alter to use scapegoating as an outlet for aggression, projection of guilt and displacement of resentment. The higher the extrapunitive tendencies of the parent, the higher will be the tendency to seek an outward avenue for aggression, resulting in the transmission of stigma to the girl. On the other hand, a high intrapunitive tendency would diminish the chances of stigma transmission because the aggression would be directed toward the self. In this hypothesis we have tried to apply to the purely theoretical formulation of stigma transmission the measuring tools devised by Rosenzweig and Fritz Heider.

The family is authoritarian in the anthropological sense, as a primary unit in a traditional structure. The definition of authoritarianism in this sense is given by Zelditch[1] as dominance of the parent (in this case the father) in decision-making in most domestic affairs. The hypothesis in the present context would impute authoritarianism to the stigmatizing parent in the sociopsychological sense as studied by Adorno, Frenkel-Brunswick and their followers. We can also avail ourselves of the further description of the authoritarian family by Frenkel-Brunswick, which is characterized by a clear-cut definition of roles in terms of one-sided expectations by the child. The interaction frame-

117

work in the family is based more on duties than affection, and there is a normative stress on stereotyped behaviour and rigid roles.

The stigmatizing parent seeks to transmit the stigma to an object (in this case the girl) symbolically associated with his deprivational change of role and status or his personal incapacitation as specified by our first hypothesis.

The normative structure of the North African Jewish family proscribes for girls the choice of role models outside the family. The members of the family therefore tend to restrict the roles to be internalized for the construction of their ego-identity to themselves, especially the parents.

This hypothesis presupposes that a girl from a North African family would tend to absorb the norms and roles imposed on her within the family without much partiality as to whether they are commendable or derogatory (stigma). In other words, if the parents, for the reasons we have specified, tend to socialize their children in a non-stigmatizing way, the children (and in this case the girl) still tend to seek their ego-identity within the family and not outside it, thus making internalization of the derogatory roles transmitted highly likely. The deterioration of the family's social position as a result of immigration could even increase this tendency "to arrange matters within the family"; the parents' control over the child would tend to be stricter as a result of anxiety and fear that they are losing their traditional authority. According to the dissonance theorists, the father's status anxiety would make his control over his family even more authoritarian.

If the stigmatizing parent is the father there is a distortion of the age and sex roles of his daughter as related to himself. This might result in overt or covert incestual attitudes of the father towards the daughter, as he regards her more as a mate as far as other domestic duties are concerned.

The change in the social position of the father or his personal deprivation in any other way is also likely to be linked with domestic strain between the parents. As our chain of hypotheses is mainly centered on the transmission of stigma by the authoritarian father, we might avail ourselves of the hypothesis offered by Spiegel,[2] according to which, in a tension-laden family, scapegoating of children tends to be transmitted to the child whose sex is identical with the tension-generating parent. Naturally, in our case, the scapegoating stigma is directed by the father towards the daughter.

The Girl

The factors predisposing the girl's being the recipient of stigma are as follows: She is significantly conspicuous physiologically, behaviourally, or by the possession of any other trait which sets her apart socially. She tends to deviate physically from the mode within the nuclear family of her immediate community or the modal image of a "good Moroccan Jewish girl." She would be either very ugly or very good-looking, physically deformed, outsized or diminutive in relation to the other members of the family, darker than the others or lighter in complexion. She might be very bright or verge on mental retardation, very introverted or very extroverted, gregarious or very detached. Conspicuity here could be in either direction and, for that matter, being the first-born, the youngest, a beautiful or an ugly child, sets her apart sufficiently to attract the transmission of stigma. It should be pointed out that physical and behavioural conspicuity are cumulative predisposing factors and are more or less objective, insofar as they can be measured by an outside observer without resorting to attitude measurements of the girl and her family.

A subjective conspicuity of the girl vis-à-vis her stigmatizing parent or other member of the family could be defined by them in their attitude towards her. Even if there is no objective conspicuity the girl may be regarded by the relevant adults as conspicuous as far as her symbolic relationship to the stigmatizer's personal or social deprivation is concerned. The literature is not very clear about the underlying processes of this attitudinal

119

definition, but a recent finding relates this definition of conspicuity to the child's (in our case the girl's) symbolic relationship to the causes of tension within the family.

The girl might be related symbolically to the physical or social deprivation of the stigmatizing adult, as a physically deformed child of an incapacitated parent or a child well-adjusted to his new environment of a parent maladjusted to conditions of social change.[3] The girl, as far as her own definition of her situation in the family is concerned, is powerless. This was conceptualized by Melvin Seeman as the expectancy or probability held by her that her own behaviour cannot determine the occurrence or the outcomes, or reinforcements she seeks.[4] This feeling of powerlessness is no doubt a subjective state of mind. Her realization that she cannot possibly influence the course of events in the family makes her more of a passive receptacle of her parents' behaviour, including stigmatizing.

The girl's feeling of powerlessness is correlated with her powerlessness in the family in the eyes of the stigmatizing parent. This is quite probable in the authoritarian North African Jewish family which guards very zealously the secretive cohesion of the family. In other words, the girl who feels powerless in a highly cohesive family which is normatively cut off from outside influences not only feels powerless, but her subjective state of mind is also inevitably perceived as powerless by the stigmatizing parents.

The tendency to be "other-directed" is another factor. David Riesman describes "other-directedness" as follows: "What is common to all the other-directed people is that their contemporaries are the source of direction for the individual—either those known to him or those with whom he is indirectly acquainted, through friends and through the mass media. This source is of course 'internalized' in the sense that dependence on it for guidance in life is implanted early. The goals toward which the other-directed person strives shift with that guidance: it is only the process of striving itself and the process of paying close attention to the signals from others that remain unaltered throughout life." We may adopt Riesman's definition of "other-directedness" but narrow its scope for our purposes to the nuclear family and a few other adults, in the sense imputed to this concept by Alfred Kuhn[5]. That means that the girl tends to be more of a hollow receptacle for the expectations of others, anchoring and focusing her own behaviour on the normative mandates of the parents and relevant others as perceived by her.

Another factor strongly linked with, and a logical result of, "other-directedness" is the probability that she would score high on conformity as measured by the Asch and Crutchfield studies[6]. In a way, her tendency to conform would actually be the measuring tool for her "other-directedness". The justification for formulating this as a separate hypothesis is methodological. The tendency to conform has been shown to be correlated with many other clusters of personality traits which could be relevant to the present context.[7] "Other-directedness", on the other hand, has hardly been studied empirically. The hypothetical link between "other-directedness" and the tendencies of individuals to conform would be useful if aetiological studies were subsequently undertaken.

The girl tends to be intolerant of ambiguity during and after her formative years, while still in a state of ego-diffusion. This personality trait, as described by Frenkel-Brunswick[8] is highly relevant to our present context, both in itself and as a linking variable which is tangentially related to most of our other hypotheses dealing with the personality traits of the girl.

The first characteristic of the family which breeds intolerance of ambiguity was held by Frenkel-Brunswick to be the social marginality of the parents.[9] Saenger adds his observation that the parents of the family experience, as a rule, status anxiety.[10] This ties up with our characterization of the North African family as experiencing status and role deprivation owing to immigration to Israel; such status anxiety could also be linked to the physical incapacitation or other personal deprivation of the father.

Another characteristic of the family which generates intolerance of ambiguity is the insistence of the father or other relevant adult on rigid familial roles. These are defined by reference to strict authoritarian mandates, by absolute demands of the parents on the child and expectancies of his absolute submission. Normative mandates and values tend to converge around the extreme poles of "positiveness" and "negativeness" with very little in between: things are either very good or very bad. Some of these characteristics are in line with our hypothesis as to the authoritarian set-up of the family; others will no doubt have to be determined by subsequent interviewing of the North African families themselves. The girl shows quite distinct compartmentalization of her ego. This is presumably linked to the extreme polarization of attitudes inherent in intolerance of ambiguity as a personality trait.

THE DYNAMIC PROCESSES OF STIGMATIZATION

The relevant processes are, presumably, initiated in the formative years, pre-adolescence and adolescence,[11] in a state which is denoted by Erikson as "ego-diffusion." The technical term is itself not crucial; the importance lies in the focus on the developmental stage of the amorphic plasticity of the personality: the no-man's-land of transition prior to the crystallization of personality. We have no intention of delving into the controversy among personality theorists as to the age at which this takes place or the processes which lead to the crystallization of the ego. We may follow the Freudian conception of the super-ego formation subsequent to the resolution of the Electra complex, or other non-Freudian personality theories dealing with the formation of the conscience and the internalization of norms. However, it would be expedient to adopt Erikson's conceptualization of ego-identity as the developmental stage in which our present dynamic process of stigma internalization is actually catalyzed.

122

Chronologically, therefore, the internalization by the girl of the derogatory images projected by the stigmatizing members of the family takes place while she is still in her ego-diffusion stage. The second connective stage coincides with her search for ego-identity as part of her developing personality.

The predisposing factors of both the parent and the girl would make the stigma of evil, pollution, inadequacy, "source of trouble", and all the other derogatory tags hurled at her in these relevant periods the most readily accessible "raw material" which the girl internalizes as the framework and anchor of her ego-identity.

It is probable that at least a part of her self-concept has been built and reinforced by the internalized evil, pollution and projected vileness cast on her by the stigmatizing others. According to Mead and the other symbolic interactionists, the girl builds her ego-identity only insofar as it is a role complementary of the expectations of the generalized or relevant others. In the tightly knit North African family, internally cohesive and relatively isolated normatively, the role expectations of the girl have optimal force and efficacy. We may hypothesize that the stigma projected would be the most relevant component with which she constructs her ego-identity in a "symbolic interaction" frame of reference.

After internalization of the stigma and partial achievement of ego-identity there is a dichotomous divergence of the facts of stigmatization as related to Rosenzweig's conceptualization and tracing of an individual's reaction to frustration[12] The possibility of the girl's reacting in an impunitive passive manner is quite remote, because the extreme stimuli to which she is exposed would presumably generate an extreme or at least active reaction and not a passive one. The latter might, however, occur if a girl experiences complete or severe ego-breakdown and deteriorates into a psychotic process, but this would exclude her from our analysis. The remaining relevant reaction would be either intropunitive, relating the causes of failure to herself, or extro-punitive relating the causes of failure to the outside world, in this case her parents and her family.

123

The presumed link between our exposition and Rosenzweig's conceptualization has further important methodological implication: Rosenzweig's exposition is related to measurable personality traits, so that predictability of our own process is therefore more feasible. Our reliance on the Rosenzweig exposition links the girl's reaction to stigma with an inevitable frustration which she tries to overcome by means of a self-defeating mechanism which operates in the following manner:

The first possibility is linked to the intropunitive type of reaction. The girl internalizes the projected derogatory image in compliance with the expectations of her socializers. She would then expect reinforcement of her conduct by the relevant adults by their acceptance of her compliance with an approving attitude towards her. This amounts to a fulfillment of her expectations of her parents. Compliance with the stigma induces her to expect acceptance, approval and a sanction of accomplishment from her parents. She expects, in a way, her parents to fulfill their part of this "dyadic bargain." Naturally it fails to materialize because most parents cannot approve cognitively of the "bad" behaviour of their daughter, even if they have prescribed this behaviour subconsciously by transmitting stigmata to her.

Here we have the initial frustration to which the girl must react. Being intropunitive, she imputes the causes of this disharmony between the expectations of her parents and their actual reaction to her behaviour to herself. She tends therefore to blame herself for not complying properly with the stigmatizing expectations of her parents. She therefore carries on compulsively and ever more extremely the derogatory behaviour prescribed by her parents, expecting thereby a complementary acceptance by them. She is geared of course to subconsciously receiving their transmissions of stigma inherent in their behaviour toward her. This is to her the actual behavioural mandate to which she imputes legitimacy. The overt vociferous rejection of the parents, which she experiences following her behavioural compliance with the stigma, is perceived by her as a dissonance. However, she again tends to blame herself for this dissonance,

124

resulting in the positive feed-back cycle of extreme negativistic behaviour, which might lead to almost ritualistic performance of the various deviations connected with sexual promiscuity and other breaches of accepted norms. Characteristically, it is not coupled with the rejection of the stigmatizing parents, however harsh they would be in their treatment of her, both verbally and physically.

The other extreme manifestation linked with an extropunitive type of reaction is as follows: After complying with the derogatory image cast on her and behaving accordingly—with sexual promiscuity, petty larceny, truancy, etc., the girl expects an initial reinforcement from the parents, When this is not forthcoming, she accuses her parents of bringing her to this cognitive dissonance. She reacts to her parents rejection of her by counter-rejection. The positive feed-back cycle in this case usually results in a complete separation of the girl from her family and a severance of all ties between them.

These are, of course, extreme instances; they are theoretical cases which rarely exist in real "life situations". Various possibilites short of the ideal type extreme reactions are also feasible, as are combinations of the two. However, our hypothesis is that these extreme, or almost extreme manifestations, are more probable. The very traits which predispose the girl to be a recipient of stigma (conspicuity, "other-directedness", intolerance of ambiguity) with her resultant compulsive over-conformity to the stigmatized roles projected on her tend to make her marginal and estranged within the family. Marginal individuals tend to show higher ego-involvment toward their roles.[13] The choice of either the intropunitive, compulsive conformity to stigma and/or the extropunitive rejection and counter-rejection of family is presumably more likely in our case.

Ambivalence toward the parents is more probable with the intropunitive solution than with the extrapunitive one. In the latter, severance of relationships quite early in the process physically separates the girl from contact with her parents. On the other hand, the intropunitive solution would most likely involve a relatively close proximity between girl and family, although the deviation process with the girl has already started. Affective links between the girl and her family probably continue, even if she has physically left the family. We presume that the intropunitive solution would be more likely with our research population of prostitutes from North African authoritarian families, whereas the extropunitive solution would tend to occur with prostitutes of European origin.

SOME OVERT INITIATION PROCESSES

By applying the stigma theory to the genesis of prostitution, we have confined ourselves to the very early levels of causality within the family during and after the formative years, but there are also social and psychological processes of association which account for the actual recruitment of the girl to the life of prostitution. We shall try to enumerate these stages in order to draw a complete aetiological picture; however, we should bear in mind that our concern is with the stigma theory as applied to the aetiology of prostitution, and the subsequent association processes, important as they are, are of secondary importance here. These overt processes of initiation may be related to current criminological theory as follows:

Differential Identification: This might be the theoretical step linking the girl from playing the "bad" role in compliance with the stigma branded on her by the family to her identification with "bad", i.e. sexual promiscuity, deviation and crime outside the family.

Daniel Glaser, who actually formulated this premise, relied on Meadean social psychology and other symbolic interactionist premises, maintaining that prior to a person's actual criminal behaviour he becomes criminal in his values and roles, he sees himself as a criminal or law violator. When his self-image is deviant he is ripe for the association with actual criminal patterns of behaviour. In our case, the role-playing of the girl in compliance

126

with the image cast on her would indeed be geared towards "evil", "bad", "dirty" behaviour. However, at this stage, it might still be amorphic, to be crystallized eventually by identification with an image of a "good-time-girl", one who stays out at night, one who gets the reputation of being an "easy girl with the boys". Identification with the role of sexual promiscuity would indeed be more likely in the present case. We have described some turbulent ambivalences of father-daughter relationships involving the marring of the girl's role as far as her age is concerned and a confusing of her role of daughter with her role of mate, bordering on incest; but cognitively sexual promiscuity is still the epitome of deviation for a girl in an oriental authoritarian family; even worse, she could become pregnant. At this stage she might leave home of her own accord or be thrown out by her parents; she is then ready for the next stage.

2. *Differential Association:* The actual initiation into criminal or deviant behaviour was believed by Sutherland[14] to materialise through association with criminal norms and criminal techniques. In our case this process will begin, presumably before, but in any case, immediately after the girl has left home. Her first boyfriend is bound to leave her. She is no longer a virgin and he would be reluctant to marry her even though he is the one who availed himself of her virginity. She lives outside home: she will move to town if she does not live there already. She then begins looking for work and for a new boyfriend. This is the stage when a pimp steps in. One of the prostitutes in our research population describes the process of actual initiation by association as follows: "When a girl has an abortion and her boy-friend leaves her and does not marry her, her folks make life hell for her and she leaves home. The pimps are after her, they have a special sense for smelling her out, they 'fall in love' with her, give her everything—money, clothes, a good time—and then she has no choice but to do what they say." If she refuses, they may use threats, violence, blackmail. Usually the girl gives in and accepts the first client sent to her: by then she is broken in. Another prostitute might be instrumental in recruiting the

127

girls: when the girl arrives in town looking for a job, the older prostitute invites her to share a room with her. The girl accepts the "kind offer", whereupon she may be urged, cajoled, and seduced into prostitution. The overt reason for the older prostitute's eagerness to recruit new ones is evident. The pimp promised her that "if you get a girl to work for us you won't have to work anymore and we will get married." The girl herself is frequently a willing partner to this process of differential association. First, because she is subconsciously favorably disposed to this process owing to her stigmatization at home and her identification with images of deviant behaviour, in this case sexual promiscuity; second, she is isolated and lonely in town, and any company, pimps and other prostitutes included, is quite welcome.

3. *Differential Opportunity Structure:* Cloward and Ohlin[15] postulate that an individual's awareness of the limited access of illegitimate opportunity may press him to be aware of the availability of illegitimate opportunities. The girl is very poorly prepared for life in town within the legitimate opportunity structures. She has had little or no vocational training; her family background would make her quite maladapted to the know-how and perseverence in achieving any steady occupation and she is alone in a strange environment. Naturally, a girl in her teens away from home, in a strange new place, subconsciously prepared for deviation and sexual promiscuity, cajoled by pimps and prostitutes, might not even go through a motion of resistance; she would most probably enter the life of prostitution as the least resistant avenue available to her. These of course are just scant empirical referents which will have to be investigated further.

These three theoretical premises bring us to the end of our theory formulation. Other areas of interest closely linked to our present formulation include the nature of the relationship between the pimps and prostitutes, the normative system of their subculture, interrelationship with other "criminal professions", and the structure of their group. However, this is beyond the scope of our present work.

CHAPTER VII

THE FORMAL STIGMA AND ITS CONSEQUENCES

> "When coal turns white
> And soot's not black
> I'll forget the prison
> That's at my back."*

We may distinguish between a formalized stigma which stems from a sanction but is not ritualistically proclaimed (as in most stigmatized pollutions inherent in sins and in the religious and supernatural attitudes towards crime), and a formalized stigma that is ritualistically proclaimed and which may follow formal sanctions (such as the Roman *Infames* or *Ignominius*).[2] A third formal effect of stigma is loss of legal or civil rights. We shall analyse the effect of formal stigma in each of these areas. Our hypothesis is that these vary in severity and external manifestations, but that the criteria for their infliction will not differ in kind from those for the branding of nonformalized social stigma. The original Mark of Cain was a formalized stigma, inherent in the sanction and dramatizing it; it was also a sign of pollution that emanates from its bearer and is transferred by sight or by contagion. Frazer cites evidence from ancient Greece, the Dobu in New Guinea, the Kikuyu and the Moors of Morocco to show that the criminal, the murderer, is not only polluted and a source of pollution, but that he pollutes the source of life itself, the earth. Therefore "it is intelligible that a homicide should be shunned and banished from the country, to which his presence is a continual menace. He is plague-stricken, surrounded by a poisonous atmosphere, infected by a contagion of death; his very touch may blight the earth."[3]

* Convict's song from Jean Genet, *Our Lady of the Flowers*

We have already shown that the pollution element of stigma stems from a religious or a supernatural philosophy of punishment: An offence against social norms (the criminal law) amounts to sin. By committing the offence, the criminal raises the wrath of the gods, by committing a sin he becomes a source of sin, or pollution. This pollution is expiated and cleansed by punishment.[4] To signify the unexpiated offender, the Mark of Cain is branded; it is a sign of pollution, a deterrent for potential offenders, and a source of a dangerous emanation.

In order of sequence, the Mark of Cain was a conspicuity signifying a pollution earned previously by an offence (sin). However, cause and effect in social phenomena have often been confused. Conspicuity by stigma is therefore linked to sin and pollution; whereas the end product, by a sort of social conditioning, could be the linking of conspicuity (physical or behavioural) to pollution sin and badness. This hypothesis appears to suffer from a bad case of disconnectedness, and becomes a false syllogism; but if at one time the polluted and therefore dangerous had to be defined by tags, it could have resulted in an association in the peoples' mind between the conspicuity and the sin, between the apartedness and the pollution. The image became identical with the thing, or to use Ogden and Richards' model, the symbol coincided with its referent.[5] The relevant model might be as follows:

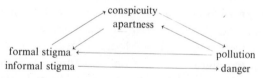

The interrelationship between formal and informal stigma is not unlike the relation between law and custom. The latter, one of the primary sources of positive law, is adopted and formalized by legislature. Conversely, a law imposed from above can become so ingrained and internalized that it is regarded more as part of one's cultural heritage than coercion originally imposed by the power of a ruler.

Informal stigma, such as the limiting of socio-economic opportunities, could thus have been the basis of a formalized loss of civil rights after conviction; on the other hand, the Censors' mark by a man's name', making him *Infames* , could have *informal* consequences far beyond its formal penalties.

By being conspicuous, one becomes socially visible. Conspicuity breeds apartness in the sense that it can be linked to an individual's isolation or even physical removal from the group. And the contrary is true: apartness, that is, social isolation by itself, can make a person conspicuous.

The polluted signified danger because of their ability to transmit evil by contagion, and conversely, the dangerous, the murderers and criminals were afflicted by supernatural pollution *because* of their destructive and offensive acts. The interrelationship between the pairs of variables in our triangular model are cyclic insofar as informal stigma is causally linked with formal stigma, conspicuity with apartness, pollution with danger, and vice versa.

The paradigm on page 132 demonstrates the interrelationships among the variables on a two-dimensional basis.

We observe four types of two-dimensional relationships among the variables. We have already noted the positive-feed-back interrelationship between the pairs of adjacent variables: conspicuity—apartness: pollution—danger; informal stigma—formal stigma, denoted as cyclic interchange. The most apparent proximity is between formal stigma and conspicuity. Here the link is direct insofar as the formal stigma itself makes the branded object physically conspicuous or socially visible. This relationship is at the lower left-hand corner of the paradigm, being the vertex of a triangle. The second type of relationships, of a lower proximity, are the indirect inferences, and are further up in the triangle. These are: formal stigma—apartness; formal stigma—pollution; informal stigma—conspicuity; informal stigma—apartness; danger—conspicuity. The relationship here is indirect insofar as the links are created by the stigmatizing processes. They can only be inferred inductively. The remotest relationship is between those that are only symbolically linked. These are: pollu-

INTERRELATIONSHIPS AMONG TYPES OF SOCIETAL REACTION TO DEVIANCE

	Conspicuity	Apartness	Pollution	Danger	Informal Stigma	Formal Stigma
Conspicuity						
Apartness	Cyclic interchange					
Pollution	Symbolic conditioning	Symbolic conditioning				
Danger	Indirect inference	Symbolic conditioning	Cyclic interchange			
Informal Stigma	Indirect inference	Indirect inference	Symbolic conditioning	Symbolic conditioning		
Formal Stigma	Direct link	Indirect inference	Indirect inference	Symbolic conditioning	Cyclic interchange	

tion—conspicuity; pollution—apartness, danger—apartness; informal stigma—pollution; informal stigma—danger; formal stigma—danger.

However, their joint appearance in the stigmatizing process links them, by a kind of conditioning. One can thus be interchangeable with the orther in the actual aetiology of stigma. The following paradigm shows a three-dimensional typology.

	Formal stigma		Informal stigma	
	conspicuity	apartness	conspicuity	apartness
Polution	Mark of Cain	Outside the camp	functional personality defects	downward vertical mobility
Danger	ostracism	heretic	"The jealous Gods"	The creative innovators

1. The formal stigma imprinted or tagged on a person with a physical conspicuity signifying pollution. These are the Mark-of-Cain type of stigma, branded on criminals and sinners in ancient and primitive societies. Historically the Mark of Cain signified a *non-expiated* murder, crime or sin. Frazer, however, cites many cases, where marks were painted on the faces and bodies of homicides to guard them against the vengeful wrath of the victim's ghost.[6]

In England gunpowder was used to brand, thieves, burglars and sodomites. Paint was used as a branding agent in Greece and ink in China. In the U.S. branding was employed for pirates, runaway slaves and horse-thieves.[7] The common denominator seems to be the derogatory nature of the offences so that the branding tends to perpetuate and formalize the pollution and turpitude of their perpetrators. The Roman Infamia also highlights the pollution element in formalized stigma by inflicting it on persons of shameful trades, dismissal in dishonour from the army, and misconduct in family relations.[8]

133

In Florence the bankrupts, the financial failures, were the most hated and despised and a degrading public flagellation was meted out to them.[9]

Ranulf cites Berger that in medieval Europe Jews, prostitutes and the hangman were branded by the necessity to wear a particular dress.[10] The common denominator of all three is presumably their turpitude and pollution.

In the Jewish community of Castilia in the 15th century the informers were branded with a hot iron[11] and the prostitutes in the Jewish community of Prague of the 17th century had to leave the community after the Day of Atonement; those who remained were branded on their forehead as a sign of pollution.[12]

In later days black signs of turpitude were posted in synagogues in Europe, naming persons who dressed extravagantly, spent conspicuously or polluted themselves by drink and entertainment in non-Jewish public houses. Here again conspicuity and pollution are represented by the formal stigma on the black signpost.

2. A formal stigma can follow the social conspicuity of successful leadership or other extraordinary exploits which spell danger to other members of the oligarchy or to ideological and political rivals. Ostracism and its modern counterparts are prime examples of this type of stigma, resulting in "the chopping off of the tallest ears of corn."

Many of the successful and illustrious leaders of Athens were ostracised: Aristides, Xanthippos, Thomisteckles, Kimon, Thucydides, Melesias, Megackles, Alcmeon.[13] Petalism in Syracuse and other institutions similar to ostracism operated in other towns of ancient Greece, such as Argos, Megara, Miletos, Delphi, Paros and Thasos.[14] The justification of this atrocity as being a means to preserve democracy is obviously a post-facto glorification.

Ranulf was more realistic when he stated that the basis of ostracism was combined resentment, jealousy and fear of the danger which the successful leader constituted to the ostracisers: "When the power, wealth and honour of a fellow citizen assumed too provoking proportions, a remedy was found in Ostracism.

When a citizen had attained the unprecedented luck of being mentioned as the victor of Marathon or Salamis, his fellow-citizens eagerly watched for the first occasion when he exposed himself, so as to fall upon him and, if possible, destroy him." [15]

A similar fate in a modern, more sophisticated form befell President Wilson after the First World War, Prime Minister Churchill after the Second World War, U Nu in Burma, and David Ben-Gurion in Israel.

3. The heretic is formally stigmatized because his *accedia,* his standing apart, spells danger to the pious flock of believers. Violators of the Roman Sacral Law were declared *ignominius* and suffered some curtailment of their legal capacities through the *pontifex.* [16] The formal declaration as *apostate* was mainly reserved for deviant clerics and especially for retracting novices. Ranulf cites Coulton as follows:

"The novice, nominally, was quite free to depart at any time; this was the whole point of the arrangement. But in fact he was regarded by all good men as one who had put his hand to the plough and looked back, as a dog returned to his vomit, as a brand plucked for one moment from the burning five, but now cast on it again. He was branded—quite illegally—with the name of *apostate*; he was a lost soul; he died in secular dress, and there was public and riotous rejoicing of devils over his soul that had been won." [17] Maimonides grades the formal stigmata used against those who blasphemed or slandered the rabbinical authorities—ghettoes both spiritual and secular. The lowest sanction was a public reprimand. The more severe was the *Nidui,* by which an individual was publicly expelled from the synagogue. If the heresy was severe, and in fact it was measured by the individual's contrariness against the rabbinical power elite, he was branded with *Shamta,* a permanent sign of infamy. [18] The *Shamta* has been described as "a prison without a lock" as "iron chains which are invisible but a person feels them binding him." [19] These are vivid and picturesque descriptions of the socially stifling effects of formal stigmata.

Excommunication in the Ecclesiastical courts in England was

to the spiritual courts what outlawing was to the temporal courts. As to the severe temporal consequences of excommunication we have Bracton's assurance that "an excommunicated person cannot do any legal act, so that he cannot sue anyone, though he himself may be sued . . . for except in certain cases it is not lawful either to pray or speak or eat with an excommunicate either openly or secretly. He is a man who has *a leprosy of the soul.*"

4. The formal stigmatization of the socially polluted by separating them from the community is a sending them "outside the camp"—in the old tradition of the nomadic tribes of Israel, who employed this measure against the polluted. The Bible mentions it as late as the Second Temple era. "Ezra rose . . . and made proclamation throughout Judah and Jerusalem unto all the children of the captivity, that they should gather themselves together unto Jerusalem. And whosoever would not come within three days, according to the counsel of the princes and the elders, all his substance should be forfeited and himself separated from the congregation of those that had been carried away."[20] This is a formalization of the apartness that one has previously professed to be by antagonizing the authorities, the princes and elders.

The Code of Hamurabi, sections 153–158, prescribes the banning from the city of the perpetrator of the universally despicable crime and sin of incest. The leges Barbarorum, the Gothic Law at the time of Ulfias (4th century), specifies the declaration as "wolf" for all who were found to be "enemies of the king, the people and God". A man formally pronounced to be a wolf could be killed on sight.[21]

In similar manner the old Saxon "Priedlos", which was equivalent to outlawry, could be slain by anyone without fear of reprisal or feud.[22] Of the same nature are the Roman *Sacer Esto* and the medieval Bannitus. All have been formally declared "outside the camp"—outlaws. The essence of outlawry has been properly described by Pollock and Maitland as follows: "He who breaks the law, has gone to war with the community; the community goes to war with him. It is the right and the duty of every man to pursue him, to ravage his land, to burn his house, to hunt him down like a wild beast and slay him; for a wild beast he is." [23] In Jewish sources the punishment of *Karet* is deemed to be by many authorities the expelling of the polluted from the camp of the respectful law-abiding and God-fearing community. [24] This formal stigma was inflicted on offenders against morality; the rules of hygiene; and other conditions or acts which signify turpitude and pollution e.g. the non-circumcised, the lepers, the witches and the venerally diseased. Maimonides states the law as to the right attitude and behaviour towards these polluted outsiders. One may not approach them closer than four yards; they should not be allowed to enter the synagogue and when they die one may not go to their funeral or mourn them. One cannot teach them or learn from them, hire them as labourers or be hired by them, sell to them or buy from them. [25] This like outlawry is a virtual sentence of death.

A Florentine law of 1398 forced the bankrupt to act as public prosecutor, [26] a typical act of transference of evil and projection of guilt. The polluted bankrupt deals with the polluted offender.

A modern counterpart of this type of formal stigmatization is the Soviet exile and banishment as laid down in the Criminal Code of 1926 (Art. 35, restricted in 1960). Exile is the expulsion of a person from the piace where he lives, with compulsory residence in a particular place; banishment is the expulsion of a person from the place where he lives with a prohibition against living in definite places. These punishment are provided for the majority of the crimes against the state. [27]

The other four types in our paradigm are related to the effects of informal stigma; we have dealt extensively with them in earlier chapters. The functional personality defects would include most of the autistically alienated. The downward vertically mobile are the escapists and retreatists. The "Jealousy of the Gods" finds its outlet by victimizing innocent objects of stigma because their success or other social conspicuity spells danger to the stigmatizing power elite. The Promethean fate of the last type—the creative innovator who is trodden upon his creative pains—is one of the central themes of this work. The last part of our present analysis will be concerned with the consequences of formal stigma, that is, the loss of rights and its relation to the other factors in society's reaction against crime and deviation.

The Loss of Rights as related to society's reactions against norm infringement. Four pairs of variables are relevant to the analysis of formal loss of rights following a conviction within the mechanism of social control: The "resistance potential" of the infringed norm, and the righteous indignation towards the infringer. Retribution, and deterrence. The sanction prescribed by the legislator, and the actual sanction inflicted by the trial judge. Loss of right itself is paired with stigma, another consequence of conviction. These eight variables have been graded according to the degree of externalization of society's reaction to the offence, beginning with the deep, subterranean "resistance potential" and righteous indignation, and culminating with the externalized and socially visible loss of rights and stigma. The variables are, therefore, graded into a scale in which the interrelationships are not necessarily symmetrical; thus the aetiological relation of retribution to deterrence is not necessarily symmetrical or similar to that of deterrence to retribution. The following Table presents the relationship of the variables in our scale; ratings were hypothetical and were carried out by the author on the basis of empirical data and theoretical considerations. The values for the links were:

1. = no link
2. = an amorphic or remote link
3. = an apparent link

1. The aetiological links between righteous indignation and the resistance potential of a norm and vice-versa are strong. Righteous indignation is one of the "safety-valve" mechanisms which permits inner aggression and negativity to be externalized and focused on a given object. By being righteously indignant against the offender the superego is strengthened in its battle against the subconscious urge to break off the normative yoke,

138

	Resistance potential	Righteous indignation	Retribution	Deterrence	Sanction prescribed by law	Sanction actually inflicted	Loss of rights	Stigma
Resistance potential								
Righteous indignation	3							
Retribution	3	3						
Deterrence	3	3	1					
Sanction prescribed by law	2	2	1	1				
Sanction actually inflicted	2	2	3	2	1			
Loss of rights	2	3	3	3	3	3		
Stigma	3	3	3	3	2	3	2	

as the offender did.[28] Righteous indignation is one of the main subconscious sources of the negative attitude to the infringer of a norm; this attitude erupts, by processes of projection and transference, from the conformist to the norm-infringer. Precisely this attitude would be the main unit of measurement of the resistance potential of a norm. The causal relationship between these two variables would tend, therefore, to be symmetrical. An illustration of this link was provided by Lord Denning in his evidence before the Royal Commission on Capital Punishment: "The punishment inflicted for grave crimes should adequately reflect the revulsion felt by the great majority of citizens for them; the ultimate justification of any punishment is the emphatic denunciation by the community of a crime."[29]

2. Another symmetrical relationship may be observed between the resistance potential of a norm and retribution. The latter, one of the objectives of normative sanctions, can be defined as the infliction of pain and suffering, not as a means to an end, but as an end in itself, for an offence or an infringement of a norm committed in the past. By stressing the past we exclude any utilitarian effect on the future behaviour of the infringer. The effect of the resistance potential of a norm on the retributive urge seems evident. The stronger the norm, as measured by the attitude of the public towards it, the stronger would be the retributive urge against its infringers. The reverse relationship would also seem to hold. The retributive urge strengthens the norm by visibly reacting negatively against its infringement. The victims or other interested individuals could take the law into their own hands were retribution not to take place. A higher urge for retribution would also presumably strengthen the resistance potential and with it the norm itself. In other words, the punitive reaction itself fortifies the legitimization of the norm by the group. This could be detected in the words of the renowned forensic psychiatrist Norwood East who states, with discernible righteous indignation, that: "Retributive justice for certain crimes arouses the public sense of the fitness of things and a demand for penalties. From a practical point of view resentment at a particularly evil form of wrong-doing is a

140

healthy reaction which recognizes the danger to social security if cruelty and injustice flourish. The retributive element of punishment has a deep-seated biological significance. In a cultural society it may be necessary and advantageous if it preserves a correct relation between the turpitude of the offence and the severity of the award."[30]

3. The effect of righteous indignation on the pressures to retaliate against the infringer of a norm would be a direct and positive one: the higher the former, the stronger the latter. The inverse relationship, although presumably strong, would be different. Retribution would presumably build up and augment the righteous indignation against the infringer until the sanction has been carried out; when retribution is consumated the righteous indignation should subside. However, if the psychoanalysts are right and righteous indignation is indigenous and feeds on inner aggressivity and is linked to the infringer by a symbolic "scapegoat" relationship, it need not subside with the execution of sanction. This alternative hypothesis must remain at this conjectural level until measurement is possible.

4. The retribution—deterrence interrelationship is not symmetrical. Deterrence may be regarded as the cognitive rationalization of the subconscious retributive urge. People do not openly admit to themselves that their attitude towards a norm infringer is retaliatory and retributive; deterrence would serve, therefore, as an appropriate, utilitarian rationalization. On the other hand, the utilitarian deterrence, the purpose of which is to prevent future infringements, cannot be causally linked to the emotionally negativistic "safety-valve" mechanism of retribution.

5. The cognitive objective of deterrence might be instrumental to a "teach them a lesson"—righteous indignation. The inverse relationship, however, is remote and vicarious. Righteous indignation is directly linked to retribution in that it is one of its subconscious sources. It is only indirectly linked to deterrence insofar as the latter is a rationalization of retribution.

6. If the resistance potential of a norm is strong, the quest for deterrence to prevent future infringements of the norm would be

141

strong too. An inverse relationship, on the other hand, would not exist here at all. Deterrence aims at preventing the punished offender himself or potential ones from offending again for fear of sanction. The degree of norm internalization aimed at by deterrence is the shallow one of sanction-orientation. The resistance potential is concerned with the deepest degree of the internalization of norms, moral-orientation. At this stage the norm becomes a personality element and sanctions are not needed for its compliance. Even the intermediate stage of the internalization of norms—identification where conformity is induced by positive sanction and compliance becomes automatically rewarding—is related to the resistance potential of the norm but not to deterrence. An individual's sanction-orientation towards a norm where deterrence applies has not reached the stage yet where the norm has any resistance potential in its internalized binding strength on him.

7. The effects of the resistance potential of a norm on the sanction prescribed by law for its infringement is bound to be amorphic and remote. Most legal sanctions in the Neo-Classic tradition are maximum penalties which leave a wide margin of discretion to the trial judge. The indeterminate sentence and its various nuances are relatively new introductions. The historian of the criminal law could possibly reveal some socio-economic and religious bases for the prescription of a given maximum penalty for a specific offence. The preparatory files of the Crown Council of the British Mandatory Government for Palestine[31] reveal some very enlightening material in this context. The High Commissioner for Palestine, General A.G. Wauchope, in a memorandum dated 17.6.1933 wrote to Sir Philip Cunliffe-Lister, the Colonial Secretary, as follows: "I am of the opinion that the provision of the adultery clause serves a useful purpose in this country, and that, among the *fellahin,* it has the effect of restraining injured husbands from taking the law into their own hands and committing acts of violence and possibly murder." It is not really important if the opinion of the High Commissioner was adopted or not. The importance lies in the approach and views which were the basis

142

of enacting and prescribing the penalties of the Criminal Code Ordinance of 1936, which is still binding law in Israel. At that time (1933), the *fellahin* were indeed the majority of the Palestinian population, but they constitute a small minority of the population of Israel today. Today most of the Israeli population would be quite lenient as far as the resistance potential of a norm against adultery is concerned! A similar opinion in the same spirit is expressed by Chief Justice McDonnell in a memorandum (8th of June, 1929) to the High Commissioner demanding the prescription of capital punishment for homicides resulting from bedouin blood feuds. Chief Justice McDonnell was also of the opinion that "flogging and whipping should be prescribed for indecent assaults on females." Another offence for which the Chief Justice advocates flogging is malicious damage to crops because: "As is well known malicious damage to crops and trees is very common in this country and calls for serious repressive measures; both Judge Baker and Judge De Freitas ask that the Court should be empowered to pass a sentence of flogging for this offence." Indeed the Chief Justice might have expressed the resistance potential of the norm against malicious damage to crops as applied to a Palestine populated mostly by Arab peasants but not by a largely urban Israel. A prime example is sec. 326(c) of the Criminal Code Ordinance, which prescribes life imprisonment for damage to a boat or any other means of sea-transport. This penalty is much higher than those prescribed for the majority of property offences in the Criminal-Code-Ordinance. This is so because we have adopted almost verbatim this section from Cyprus which imported it from Britain. Both Britain and Cyprus are islands, the life line of which is marine transport. A person who damages an old punt is still liable for a harsher sentence than someone who steels a necklace worth $100,000 from a jewellery shop. This illustrates our premise that historically the resistance potential of a norm, as conceived by the legislating organs, did affect the penalty prescribed by law, but the latter, being formal, conservative and rigid, very rarely shifts with variations in the resistance potential of a norm caused by time and social change. There

143

could not be any discernible influence of the penalties prescribed by law on the resistance potential of a norm, because the former are hardly known even to lawyers and judges. The public at large is virtually ignorant of the penal dosages in the law book, although everybody is presumed by law to know them all.

8. It seems feasible that at the time of enactment or prior to it righteous indignation might have been strongly linked with the maximum penalties fixed by law. We might resort again to the preparatory files for the Palestinian Criminal Code Ordinance 1936. Judge Copland very righteously indeed demands: "It is time that something should be done to stop the offence of sodomy, which is appallingly rife." As to begging, Judge Copland says: "Judge Webb expresses the opinion that it is cruel to prosecute beggars. Judge Baker and Judge De Freitas are in favour of the retention of these clauses, and I confess that I am in agreement with them, especially in a country such as this where mendicancy of a rather revolting kind is very rife." The emotionally loaded expressions of "appallingly rife" and "revolting" reek with righteous indignation. This victorian puritanism was no doubt of prime importance at the time of enacting the Criminal Code Ordinance, but not today. The offence of homosexuality is still binding law in Israel, but if it is done between consenting adults there is a standing regulation by the Attorney General not to prosecute. Here again, as with the resistance potential of a norm, the righteous indignation which might have been quite strongly linked to the prescribed penalty at the time of enactment very often disappears, or lags behind the changing mores. The inverse relationship does not hold here because the maximum penalties prescribed by law are dead words as far as "the man in the street" is concerned.

9. The grading of the penalties in the criminal laws by the legislator seems to be largely retributive. It is determined by the objective severity of the offence. The effect of the penalty on the future behaviour of the punished offender, the main attribute of the utilitarian objectives of punishment, is excluded here because at the time of enactment the identity of the offender and his per-

sonality factors are not known. The retributive nature of the penalty dosage of the law stems also from its ideological similarity to Lex Talionis of the XII Roman Tables, which strived to equate the severity of sanction with the severity of the objective damage caused by the offence. Insomuch as the legislator grades the penalties according to the severity of damage caused by the offence, we may assume that he does so by assessing the severity of the reaction of the victim where the latter could have retaliated himself against the offender. The legislator, thus, places himself in the victims stead and quantifies the retributive reaction according to the possible harm (hypothetical at this stage), as assessed by the actual victim.

Timashef also stresses the retributive nature of the penalties fixed by law. "By studying criminal codes from the earliest times down to our own days, all of them are constructed in the form of catalogues of possible crimes and of social reactions against them; the higher the socio-ethical value injured by a crime, the stronger the social reaction . . . . In actuality no other explanation of criminal codes than the retributive one is possible; they were and still are constructed in accordance with the idea of retributive punishment."[32] There is no clearly discernible feed-back effect from the maximum penalties fixed by law to the retributive urge of the legislature or the public at large.

10. As we have noted in the previous section, the sanction prescribed by law is largely of a retributive nature but in special cases the element of deterrence is also relied on. Sec. 317 et seq., for instance, of the Criminal Code Ordinance specifies heavy penalties for arson. In a period where most of the constructions were of wood and other inflammable materials the deterrent heavier penalties for arson were deemed to be imperative. In sec. 326(a) we find a general penalty for damage to property, but if the object of the damage is agricultural tools the deterrent protection is higher, seven years imprisonment (sec. 326(b)). Presumably the legislator considered the vital importance of agricultural tools in a country largely populated by *fellahin*. A further deterrent protection is provided by prescribing 14 years

145

imprisonment for the destruction of wills, deeds and other property identification papers (sec. 326(d)). The protection of dwelling houses following the British tradition of "my home is my castle" reaches a peak of life imprisonment for damage to dwellings. Other deterrent considerations are linked to a specific mode of perpetration of offences which the legislator regards as particularly dangerous and intends to prevent them by special heavy penalties. These are, for instance, committing a burglary while being armed with firearms (sec. 288), and being drunk while carrying firearms (sec. 101(b)). However, most of the sections are motivated by a retributive retaliatory spirit and relatively few have a deterrent basis.

11. The sanction inflicted by the trial judge on the offender before him would only partly be determined by the resistance potential of the norm. The sentence imposed on an offender is influenced by three complex groups of factors:

    a. The offence and its circumstances. In relation to this factor there must be considered the specific law declaring a certain act or omission to be an offence; the punishment prescribed for those who commit the offence; the harm that the offence is likely to cause the victim or the public at large; the aggravating or mitigating circumstances of the offence, and the actual harm or damage caused by it.

    b. The offender and his background. The offender's economic means and position, his family, age, social background, physical and mental health, his criminal record or lack of previous convictions are all included under this heading.

    c. The third factor is the most elusive and indefinite element in any sentencing policy, namely, the attitude of the trial judge.[33]

The resistance potential of the norm could belong both to the first group—the offence and its circumstances—or it could be reflected by the third—the personality of the trial judge. The latter is no doubt part of the social system and controlled by the

146

normative system of which the specific norm is an integral part. The sanction actually inflicted on the offender would serve, no doubt, as a reinforcement to the resistance potential of a norm, because the public at large would feel that the inner binding of a norm is supported by sanctions against its infringement. On the other hand the resistance potential of a norm is, as we have seen, more a function of its internalization by an individual so that it is legitimized as "just", "right" and "true", and is less dependent on the sanction for its infringement.

12. The link between righteous indignation and the sanction inflicted by the trial judge, or, for that matter, the link between the latter and other factors influencing the type and severity of legal sanction, could be gleaned from the sentencing grounds. These, as employed in the Israeli sentencing policy, are the means by which the judges justify in their sentence the infliction of a particular punishment.

The sentencing grounds represent the individual judge's attitude towards punishment, and the Israeli judge thus conveys to the public (and to the court of appeal) his particular reasons for inflicting a certain method of punishment on an individual offender. We must bear in mind, of course, that the sentencing grounds do not reflect the whole of the judge's reasons for inflicting a certain punishment, nor do they represent the inner subjective reasons, which are mainly determined by the judge's disposition and his personal outlook on life; moreover, the sentencing grounds are sometimes given very briefly and sometimes not given at all; but these grounds are the only explicit declaration of the judge's decision, which is obviously the most important factor in a sentencing policy.[34]

Many sentencing grounds in the judgements of the district courts of Israel examined by the author included the following emotionally loaded grounds:

"We are dealing with an *infamous deed*"
"This is *abhorring*"
"These are an assortment of *obnoxious* offences"

147

"The defendant does not deserve leniency because he has committed a *lowly act*".

These expressions, and especially the words italicized, reveal the righteous indignation of the judges and radiate emotional negativity against the defendant. The link between the actual sentence inflicted on the offender and these righteously indignant expressions may be apparent from the choice of these specific words by the trial judge; as Andenaes rightly says: "The choice of terminology may influence our attitude; if a person is described as 'a ruthless egoist, cynically exploiting others for his own ends', the moralizing terms used create an impression of a high degree of guilt and a well merited punishment."[35]

However, as we have noted before, many other factors determine the type of severity of the actual sanction inflicted by the trial judge.

The inverse relationship is also a medium one because, although the sentencing policy of courts does influence the emotional attitude of the public against the infringement of legal norms, it is rather difficult to determine cause and effect relationships and so the link may be rated, for the time being, as amorphic.

13. The retributive element of the sentencing policy of criminal courts, at least as judged by the data from Israel, is quite pronounced. It ranges from an overt advocation of talionic retaliation, through stressing the objective severity of an offence, to stressing the excessive criminal intent of the offender which deserves a harsher retributive reaction.

Instances of clear talionic sentencing grounds are the following:

"The defendant has deprived the complainant of the most important sense, his eye-sight; a human being derives the utmost delight and pleasure from his eyes. Our ancient Torah decreed in this case, an eye for an eye."[36]

"The defendant defiled the honour of a married woman, on her way to rejoin her husband—this calls for a heavy penalty."[37]

"We are of the opinion that such despicable acts as the simulation of a theft in order to swindle insurance money are extremely abhorrant and call for the severest penalties."[38]

148

Grounds which stress the objective damage caused by the offense are illustrated by the following:

"The value of the stolen property is considerable".

"The defendant has injured the complainant's body very severely".

"When a man's life has been taken, fines do not suffice as punishment".

These grounds display the retributive symptoms: they are solely concerned with the objective outcome of the offense; they refer to the past and not to the possible effect of the penalty on the future behaviour of the offender or of potential offenders. Other retributive grounds take the victim's point of view: "The appellant stabbed a social worker who for a long time had taken care of him and arranged jobs and lodgings for him and his family. The penalty should be raised therefore from four to five years imprisonment."[39]

"The appellant committed his offence while being a member of a public body. The victims were 14 families of new immigrants who gave him their trust; we feel that these circumstances call for a severe punishment."[40]

Still another group of retributive sentencing grounds stress the excessive criminal intent which a defendent had while committing the offence. This is superfluous as far as substantive criminal law is concerned. The proof of *mens rea* is imperative at the conviction stage; without it guilt has not been proved. The mentioning of an excessive *mens-rea* at the sentencing stage could only be interpreted as a retributory attitude towards the defendant.

The inverse relationship holds here too, because a judical punishment is largely interpreted by the defendant himself and the public at large as the retaliatory mechanism against crime. The public through the press might even clamour and lament what seems to it the over leniency of the courts in certain cases. Moreover, the retaliatory attitude does not subside with the conviction and sentence; the stigma of an "ex-con" trails the offender and limits his socio-economic opportunities long after he has served his sentence and presumably paid his dues to society.

14. Deterrence, although less prominent than retribution, seems to affect considerably the sentencing policy of the courts. If we resort again to the Israeli courts, we find deterrent grounds which stress the necessity of deterring the *convicted* offender from committing further offences in the future, so called "individual prevention".

"It is necessary to deter the defendant by a heavy penalty from committing further offences."

"The punishments inflicted on the defendant in the past were too light and apparently they were not sufficient to teach him a lesson."

The "general prevention" grounds stress the presumed deterrent effect of punishment on potential offenders:

"It is necessary to eradicate the 'knife-culture.'"

"A light punishment will create 'a paradise for criminals'."

"Orderly life in society necessitates that the public's confidence in its banks should be stable. This confidence may be guarded only by severe penalties against its infringements."

"The management had full confidence in the appellants, but the latter conspired against the management and the factory. It is necessary that this kind of confidence breakers and their like should understand that amassing fortunes in this way is not profitable."[41]

"Punishment of motoring offences should be severe enough to curb the harvest of blood and the havoc on the roads that we are witnessing daily."[42] The inverse relationship is quite problematic. Although nobody doubts that punishment does have a deterrent effect, the greatest enigma of modern penology is still the effective scope of deterrence and the range of its effect as far as type of offence and type of offender are concerned.

15. There seems to be no link between the penalty prescribed by law and the actual punishment inflicted by the trial judge. We examined the relationship in the sentencing of the district courts of Israel and found that the peak of severity of actual sentences was for offenses the maximum penalties for which were five and seven years. The severity of actual punishments tended to decline

towards both tails of the curve, i.e., when maximum penalties were less than five years or more than seven years.[43]

The inverse relationship does not seem to hold. There is apparently no effect of the sentencing policy of courts on the penalties fixed by law.

16. The effect of the resistance potential of a norm and the formal loss of rights after the conviction for its infringement have been historically quite pronounced.

Wolfgang tells us, for instance, that in medieval Florence:
"The bankrupts were considered public delinquents . . . The grandfather, father, sons and descendants of the honest bankrupt were held answerable for him in goods and person . . . The sons afterwards, were declared infamous, and deprived of all civic rights and all male descendants of fraudulent bankrupts, though born and privileges as Florentine citizens, including eligibility to public office, their wives, children, servants and even their neighbours, might . . . be arrested and punished at the magistrate's discretion."[44]

In the money lending, commercial and fiercely lucrative medieval towns, a bankrupt was indeed anathema. Similarly, according to the 17th century regulations of the Jewish Ghettoes in Lithuania, the bankrupt, the gambler and patron of gentile houses of entertainment lost their community rights.[45]

Bankruptcy injured the mainly commercial economic structure of the European Jewish communities, whereas the other two are against the religious and moral core of Jewish life. It is doubtful, however, whether the modern instances of loss of rights specified in the penal codes of France,[46] Germany,[47] and Italy,[48] restricting electoral rights, some familial rights, and the civil and social rights of convicted offenders reflect the present day resistance potential of the norms as measured by the attitudes of the modern populations of these countries.

The formal loss of rights after conviction might have a feedback effect on the resistance potential of a norm but its nature and magnitude seem quite uncertain.

17. The link between righteous indignation and loss of rights

151

seems quite discernible. Eden, that old self-proclaimed crusader for harsh punishments, favoured the pillory and the loss of civil rights of offenders because: "The idea of shame should follow the finger of the law."[49]

Again in Florence: "The general extravagance in the dress of all ranks and both sexes had early called for Cosimos' interference by the Law of October 19, 1546. . . . citizens who did not comply with the dress habits were punished by forfeiting their eligibility to office."[50] The loss of rights here followed a seemingly super-Victorian fervour against conspicuity and extravagance in dress and manner.

When we turn to modern penal codes we find, for instance, in the French Code that loss of civil rights was antecedent to infamous offences which were followed by *infamous* punishments.[51]

"Infamous", "involving or indicating moral turpitude": the link between these emotionally loaded epithets and righteous indignation becomes therefore apparent. The inverse relationship, although tenable, is less apparent because the whole idea of the loss of civil rights following conviction is a diminishing legal phenomenon. In England, the U.S.A. and other Anglo-Saxon countries influenced by the Common Law, it has never been extensively resorted to. In Sweden, this formal loss of rights was abrogated in 1930. In France, Germany, Italy, and Switzerland it gradually but systematically diminished in scope. The Council of Europe, in its resolution of 1st February, 1962 reproduced in extenso in the notes below,[52] proposes to limit to a bare minimum the loss of electoral, civil and social rights of convicted offenders.

18. The retributive basis of the loss of rights is already apparent in the wrath of Ezra when he decreed the loss of rights of all those who did not come to the gathering in Jerusalem.[53]

If we scan the legal provisions in some codes prescribing the loss of rights following a conviction we find in the French Penal Code the deprivation of the right to wear medals and decorations, disqualification from being a court-appointed expert, a witness to legal instruments, a guardian, prohibition to bear arms, to be a member of the National Guard, to serve in the French Armed

Forces.[54] The German Penal Code decrees that the loss of civil rights entails the disqualification for the period provided by the judgement to acquire public offices, honours, titles, orders and medals, to vote, to be a witness, to be a guardian.[55] The Italian Penal Code of 1930 specifies the loss of the husband's familial right, the rights to vote, to hold office, Government pensions, medals and academic titles.[56] These seem to be less utilitarian preventive measures than retaliatory and retributive ones. The loss of rights here is more a loss of status, honour and titles. Being a witness, making a deed and performing other formal rights are also abrogated because of their honorific and ritualistic nature.

The inverse relationship will also hold, because the loss of rights is bound to be interpreted by the defendant himself and the public at large as a retaliatory measure, in addition to the ordinary punitive measures which have already been inflicted.

19. The abrogation, curtailment, forfeiture or annulment of licenses and permits to practice the professions a trade or an occupation are more of a utilitarian nature involving deterrent and preventive considerations.

The last interrelationships, between stigma and the other variables in the scale, have been widely discussed and analysed in previous chapters. We have seen the strong reciprocity between stigma, the resistance potential of a norm and retribution. The latter kindles the subconscious and subterranean reservoirs of aggressivity and negativity which erupt into the scapegoating fervour of stigma. We have also seen that in many instances the most potent deterrent is the stigma of conviction, and its socio-economic effects. A somewhat less pronounced relationship exists between the sanction prescribed by law and stigma. The former is a formal legalized construct whereas the latter is a group-behavioural entity, and the two do not always harmonize. We have also seen in the previous chapters that there is a strong inter-relationship between stigma, the sanction actually inflicted and the loss of rights.

CHAPTER VIII

THE EFFECTS OF SOCIAL STIGMA

If people know I'm a criminal they won't really accept me; and if they don't know (when you take one of your friends, for instance), well, if they did know, they wouldn't accept me...Whether I look upon myself like that or not, other people certainly do. Other people's opinions shouldn't matter, I suppose, but they do . . . *

THE STIGMA OF CONVICTION

The stigma of conviction or of social deviation limits a person's social and economic opportunities, and his status and role are forcibly changed. At first, he may reject some of the group's norms and seek the company of others with similar "adjustment" problems. Eventually, he may adopt the norms and values of the deviant group, where his stigma becomes a status symbol.

The branding of a person as socially deviant is very similar in its dynamics to W.I. Thomas' basic theorem: "If men define situations as real, they are real in their consequences." Merton illustrates the effect of this in his "self-fulfilling prophecy".[1] If people say a bank is insolvent, the bank becomes insolvent when all the depositors rush to withdraw their deposits. When a group declares a person to be deviant, the prophecy fulfills itself and he becomes deviant (irrespective of his initial beliefs and behaviour). This is well known to rumour-spreaders and gossip-columnists (who are most powerful social stigmatizers): they spread the "news" that somebody is "anti-social" or "neurotic," and everyone then treats him accordingly. The branded individual is upset by the change of attitude toward him, and this in turn is interpreted as partial corroboration of the rumours; a positive feed-back cycle operates on ego

* Tony Parker and Robert Allerton, *The Courage of his Convictions*

equilibrium of the individual and eventually he does become anti-social.

We shall pursue our analysis on two levels: the effects of stigma on the individual and the way he perceives it, and the relevance of social stigma to the formation of deviant subcultures.

The Powerful Tags

Tannenbaum recognized the effects of social stigma: "There is a gradual shift from the definition of the specific acts as evil to a definition of the individual as evil, so that all his acts come to be looked upon with suspicion. In the process of identification, his companions, hangouts, plays, speech, income, all his conduct, the personality itself becomes subject to scrutiny and question. . . The first dramatization of 'evil' which separates the child out of his group for specialized treatment plays a greater role in making the criminal than perhaps any other experience . . . he has been tagged. A new and hitherto non-existent environment has been precipitated out for him. The process of making the criminal (or the anti-social person) therefore, is a process of tagging, defining, identifying, segregating, describing, emphasizing, making conscious and self-conscious. It becomes a way of stimulating, suggesting, emphasizing and evoking the very traits that are complained of. . . It identifies him to himself or to the environment as a delinquent person. . . The person becomes the thing he is described as being." [2]

An excellent example of the effects of stigma on the self-image of an ex-convict was provided by the hero of the film *The Mark*. An ex-prisoner who had served a sentence for indecent assault on a child managed to get a job, lodgings and a girl friend, until a sensation-seeking journalist publicized his story, warning the public that a sex maniac was at large. The ex-prisoner came to his prison psychiatrist begging to be re-admitted to prison, saying: "Look, Doc, everyone says I am a sex maniac, so I must be one: they can't all be wrong, can they? And surely a sex maniac's place is in prison."

155

Tappan cites a case of a delinquent who "went straight" for a while after being adopted by a wealthy foster mother: "He returned to school and completed the first year of high school which ended his formal education. The record indicates that he became much disturbed at school when a woman from the Parent-Teacher Association objected to his taking part in a school play because he was illegitimate. The principal reminded him of his past and took him out of the play."[3] The boy then ran away and cashed forged cheques.

An ex-prisoner who spent more than ten years in prison said in an interview that an "ex-con", even a very intelligent one, who wishes to "go straight", is subject to tremendous stigmatizing pressures and barriers. "A guy," he said, "might be accepted for a while by the squares, for the novelty of the thing; he is treated like an exotic animal, he has some interesting stories or experiences to relate, after all, a criminal alive and kicking is more interesting than a detective story. But the novelty wears off, the squares have enough, the ex-con is not really accepted and he must find other company, where he is treated on equal terms. This, and not the economic difficulties, is the main reason for the renewed association with ex-cons like himself; nobody there can snub him or look at him as if he were a monkey in a zoo, and this, of course, is a sure way to go back to jobs and to prison."

Another "ex-con" said in our interview: "The hell with them, they won't leave a fellow alone, what do they (the police) want of my life. O.K., so I go around with crooks, and my girl friends are whores, but where can I get another crowd to mix with? If I go with a straight fellow, they immediately come over and squeeze the hell out of him. If I go with a straight girl they come over to her and say: Going around with a criminal, eh? Don't you know who he is? And of course she does not want to go out with me anymore. It's only with whores they can't mess up things for me, so I hang around with them." Different versions of this have often been voiced; it is not really relevant if the facts are well founded or not. The point is that the released convict usually defines his situation as a stigmatizing one that will push him to continued association with the criminal subculture.

The author recently interviewed a highly-skilled ex-burglar who, though he had abandoned his criminal trade five years earlier, was still maintaining his social contacts with his former criminal mates: "The others don't invite me, and if they do, they put on an act, over-polite, careful with their words and all the rest of the crap; I feel better with old Nissim, Zaki and Dodo—they are after all the only friends I have." The most remarkable aspect of the case is how this fellow managed to "stay clean" for five years while maintaining social contacts with his underworld friends.

This case, of course, is quite characteristic of the effects of social stigma. By abstaining from crime for a considerable period, he clearly showed his desire to lead a law-abiding life; but his mannerisms, expressions, emotional affiliations and personal preferences were with the criminal subculture. He tried to emerge from the latter, but was sharply and rudely driven back to "where he belongs". The pressures to conform within the criminal sub-culture, i.e. to join the crowd in committing "jobs" was, of course, tremendous. His ability to withstand, for any length of time, the pressure to belong not only socially but also professionally to his actual membership group is, unfortunately, a matter of uneven (and unfair) odds.

In a detailed study, Kelner quotes a prostitute's conviction that, "people never help you to go straight; on the contrary, they'll always push you back to the gutter. I tried to help myself. I tried to go straight, and began to work in an orange grove. Everything went fine, until somebody told the foreman who I was, and I was chucked out immediately; the foreman, never-theless, tried to get it for free. I went to the labour exchange, but what was the use? Somebody recognized me, talked or hinted, and I was out of a job again." When she finally found herself a boyfriend, she decided that if they would be true to each other, she had to tell him of her past. This, she felt, would purify and expiate her and make her worthy of his love. He left her immediately and wrote her a letter saying that she was much worse than she told him, because she was a "fake and a phony, and all the love she had shown him was not love at all, but mere routine of a professional."[4] It was indeed a freak of nature, and certainly to the credit of the treatment she received, that this prostitute was finally rehabilitated.

The effect of stigma on an individual offender, from the first offence onwards, is a vicious circle, a positive feed-back cycle between society and the criminal. The first step is presumably taken by society in three directions; economic, domestic and social. The narrowing of job opportunities, the severing of business links, the withholding of financial credit, are some of the wide range of economic effects of the stigma of crime. Domestic difficulties—divorce, separation and disruption of relationships between parents and children or the criminal and other members of his wider family—are common consequences.

The most potent effect of stigma is apparent, however, in the "general attitude" of society, the "man in the street," by whom he is treated with suspicion, unnatural courtesy or perverse curiosity. If the effects of his stigma become uncomfortable, burdensome or even unbearable to the individual, he will tend to react along the lines of least resistance. As far as economic problems are concerned, if the effects of the stigma have been severe enough objectively or have been perceived as such subjectively by the individual, the outlet can be to do another "job" with the crowd. The road to recidivism is lengthy, and involves the differential association process with the criminal group and learning the technique of crime.

However, frequently further crime is the most handy trade for an ex-con just out of prison who has had some failures in securing himself a legitimate trade. Quite often crime is the sole occupation, and it seems feasible and "proper" to a stigmatized ex-convict who has recently left his prison cell and whose only social contacts are inmates or ex-inmates. The easiest alternative for domestic relations which have been severed or damaged as consequences of "how can I show my face in public with a criminal husband?" or "what are people going to say?" are transient relationships with women who are not deterred by social stigma. Mostly these are women who are stigmatized themselves, such as hostesses, call-girls and street-walkers. The reaction of the stigmatized individual toward the stigmatizing "generalized other" is a tough task, and it involves the formulation of a *ressentiment,* a "sour grapes" attitude. It is quite irrelevant whether this attitude is based on rationalizations or facts.

The empirical findings on the social effects of convictions are quite meagre; Reitzes' study as to the effect of social environment upon former felons[5] is noteworthy, and it contains data which are relevant to the three main areas of adjustment: employment, domestic relations and social contacts. In employment, those who were more skillfull or fortunate in hiding their previous criminal records could hold their jobs longer, and their resultant stability at work contributed to a lower proneness to recidivism. The domestic relations of non-recidivists as compared to recidivists were characterized by fewer divorces and separations, and less conflicts with spouses in those cases where they lived together. They had more contacts with parental families, and these contacts were of a more harmonious nature. The cause and effect here are interchangeable, but this is less relevant than the fact that families of the non-recidivist felons were less exposed to the derogatory effects of convictions than the families of recidivists. The social contacts of non-recidivists were overwhelmingly from legitimate opportunity structures, and they were, as a rule, members of non-criminal organizations. Here again we cannot point out clearly the dependent and independent variables, but the prior rejection of recidivists by non-criminal contacts and organizations fits the present finding. A wide-scale study is being carried out at present as to the social effects of convictions by John P. Martin under the auspices of the Cambridge Institute of Criminology. This study, which at the time of writing is at its data collection stage, intends to provide a detailed empirical answer to problems of the extent and nature of the effects of conviction on offenders' social position, that is, status and roles in his employment and family life. The study itself is being conducted on three-hundred men charged with offences committed in the County Borough of Reading.[6] Some of the initial hypotheses of this study relate to the disintegration of many marriages following conviction, and the resultant short-term purely hedonistic and more casual relationship with other women. Social relationships become less enduring and more shallow; they tend to cut off their relationship with more people in law-abiding society with every new conviction and "drift into the half-world of pubs, clubs, cafes, betting shops, etc., which would offer undemanding relationships. Having 'done time' would no longer be a disadvantage and, sooner or later, the chance of taking part in a further 'job' might present itself".[7] These hypotheses are strongly linked to some of the premises in our work and their empirical testing will shed light on the validity of some of our hypotheses as to the effect of stigma on the future behaviour of convicts. The National Council on Crime and Delinquency in the U.S. has recently drafted a Model Act to annul convictions for crime. This would result, in appropriate cases, in cushioning or even preventing the presumably stigmatizing pressures towards recidivism on first offenders.

THE STIGMA OF DEVIATION

In the first part of our analysis we dealt with the effects of stigma on the genesis of recidivism; we shall now proceed to examine the effects of stigma on social deviation.

Merton, who initiated much of the study and research on anomie and social deviation, tries to differentiate in his *Continuities in The Theory of Reference Groups and Social Structure,* between non-conformist and criminal behaviour. He notes the "moral indignation" which, in his view, is one of the most forceful reactions of the public towards social deviation. Moral indignation was conceived by Merton as follows: "The orthodox [conformist] members of the social system ... respond with hostility, [towards the deviant], since they have internalized the moral norms now being violated and experience the behaviour which in effect repudiates these norms, or threatens their continued social validity, as a denial of the worth of what they, and their groups, hold dear. The form which such reprisals take is best described as 'moral indignation' ... Were it not for this reservoir of moral indignation, the mechanisms of social control would be severely limited in their operation. They would be confined only to the action of people who are directly disadvantaged by non-conformist and deviant behaviour. However, moral indignation to deviant behaviour lends greater strength to the mechanisms of social control, for not only the relatively small number of people directly injured by deviance,—but also the large collectivity, adhering to the culturally established norms are activated to bring the deviant [and by anticipation, other prospective deviants] back into line".[8] What Merton prefers to denote "moral indignation"[9] has most of the components and characteristics of social stigma. The anxiety generated by the deviant act, the threat to the normative-system, and, therefore, to the status and roles of the conformist gives rise to a reaction, *quite distinct from any other sanction formal or otherwise,* which is apparently a generic tool of social control and which we have identified as social stigma.

We claim, however, that the mechanisms and effects of stigma both as an accelerating pressure towards further deviation, and as an inner control for those who do keep to their normative grooves, transcend the isolated areas referred to by Merton. Stigma operates through the vast machinery of trial by press and more widely through trial by gossip. The individual who finds himself libelled by the former soon realizes that unless he has the resources of a Rockfeller and nerves of steel, he has already lost the battle. If, however, he decides that the legal avenues are too costly or laborious and tries to fight back through the same medium, he will remain forever as "the one who raised this scandal", irrespective of whether he is right or wrong. By the mere fact of being outrageously conspicuous he is guilty. Trial by gossip is even more effective. We assume that the necessary elements for the genesis of stigma towards a certain individual, as elaborated previously, are indeed present in a given case. The act of stigmatizing consists of tagging the individual by an adjective which would make any material evaluation of his acts or personality superfluous. If the informal groups of stigmatizers brand somebody as an idiot, this settles the argument because obviously an idiot is capable of idiocy only; the verdict by gossip would probably hold even if the culprit presented a certificate from a trained mental tester that he was a genius. This, of course, is a simple example; more elaborate, subtle and effective are instances such as following: "Jones is all right, of course, but I have seen his hands shake, I hope to God he isn't a secret drunk." "Smith is first-class, I'm sure he is one of us, but Chris told me he has seen him at the bar with Wilson, that red bastard." Jones would find it hard to prove that he is not a secret drinker, and Smith cannot prove that he is not a red sympathizer because formally nobody said he was; they might as well try and prove that they are not homosexuals, do not beat their wives or do not drink the blood of children at Passover. What they have to do is attack the source of their stigma, that is, to renounce their conspicuity, adopt the cult of mediocrity and "participate", "adjust", above all be a "joiner" and more or less fit the description of the "socialized" individual portrayed by C. Wright Mills: "He conforms to middle-class morality and motives and partakes in the gradual progress of respectable institutions. He does not brood or mope about but is somewhat extrovert, eagerly participating in his community's institutions. His mother and father were not divorced, nor was his home ever broken. He is 'successful'—at least in a modest way—since he is ambitious but he does not speculate about matters too far above his means, lest he become 'a fantasy thinker', and the little men don't scramble after the big money. The less abstract the traits and fulfilled 'needs' of 'the adjusted man' are, the more they gravitate toward the norms of independent middle-class persons verbally living out Protestant [or Catholic, or Moslem or Jewish or "good-communist") ideals in the small towns of America [or throughout the world.][10]

Albert Cohen, in his analysis of the *Sociology of The Deviant Act,* feels that something is amiss in the current expositions of Anomie. He says: "The starting point of anomie theory was the question: 'Given the social structure, or ego's milieu, what will ego do?'. The milieu was taken as more-or-less given, an independent variable whose value is fixed, and ego's behaviour as an adaptation to that milieu. Anomie theory has come increasingly to recognize the effects of deviance upon the very variables that determine deviance. But if we are interested in a general theory of deviant behaviour we must explore much more systematically ways of conceptualizing the interaction between deviance and milieu."[11]

Our present stigma theory is one such attempt to explain the effects of social branding on ego's deviance, further deviation, and the normative structure as a whole. We shall begin by stressing the functionality of social stigma. This is in line with the teachings of George Simmel and his modern exponents, especially Lewis Coser, as to the functionality of social conflict.[12]

We have already shown that social stigma serves as an outlet for accumulated aggression and frustration, a kind of "letting off steam" through a safety-valve mechanism, which is indeed embodied in the operation of social stigma. It serves to delineate the rules and strengthens the in-group by stigmatizing and excluding individual outsiders or the out-groups. This analysis imputes functionality to deviance insofar as it serves as an object to stigma. Cohen realizes this when he says: "Since other's wickedness sets off the jewel of one's own virtue, and one's claim to virtue is at the core of his public identity, one may actually develop a stake in the existence of deviant others, and be threatened should they pretend to moral excellence."[13]

Genet puts it more bluntly by pointing out that without criminals there would be nobody to judge. The judge is therefore, dependent, for his very existence, on the criminal.[14] Nobody seriously

163

argues the contention that the so-called progress of civilization has mostly been brought about by a continuous chain of innovations. We have already pointed out that innovators are the ideal objects to be branded as deviants. The process of stigmatization, as stated in chapters 2 and 3 is not necessarily linked with the specific mode of innovation or deviation, but displaces and substitutes some aggression or deficiency of the stigmatizer, who imputes them by projection and transference to the innovator or deviant. In these cases, the innovator cannot grasp the reasons for his being stigmatized because he cannot comprehend the link between his behaviour and the group's attitude towards him. There is of course, no direct link, and the stigmatized innovator is driven to a wide range of reactions within a dichotomy. He can choose to renounce legitimacy from a society which stigmatizes its innovating benefactors and devote his life to dissect and abuse its absurd social and normative structure. He can do his best to change, injure or overthrow it. Another way leads to self-doubt, depression, autism, and self-destruction.

We propose now to analyse the effects of stigma on the various modes of social deviations examined by us previously. Of the four types of deviation in our paradigm which have been tagged with stigma, one, the "true" deviant can be excluded in the present context, as this category includes mostly the criminals and some types of deviants formally stigmatized by official organs, and we have already dealt with the effect of stigma on them.

THE EFFECT OF STIGMA ON THE VICTIMS

In their ideal type, these are the scapegoats, and are innocent in as much as they are factually unrelated to the act or acts imputed to them, but they are indeed guilty as far as their symbolic relation to stigma is concerned. The human scapegoat has been magnificently portrayed recently in Bernard Malamud's novel *The Fixer*. This work is semi-historical because it is based on the

Beiliss case, one of the notorious "ritual murder" trials in Russia at the beginning of the century. The victim, whom Malamud calls Bok, (literally "goat" in German and in Yiddish) is accused of killing a Christian boy and using his blood for the Passover feast. What makes Bok fit for the role of victim and scapegoat is his being a stranger not only to Russia but to the Jews as well. He has left Judaism for Spinoza and his wife left him for a *goy*. He chastises the Christians for not being good Christians and he, himself a Jew, makes a living by working for an eminent anti-Semite. In his cell, he reads the Beatitudes on his knees for a Christian cell-mate who committed suicide.

Malamud depicts here, with theoretical sensitivity that good novelists often possess, the actual criteria of choosing a scapegoat, the chronic angularities protruding from all the social structures which are normatively streamlined by nature. The odd ends are disgustedly thrown to the garbage pile by the regulating mechanisms of stigma. The disgust is greater when the symbolic essence of the scapegoat to the stigmatizer is more relevant. Then the horror is complete.

The effect of stigma on the victimized is more extreme, and is manifest in the severity of sanction. A partial explanation for this extreme reaction can be found in the symbolic and sub-conscious sources of scapegoating. The covert, non-rational and cognitive incomprehensibility of a person's hatred and violent negativity towards a prospective victimized scapegoat fill him with fear and anxiety. These presumably augment the violent attitude towards the victim through the various mecha-nisms of reaction formation and projection of guilt; criminals or deviants whose behaviour is cognitively more comprehensible will presumably encounter a less violent reaction than those whose behaviour seems incomprehensible.

An instance in which the results of stigmatized victimization became an orgy of torture and horror was, of course, the treatment of heretics by the Inquisition; the victims paid dearly for the anxiety and even sheer terror of the established theocratic sects from the rival paths to salvation. The *prima facie* plausibility of the rival sectarian doctrine was a direct threat to the existence of the established theocratic power elite. Runciman's pious observation that "The church was narrow-minded because the true path is narrow and it knew that for Christians no other path led to Salvation"[15] seems hopelessly facile. The contrary is true. The Gnostics, the Manichees and Cathars were persecuted so furiously because their proposed path to salvation did seem at least as feasible as the official one.

The danger and anxiety in this case were less symbolic and more imminent, because the schismatic sectarians were professed heretics against the accepted dogma. However, the treatment of the various social deviants by the Inquisition under the blanket-pretext of heresy is of more direct interest to us. Lea tells us that, as from the 13th century, all Christians were ordered by the Church to denounce heretics to the Inquisition. No familial, social or amorous ties were regarded as an excuse, and in some cases parents and children, husbands and wives denounced one another. The only sin which the confessor priest had to report to the Inquisition was heresy, thereby breaking his vow of secrecy.[16] The procedure before the Inquisition started with the report of the confessor priest; names were given by other heretics or witnesses who appeared before the Inquisition or by any other individual who volunteered to give evidence of heresy. Any jurist, civil rights activist or social worker who has doubts as to the slow but nevertheless evident evolution of modern trial procedure should consider the following: after the hearing of fragments of gossip, confession by a husband as to his wife's heresy, or the evidence offered by a jealous business associate, the defendants were brought before the Inquisitors. These unfortunates had then a miserable choice: they could either confess and be punished by heavy penance, or deny their guilt and be turned over to the secular authorities to be burned on the auto-da-fe. One can infer from the register of Carcassonne that no other choice existed. Of the two-hundred cases dealt with by the Inquisition of this town from 1249 to 1258 *not one was found to be innocent*.[17] The results of the stigma of heresy were, therefore, uniform in their finality. Escape was impossible, the tightly knit mediaeval society was covered by the intelligence net of the Inquisition. The word was spread throughout Europe "putting the authorities on the alert to search for every stranger who wore the air of one differing from the ordinary run of the faithful".[18] The different, the strange, the unfamiliar, the odd-looking, the out-of-place had most of the characteristics we have attributed to the objects of stigma. Their conspicuity and apartness aroused anxiety; they are different and powerless. They would be, therefore, tagged as heretics, snared, hunted and turned over to the Inquisition to do penance or be burned at the stake.

The second factor determining the effect of stigma on the victim is the social proximity of victim and stigmatizer: The greater the proximity the harsher the effect. If both belong to the same membership group, reference group or belief system, the effect of stigma was notoriously extreme. This premise is quite close to one of the rules formulated by George Simmel on social conflict. "People who have many common features often do one another worse wrongs than do complete strangers. The more we have in common with another as whole persons, the more easily will our totality be involved in every single relation to him. Therefore, if a quarrel arises between persons in such an intimate relationship, it is often so passionately expansive. This hatred is directed against a member of the group, not from personal motives, but because the member presents a danger to the preservation of the group."[19] Here, of course, the hypotheses for conflict and for stigma diverge. The stigmatized, especially the victim, does present a symbolic danger to the stigmatizing individual. With stigma, unlike open conflict, the danger to the group is amorphous and the anxiety of individuals is the prime mover of the branding mechanisms. Of further relevance is Simmel's observation on the renegade: "The recall of earlier agreement has such a strong effect that the new contrast is infinitely sharper and bitterer than if no relation at all had existed in the past . . . respect for the enemy, is usually absent where

167

the hostility has arisen on the basis of previous solidarity."[20] Coser, one of Simmel's contemporary disciples, also stresses the violence which erupts from the group towards the heretic, a violence which is more destructive than against that levelled at the non-believer or the apostate. Coser attributes this harsher reaction against a deviating ideological sibling to the actual and imminent danger which he constitutes to the established part of the ideological family. Heresy is a competition for ideological loyalties and this is the reason, according to Coser, "why Trotsky appeared to Stalin as a more serious danger than General Vlasov, and why Lenin's most violent denunciatory language is not directed against any capitalist but reserved for Karl Kautsky".[21] Here again our proposition is similar to the one reformulated by Coser as far as their factual manifestations are concerned. However, we differ in the interpretation of the greater violence against deviants from a very close ideological proximity. We hold that the actual danger afforded by the exiled and ailing Trotsky at the time of his assassination to the then all-powerful Stalin was next to nil. One could be a Trotskyite by adopting Trotsky's teachings, as one could be a Marxist decades after the death of Marx. The frail and practically powerless Madame Sun-yat-Sun did not present any actual danger to the Red Guards in Peking who nevertheless abused her violently. As Coser himself notes, there are realistic and non-realistic elements in conflict situations.[22] The stigmatized victim can, therefore, be more of a non-realistic antagonist. Trotsky was as good as dead many years before he was assassinated. It was Stalin's primaeval fear which necessitated the final ritualistic sacrifice of the "Enemy of The People". Victims are household necessities for any solidarist group; but the more a group is cohesive, the more is it anxious and jealous of its cohesion,[23] the more it needs to stigmatize real or imaginary deviant victims, and the harsher is the treatment of these victims. This premise may be considered as quite satisfactorily documented and tested by the works of Back,[24] Festinger,[25] Schachter,[26] Berkowitz and Howard,[27] and Weller[28].

168

STIGMA AND INNER CONFLICT

A comprehensive prognosis of the effects of stigma on the syndrome which we have described as inner conflict is a practically impossible. All that we have done is to trace a relatively narrow segment of the wide and complicated process related to the internalization of social norms by individuals. This segment deals with the special case of individuals internalizing the social norms in their literal sense. They are not unaware of the flexible relativity of the compliance of most people to these norms, and for them these norms are, so to speak, the essence of life, without which all existence seems empty and absurd. The inner conflict here would be, presumably, a developmental phase: the discord between the internalized ideal of a norm by ego and his perception of the partial or non-adherence to this norm by most of the relevant alters. This conflict is resolved into diverse types of deviations and alienations depending on the personality in each case. Our hypothesis on the effect of stigma on this transitional inner conflict falls into two complementary parts: first, the stigma itself is relatively strong, and second, the stronger the stigma, the shorter the period of inner conflict. The first part stems from the very nature of our brand of inner conflict. An individual who does insist on adhering to norms that others prefer to pay lip service to, is an irritating *j'accuse* of their hypocrisy. If someone does not understand that adultery is acceptable if not too public and with the "right" kind of woman he is a prude. If someone takes too literally the honesty and propriety slogans of his local Chamber of Commerce or Rotary Club he is not only a bore but also not a businessman, and he will probably not last long as a member of the chamber. Scheller assured us many years ago that this dual-moral accountancy is a sheer necessity for the world of commerce and industry. "The qualities that enable [the businessman, the industrialist, the executive] to succeed are set up as generally valid [indeed the "highest"] moral values. Cleverness, quick adaptability, a sense for the 'calculability' of all circumstances."[29] If someone positively affirms the deflated norms which have become mere banalities in inaugural addresses and sermons he is unacceptable; he is unearthing the normative skeletons in the groups' moral junk-and the reaction, depending on the degree of inner cohesion, will be harsh indeed. The second part of the hypothesis is linked to the violent push of a stronger stigma on the individual to leave the no man's land of inner conflict towards conformity or a more definite pattern of deviation. If an individual displaying our present syndrome is being dismissed by the group as a mild case of Jesuitis or moral ossification he will be left alone to a life-time of pondering on the relative merits of his moral rigidity and everybody else's double-thinking flexibility. He himself will probably evaluate his moral stance as absolute, having selectively remembered or retained the instances which reinforce his moral self-concept. This is as relevant (or irrelevant) as a camel seeing the humps of every beast in the herd, but not its own. The crucial point is that the conflict between ego's subjective legitimization of the ideal of a norm and its mass infringement or adulteration by most of the relevant others, although accompanied by verbal tribute, is resolved more unilaterally by the group's stigma than by ego's introspection. A strong stigmatizing reaction will tend to buffet the individual more quickly to conformity, in this case to realize the all important difference between formal, external and verbal support of the norm and the far less prevailing behavioural adherence to it. This is how most adolescents are "broken in" by the adult world. They are socialized into discarding their "intolerance of ambiguity" so that they internalize an amorphic, ambiguous, flexible and therefore "mature" normative system. Another direction to which an individual is pushed after even a shorter period of inner conflict (depending on the violence of the stigmatizing reaction) is towards behaviour deviation. It is impossible and superfluous to enumerate the various modes of deviation that can follow the inner-conflict phase. However, one typical example can be given for illustrative purposes. A very common sequel to inner conflict in our present sense is likely be "social marginality". The "Marginal Man",

170

as originally conceived by Park[30] and Stonequist[31], was an individual who sat between two or more cultural chairs without being able to claim any of them as his own. These were generally individuals entangled in inter-racial relationship or culture conflict due to migration and ethnocentrism. The marginality in our case, being a matter of different origin, would probably manifest itself by marginality of a higher social visibility. The individual being disgusted with one group for failing to come up to his internalized normative absolutes, tries to affiliate himself to another group, only to find out sooner or later that the second is no better than the first as far as compliance to his inner normative image is concerned. He then turns to a third, a fourth, a fifth group, realizing to his growing dismay that these are no better than the previous ones. After he has passed the initial stage of inner conflict at which he was still capable of confronting his own idealized norms with the moral flexibility of the group, he is no longer able to grasp that he is chasing a mirage. He would enter a vicious circle of changing group affiliations in rapid succession, probably involving instability of employment and breakdown of family. This person can be likened to the the nymphomaniac who chases the n'th male who, she hopes has for her the coveted orgasm she has never attained. The marginality in our case could lead, by a positive feed-back cycle, to the breakdown of ego control and even culminate in a psychotic process in which an individual's absolute norms reign supreme in his private hallucinatory world. To conclude this part of our analysis we shall return to the best source of all, the Greek tragedy. In Sophocles' *Phoenician Women,* Eteocles, one of Oedipus' sons who refuses to hand over sovereignity of Thebes as agreed beforehand to his brother Polyneikes, confesses candidly: "Among men equal rights exist merely in name, not in reality. . . If wrong must be done, it should be for Royal power; in other matters, pious conduct should be observed."[32] This is a "realistic" and "mature" flexibility of norms. The inner conflict of an Oedipus might, therefore, be interpreted with a novel hue: he took *too* literally the norms and the mandates imposed by the Gods.

171

THE STIGMATIZED DEFIANTS

The difference between inner conflict and defiance are both material and formal. Defiance is value deviation inasmuch as not only the relevant group values are rejected but also the individual's own are adopted in their stead. In inner conflict the norms of the group are adopted, but in a too literal manner and with abstract rigidity. Formally, inner conflict is a transitional phase whereas defiance is more of the solidified outcome of inner-conflict itself. The effects of stigma on the defiant can be and very often are the renunciation of value deviation in favour of conformity. The pressures to conform combine with stigma to weaken the conviction in the specific brand of value deviation. Asch reports that value deviants, when confronted experimentally with group pressures to conform, felt that: "There was a lurking fear that in some way I did not understand I might be wrong . . . I felt disturbed, puzzled, separated, like an outcast from the rest. Every time I disagreed I was beginning to look funny . . . It is more pleasant if one is really in agreement."[33] Once self-doubts have crept in as to the veracity or feasibility of defiance, the first step back to conformity has been made. The outsider's dilemma is apparently voiced here too: In one's value judgement one stands apart, but how much nicer would it be to be accepted, together with the crowd, the "us". The reduction of anxiety by "togetherness" is a truism. The menacing reef loses much of its danger if another skin diver is present. A lone pleasure seeker in Pigale, Soho or the Ripperbahn is a jittery and timid soul, but he becomes full of bravado in the company of others. Value deviation is an even lonelier affair. The defiant's ability to combat self-doubts is quite erratic. Even if he does not succumb to the group's stigmatizing pressure he experiences a gradual loss of certainty as to the validity of his stance. He becomes less certain about his judgments even in relation to his values and norms which are not opposed to those of the group.[34] This deterioration of the normative defences coupled with growing anxiety and self-doubt will often lead, jostle or push the defiant, depending on the strength of stigma, back to value conformity. However, the movement can be away from conformity towards a more pronounced and bitter defiance. It is beyond the scope of the present work to distinguish between factors which move an individual one way or the other. Some outstanding research findings may, however, be referred to: the Asch-Crutchfield conformity studies revealed that conformists were more submissive to authority, narrow of interest, over-controlled, plagued by anxiety and intolerant of ambiguity.[35] Linton demonstrated that persons who tend to respond acquiescently to problems and statements posed to them irrespective of their meaning also yield readily to the pressures of the majority towards conformity.[36] Moreover, those who tend to conform in one situation tend to conform in other situations as well.[37] Anchoring oneself on the majority, and the tendency to conform is more of a personality trait than a cognitive problem-solving process. On the other hand, a tendency towards deviance and, for our purposes, defiance, has also been identified as a personality trait. Berg examined the hypothesis that persons who are clearly deviant in their responses to some social norms also tend more to deviate from other norms so as to display an ever-enlarging pattern of deviance as a personality trait.[38] That means that the former personality traits studied by Crutchfield and Linton, if present within an individual personality structure and confronted by stigma, will tend to break down a defiant and lead him back to conformity. On the other hand a personality displaying Berg's pattern of deviance tends more to perpetuate and strengthen its defiance by a positive feed-back cycle.

The "authoritarian personality" who is intolerant of perceptual ambiguity tends more to conformity[39]; those whose initial level of certainty in their attitudes is high tend more to abide by their defiance.[40]

The effects of stigma on the defiant individual will depend on characteristics of the group: its size, inner cohesion, whether it is membership group or the reference group of the stigmatized defiant, whether the "resistance potential", that is, the inner strength of norms defied, is high or low, whether the defiant's dissent has little effect on the achievement of the group's goals or is regarded as crucial to the group's welfare.[41] These are but a few of the many variables which would determine the effects of stigma on the defiant.

CHAPTER IX

SOCIAL STIGMA
AND THE CRIMINAL GROUP

We are what they want us to be. We shall, therefore,
be it to the very end, absurdly. Put your masks on
*again before leaving. Have them escorted to Hell.**

SOCIAL STIGMA AND THE GENESIS
OF CRIMINAL AND DEVIANT SUBCULTURES

Theories on the aetiology of delinquent subcultures are many, varied and inconsistent. It is, however, imperative to trace the relationship of these with stigma apart from the effect of stigma on the future behaviour of the individual delinquent and deviant. One may crudely classify the delinquent subculture theories into three. This is an *ad hoc* taxonomy, and only the most representative theories have been included. The first group can be called "the class-centred" theories. They stress the divergent roles of youth caught between the clashes of class structures and the discrepancy between the normative system of the upper classes and the performance level of the lower-class youth. Most representative in this group would be the now classic theory of Albert Cohen[1] and the expositions of Whyte,[2] Miller,[3] and Cloward and Ohlin,[4] The second group of subculture theorists have linked the delinquent solution processes to various flaws in the primary socialization of the youth. These include Thrasher,[5] Parsons,[6] Bloch and Niederhoffer,[7] Erikson,[8] and Shoham.[9]

The third group of theorists see the delinquent gang as a corollary and receptacle of normative discord among individuals and groups in society and an outcome of a disjunction between the evaluations of an individual's behaviour by himself and by his membership or reference group. These are represented

* Jean Genet *The Blacks*

by Merton,[10] Tannenbaum,[11] Zorbaugh,[12] Landesco,[13] Kvara-ceus,[14] Yablonsky,[15] Sykes and Matza,[16] and Downes.[17] We shall start our analysis of the class-centred theories with the pioneering exposition of Albert Cohen. He regards the aetiology of the delinquent subculture as based on the discrepancy between middle-class norms and the achievement of lower-class boys; indeed, it is quite feasible to assume that a receptacle is needed for the rejects and failures among lower-class boys who lagged behind in the "rat race", the rules of which have been set by the middle-and upper-class elite. However, the causal chain here is, to say the least, disconnected. This group has to be organized and defined as criminal or deviant both by its members and "legitimate" society. This process of definition and self definition, the division between the in-group and the out ("legitimate") group, the delineation of the dividing barricade, is mostly an attitude forma-tion, and a name calling, a branding procedure, which operates in a closed cycle from the larger society to the subculture and vice-versa.

Cohen himself raises this point. He says: "Within the framework of goals, norms and opportunities, the process of deviance was conceptualized as though each individual were in a box by himself. He has internalized goals and normative, regulatory rules; he assesses the opportunity structure; he experiences strain; and he selects one or another mode of adaptation. The bearing of other's experience—their strains, the conformity and deviance—on ego's strain and consequent adaptations is comparatively neglected . . . *Deviant action is typically not contrived within the solitary psyche, but is part of a collaborative social activity, in which the things that other people say and do give meaning, value and effect to one' own behaviour.*"[18] Cohen feels, apparently, that there are some missing links between the failure experiences of a lower-class boy struggling with middle-class norms and the emergence of a delinquent gang or, for that matter, joining one. Cohen, to be sure, did not deal in his theory with the process of an individual's initiation into the life of crime and his association with criminal patterns of behav-iour, which was dealt with by Sutherland and his disciples.[19] Cohen expressly confined his analysis to the sociological function of the delinquent group and the social processes which give rise to it. Even in this relatively limited definition, Cohen himself feels that a process of tagging the group as deviant and the reaction of its members to his stigmatization should take place before its image is finally shaped. In other words, had Cohen formulated his criminal subculture theory today, he would have agreed that the stigmatizing pressures of the law-abiding society on the lower-class juveniles—and the latter's subsequent self-definition as delinquent gang members—play a major role in the aetiology of the delinquent subculture. Whyte's study of the gangs in the Italian slum in Cornerville has been heavily relied on and actually incorporated in Cloward and Ohlin's exposition of the differential opportunity structure. The limited access to legitimate opportunities as perceived and experienced by a lower-class boy or a slum kid may press him to be aware of the availability of illegitimate opportunities and try to find access to them.

The sociological function and structure of the delinquent subculture which an individual associates with would be classified, following Cloward and Ohlin, as follows:

1. *The Criminal Subculture:* (mainly property offences). Here the subculture members have been rejected from the legitimate opportunity structures. The avenues from a relatively organized slum to the illegitimate opportunity structures are readily accessible. The delinquent subculture is linked with the adult organized crime by means of a liaison man, usually the "fence". The young delinquent subculture serves as a recruiting depot for the adult "underworld".

2. *The Conflict (Violence) Subculture:* Here the young Puerto Ricans, or the violent gangs in the old immigrant camps in Israel, are detached both from the legitimate and illegitimate structures. They are not eligible for either because of language, ethnic origin and other socio-economic barriers. They form, therefore, their *delusive make-believe* worlds of kings, dragons and magicians; they also carve out "territories" for themselves, where fights

177

can be held, and status gained without resort to the inaccessible adult world.

3. *The Retreatist Subculture:* The retreatists have been rejected by and in turn rejected the legitimate achievement pyramid. They either had inner normative barriers against joining the illegitimate structure or been also rejected by the latter so as to become "double failures". Their solution became a collective fringe existence, where the main interests in life are "kicks" and euphoria.

One of the salient questions to be asked concerning the genesis of the delinquent subculture is the prevailing basis of rejection from the legitimate structures. This is readily answered by Cloward and Ohlin themselves: "The initial contest between the individual and the authorities over the legitimacy of certain social norms and the appropriateness of certain acts of deviance sets in motion a process of definition that marks the offender as different from law-abiding folk. His acts and his person are defined as 'evil' and he is caught up in a vicious cycle of non-violation, repression, resentment, and new and more serious acts of violation. The process of alienation is accelerated, and the chasm between the offender and those who would control and reform him grows wider and deeper. In such circumstances he becomes increasingly dependent on the support of others in his position. The gang of peers forms a new social world in which the legitimacy of delinquent conduct is strongly reinforced."[20] This obviously supports the stigma premise, but then they delve into an argument as to the relative importance of the youth's predisposition to deviance and the group's reaction to it in the genesis of the gang. They impute primacy to the former over the latter. This seems to be superfluous. We shall show that these two factors belong to different levels of causal analysis which we shall synchronize in one model. The first is a configuration of predisposing factors and the second belongs to a chain of dynamic pressures which lead a given individual to association with criminal and deviant groups and to absorption of their patterns of behaviour. Miller's theory as to the formation of the delinquent subculture could be summarized by the seemingly far-fetched contention that part of the normative system of the lower classes by itself is geared towards law violation. These "criminal norms" become the nucleus for a normative system for the delinquent subculture. "Engaging in certain cultural practices which comprise essential elements of the total life pattern of lower-class culture *automatically* violates certain legal norms."[21] We may note that whereas Cohen sees the delinquent subculture as the outcome of a *clash* between the lower-class boys' performance level and the middle-class norms, Miller regards part of the lower-class normative system as delinquent per se.

Our contention is that Miller's theory by itself is a powerful demonstration of our stigma thesis, as his thesis amounts to claiming that the lower classes are less morally oriented than the middle or the upper classes.

Miller bases his exposition on some "focal concerns", values and behaviour patterns of the lower classes which are tightly linked, in his view, to law-violating and delinquent behaviour. These are trouble, toughness, smartness, and excitement.

Trouble: "Concern over trouble" says Miller "is a dominant feature of lower-class culture . . . Trouble in one of its aspects represents a situation or a kind of behaviour which results in unwelcome or complicating involvement with official authorities or agencies of middle-class society . . . Expressed desire to avoid behaviour which violates moral or legal norms is less often based on an explicit commitment to "official" moral or legal standards than a desire to avoid getting into trouble, e.g., the complicating consequences of the action."[22]

Indeed, one could similarly investigate the middle-class business-man, or the upper-class power elite. They would be concerned about trouble connected with income-tax returns, infringement upon corporation laws, raising prices and lowering the quality of goods by forming official or secret cartels and making "delicate" connections with City Hall.

Then, and only then, would Miller's thesis be tenable. Also we have a strong suspicion that . . . might even serve as an alternative

179

to Miller's hypothesis—that the incidence of sanction-orientated individuals, i.e., those who refrain from infringing rules to avoid "getting into trouble" among the middle and upper classes, is at least similar to that among the lower classes.

Toughness: Among its most important components are physical prowess, evidenced both by demonstrated possession of strength and endurance and athletic skill. The model for the 'tough guy'— hard, fearless, undemonstrative, skilled in physical combat—is represented by the movie gangster of the thirties, the 'private eye' and the movie cowboy. [23]

It should be pointed out that toughness, endurance and masculine courage, as demonatrated by skin-diving, skiing mountain climbing, and duelling fraternities, are institutionalized for middle and upper-class youth and less so for the lower classes, but this does not mean that toughness and endurance as values are not cherished by the middle classes. The image of a tough administrator or executive is a highly coveted one to the power elite. Also, where is the evidence to support the conclusion that Buck Jones, the Lone Ranger or Perry Mason are idealized models for lower-class children only?

Smartness: According to Miller, this involves the capacity to outsmart, outfix, outwit, "take" others and the concomitant capacity to avoid being outwitted or "taken" oneself. [24]

Is this an idealized picture of the "smart" salesman? The "smart" businessman, who manages to outsmart his competitor, or a "smart" executive who manages to outwit his peers for "the room at the top?" "The survival of the fittest" (or smartest) is not a maxim appropriate only to the jungle and the lower classes, but also apparently to the middle and upper classes and the power elite.

Excitement: "Many of the most characteristic features of lower-class life are related to the search for excitement or thrill"— a patterned set of activities in which alcohol, music, gambling and sexual adventuring are major components. [25] If we accept Miller's thesis here, it would seem that boozing is shunned or almost unheard of with the middle classes, that sexual promiscuity is the exclusive domain of the lower classes, and that the gambling resorts in Monte Carlo, Nice and Las Vegas are patronized by slum dwellers. Miller's hypotheses are more relevant to our present context than Cohen's or Ohlin and Cloward's.

The latter, as we have seen, deal with the pressures that explain the sociological function of the criminal subculture. They also try to describe some of the processes which cause a given individual to be "recruited" to the life of crime. Miller, however, formulates a theory which is stigmatizing in its essence.

In branding part of the normative system of the lower class as virtually delinquent, he replicates the less scientific manner by which society at large and many of its social institutions operate the branding mechanism of stigma. This strengthens and quickens the positive feed-back cycle of defining and redefining a given group as delinquent or deviant. It should be stressed, however, that we do not claim that stigma, the social branding mechanism by itself, is responsible for the creation of the delinquent or deviant subculture. It is a factor in an aetiological configuration the relative importance of which we shall demonstrate later in our causal model.

The inadequate-socialization-centred theories include Thrasher's exposition insofar as he sees the gang as a substitute for the failing socializing agencies where the family, school, church and other agencies fail to hold, attract and regulate the necessities and leisure time; whether out of neglect, repression or inadequacy, the youth would unite spontaneously, according to Thrasher, to form an alternative existence and play-medium by themselves and for themselves, that is, the gang.

"It offers a substitute for what society fails to give; and it provides a relief from suppression and distasteful behaviour."[26] However, when describing the process of individuals affiliating themselves to gangs, Thrasher notes that its triggering impetus was the boy's reaction to the deprivation and rejection by the society of adults. They somehow realized that they have been pushed outside the existing structures, including their own families. They felt abused by their own parents so they had to seek a new identity.[27] This points to a process of defining and isolating

181

by stigma. On the boys' side another process of tagging and name calling helps to create and accentuate the new self identity; "Dirty Dozen", "Vultures", "Forty Thieves", were some picturesque and expressive tags used by the boys. There are also tags and nicknames which help to ascribe the status of the boy in the gang: "Personalities are recognized by the names applied to the members of the gang. Individual peculiarities, which have an important effect in determining status, are likely to give colour to the boy's whole personality. He is named accordingly, and his name often indicates the esteem in which he is held by the group."[28] When finally he complies with the image of a gang member he is finally at peace with himself: "It not only defines for him his position in the only society he is greatly concerned with, but it becomes the basis of his conception of himself."[29] Thrasher, therefore, seems to rely on the stigma premise as one of the links in the causal chain of his theory on gang formation.

Bloch and Niederhoffer trace the delinquency of both lower and middle-class youth to a faulty process of adolescence.[30] Here the hypothesis is based, partly, on Erikson's personality theory, according to which the end-product of a socialized and "adjusted" adult is ego-identity, i.e., a persistent sameness within oneself and a persistent sharing of some kind of essential character with others,[31] whereas the period of adolescence is characterized by "ego-diffusion" which manifests itself by a diffused sense of time, preoccupation with looks, being vain and touchy, inability to develop a deep intimacy with other human beings, periods of "work paralysis", continuous experimentation in various roles (by means of actual behaviour, and day-dreaming) and uncompromising and belligerent loyalty to his ideas.

An adolescent in a state of "ego-diffusion" may be ripe for the various processes leading to gang membership because "gang membership ... often helps the vacillating youth to act. It reinforces his sense of identity." His assignments in the gang overcome the feeling of work paralysis, and as a gang member he can safely assert his masculinity and his defiance of authority.

An empirical proof for this hypothesis may be found in the data

182

brought by Lewin according to which the emotional tension of adolescent youths was greatly diminished when they finally became members of a criminal gang[32] and there they found presumably their coveted "ego-identity".

Several questions must be raised: Why does an individual youth share his "inner-sameness" with the gang and not with his family or the boy scouts? Is it because he was covertly rejected by his family by stigma? And how does he achieve his coveted "ego-identity" which in this case is delinquent? The stigma may supply the missing link of rejection by the (legitimate) group and crystallize the "bad", "delinquent" self-concept as a partial compliance with the image thrust on youth. Talcott Parsons formulated the "Masculine Protest" hypothesis which is based on his analysis of the structure of the middle-class American family. The mother is the main socializing figure in this family, whereas the father is most of the time outside the home taking care of his business and other affairs. This causes the boy's identification with the "role-model" of his mother; when the boy seeks his masculine identity he may turn to the unrealistic extreme of being tough and unsentimental.[33] An obvious way to be "tough" and "become a man" is to commit delinquent acts.

Cohen also subscribes to this hypothesis while dealing briefly with middle-class delinquency. He adds that "good" behaviour is symbolized by (mother's) femininity, whereas "bad" acts stand for masculinity, and a lad who grows up in a family dominated by feminine figures and images thus asserts his manhood by being "bad", that is, delinquent.[34]

Parsons did not claim for his hypothesis the stature of a comprehensive theory (we may therefore point out that the image of "badness" could not have been invented by the boy); some processes must have presented to him these "tough" and "bad" images. On the other hand, we have to know more of the ways this image has been internalized and complied with. The tagging by stigma and the boy's subsequent compliance with it might be a possible answer.

My own hypothesis is that the higher the intensity and the extent

183

of conflict situations in the socialization process, the greater the shift on the continuum from moral orientation to sanction orientation, the final product being that the normative barrier against a given crime is completely shattered and the crime then is in being caught and not in committing the offense.

We have already described the variables which might be relevant in testing the link between "conflict situations" in the primary socialization process and delinquency: 1. degree of marital maladjustment measured by scales of conflicting roles in the family; 2. discord of parents towards main values and norms; attitude towards authority, private property, education, and resort to violence, which might be relevant to forming the children's attitude towards delinquent or nondelinquent behaviour; 3. value and norm conflicts between parents and children; 4. degree of consistency of parents in disciplining their children. The scaling of this variable is based, of course, on current theories of learning as to the possible effect of contradictory or inconsistent responses: reward, withdrawal (punishment) to the same (or similar) behaviour of the child; 5. value and norm discord between the parents and other socializing agencies, such as church, youth club, etc.

Conflict situations might also occur between verbally transmitted norms and the actual behaviour of parents. Paying lip-service to legitimate behaviour but behaving contrary to those same norms create conflict situations which may explain some of the middle and upper classes' juvenile delinquency.

If we turn now from the family to the various norms imbued in a given culture which are supposed to be internalized by juveniles, we find numerous conflict situations produced by contradictory norms. The child's inability to integrate grossly contradictory norms, his inability or refusal to use double standards, or a selective approach to norms may indeed cause an attitude toward the child's personality as being "rigid", with a higher probability of not only emotional derangement, but delinquent solutions. [35]

One type of solution of the conflict situation in the norm-sending process is to turn to street corner gangs, or to openly delinquent gangs for clearer norms and clearly defined non-ambiguous values and patterns of behaviour. Newcomb points out this possibility of conflict solution by citing with approval that: "adolescents frequently find relief from puzzling inconsistent and confusing situations by . . . anchoring themselves to an age-hate world." [36]

This type of solution (in the absence of a restraining normative barrier) becomes more probable with adolescents whose roles are bound to be ambiguous because of the biological changes which place them in the no man's land between childhood and adulthood. By closely associating with (anchoring on) his age-mates an adolescent joins a group composed of individuals who have similar adjustment problems and gains thereby further emotional security.

However, the process of self-definition following a definition by others is lacking. This missing link is readily supplied by the stigma premise.

The norm-conflict-centred theories are the closest in their conception and formulation to the ideas expressed in the present work as to the function of stigma in the genesis of the criminal and deviant subculture. Merton's classic exposition of the various modes of personal anomie as a disjuncture of cultural goals and institutionalized norms and means to achieve them [37] has been a starting point for various subculture theorists.

We have pointed out previously the applicability of Merton's typology, in a modified version, to the description of the *outward manifestations* of some criminal and deviant groups. The criminal crime-for-gain group is characterized by the acquisitive type of innovation insofar as the latter is concerned with the achievement of property or other material gain, i.e., accepted cultural goals by illicit means. [38] The acquisitive type of offence should be sub-classified into occasional and professional, the latter being perpetrated by a distinct type of offender, who looks upon crime as his trade. This type of offender is often highly skilled and the training for his profession is relatively lengthy and arduous. The semi-professional type may be introduced as standing halfway between the two; but this type is not yet a full-time professional.

185

The retreatist "kick" group is characterized by the rejection of goals, norms and means, the pursuance of hedonistic pleasure, and euphoria by means of drugs or alcohol. The violent groups consist of "chaotic rebels",[39] the increasing number of "rebels without cause", the hordes of aggressive teenagers all over the world, who indulge in meaningless aggression and destruction. They have rejected the conventional cultural goals, but their goals are either confused or non-existent. Those offenders are in many ways ritualistic because they have their own norms and ways of acting, i.e., special clothes and mannerisms, but they are mainly concerned with form, directed apparently toward no goal whatsoever. This is, to be sure, only an external description of the activities of the groups. Of deeper relevance to the criminal and deviant group formation is Merton's Reference Group Theory[40] in which he states: "What the individual experiences as estrangement from a group of which he is a member tends to be experienced by his associates as repudiation of the group and this ordinarily evokes a hostile response." In our conceptualization we may observe stigmatization by the group following value deviation. Merton vicariously stresses the importance of stigma by pointing out that: "What is anticipatory socialization from the standpoint of the individual is construed as defection and noncomformity by the group of which he is a member. To the degree that he identifies himself with another group, he alienates himself from his own group.[41] Yet although the field of sociology has for generations been concerned with the determinants and consequences of group cohesion, it has given little *systematic* attention to the compulsory subject of group alienation. When considered at all, it has been confined to such special cases as second-generation immigrants, conflict of loyalties between gang and family, etc. In large measure, the subject has been left to the literary observer, who could detect the drama inherent in the situation of the renegade, the traitor, the deserter. The value-laden connotations of these terms, used to describe identification with groups other than one's own, definitely suggest that these patterns of behaviour have been typically regarded from the standpoint of the membership group (yet one

186

group's renegade may be another group's convert). Transfer of loyalty to another group is regarded primarily in affective terms of sentiment rather than in detached terms of analysis. The renegade or traitor or climber—whatever the folk-phrase may be—moreover becomes an object of vilification rather than an object of sociological study."[42] The processes of an individual's secession from the legitimate society and his crossing to the illegal side of the barricade have been analysed and documented. We shall examine later the process of differential association and identification as related to the causal scheme of the criminal and deviant subculture formation. Merton realises the importance of stigma and deplores the absence of its theoretical incorporation into the deviant group formation and the individual's recruitment into it. The present context is one such attempt to supply the missing theoretical link. In all fairness it should be mentioned that some of the earlier expositions which might have escaped the attention of Merton did indeed stress the importance of stigma in the delinquent and deviant group formation. Zorbaugh describes in his study of the late twenties the way a boy's family or neighbourhood are defined for him as "dago", "wop", "foreign", etc. and by "these same *definitive epithets, he is excluded from status and intimate participation* in American life. Out of this situation arises the gang, by conforming to delinquent patterns he achieves status in the gang, and every boy in Little Hell is a member of a gang."[43]

Landesco relies heavily on his observation that at some stage of the process of gang formation a stigma is applied to legitimate occupation—and the stigma that society brands on an individual as an "ex-con" identifies him the more with the underworld.[44] We have already mentioned the extreme significance that Tannenbaum imputes to the tagging by others as an almost self-perpetuating image of delinquency and deviance.[45] The most recent theoretical expositions include the works of Kvaraceus, Downes and Matza. The first claims that the modern social structure makes youth a surplus, a superfluous commodity: "Automation with its elimination of routine chores that once depended upon youthful hands, labour laws written in the spirit of safeguarding children and

187

youth, and labour unions organized to protect the adult worker have all combined to diminish the need for strong young hands. Even the compulsory classroom, now extending through the teenage years, has tended to shunt the young learners from the main stream of social, civic and economic life activity of family and community, thereby retarding the process whereby youth join the adult world. In a sense, the youth now experience an organized isolation from the regular community."[46] Youth becomes, therefore, the modern involuntary leisure class, with an excess of leisure. Forced leisure as claimed by Kvaraceus, a re-affirmation of the traditional working idea of "good time" leisure as described by Downes,[47] or a "soft-indeterministic drift into leisure"[48] are considered to be the social *conditio sine qua non*, the structural background of modern delinquent and deviant groups.

"The Leisure Class" theorist Veblen noticed the "good-time spender" aspect of delinquency and he compares "the ideal pecuniary man" with the delinquent who is characterized mainly by an unscrupulous conversion of goods and services.[49] Sykes and Matza elaborate this view by pointing out that the delinquent does not really deviate from the prevailing values in society.

A recent exposition of the delinquent as belonging to the welfare-state leisure class is found in Fyvel's work on delinquency in Britain and other countries. He paints the picture of the delinquent as a lad who has lost almost all values except entertainment and other pleasures which may be bought from the juke box, treble-chance pool and other glittering neon-lighted establishments of the city and suburbs. In keeping with the spirit of the age they shun middle-class bourgeois values which have already disintegrated and have lost their grip on society and its smallest unit, i.e., the family. The latter no longer fulfills its socializing function, and the boys are brought up with an amorphous set of moral values with the result that they regard life as a vacuous adventure riddled by recurring boredom "where nothing mattered but money and the smart thing at all times was to give as little as you could for as much as you could get; in short, as they [the delinquents] saw it, a distorted materialistic society without purpose. On this soil luxuriant visions could flourish where fact and fancy were apt to mingle."[50]

Backgrounds, however, cannot be confused with the actual dynamics of the delinquent and deviant group formation. Kvaraceus goes on to describe one of the possible outcomes of the structural superfluity of modern youth. They are excluded by the adult world from significant roles and tasks which are scarce and become more so with the growth of technology and specialization. They feel unneeded and unnecessary and worst of all they are "stigmatized, infantilized, down-graded and disengaged".[51] One of the reactions is the formation of their own membership and reference groups, i.e., gangs. Sherif supplements Kvaraceus' formulation by describing the sense of deprivation, the insecurity, the feeling of being tossed around by the adults, all of which disappear entirely once a youngster joins a gang—this alleviates their psychological crisis situation and anchors them on groups of peers with kindred soul.[52] Matza presents us with a normative no man's land in which the delinquent drifts in suspended animation in the midst of a value vacuum. We could be led to visualize a normative Shangri-La where the delinquent in a fit of free-will hedonistically grabs and lives it up in a permissive environment. This, no doubt, is an illusion; a normative vacuum is a myth. One is not left alone to drift in a sociological value-vacuum. One is jostled, coerced and pushed around. One is not abandoned to drift in a sociologically absurd normative neutral area—one has to commit oneself not by a "soft indeterminism" but by a harsh determinism; either one is with us (the legitimate structure) or not with us—and then one is against us. A normative moratorium is an illusion. Matza himself realizes this elsewhere. "[The delinquent] is transformed in the situation of company to a committed quent by dint of the cues he has received from others."[53] This is actually an internalization of an image thrust upon one by the relevant others, i.e., stigma. The importance of stigma in the aetiology of deviant groups should also be evaluated in the light of conflict theories.

According to the latter, stigma is a non-realistic conflict situation

189

insofar as it imputes to the stigmatized, through the "scape-goat" or "safety-valve" mechanism, derogatory attributes which he does not possess. On the other hand, there is indeed a realistic conflict situation insofar as the delinquent or deviant displays value or behaviour deviation.

Here we have Simmel's and Coser's assertion that this admixture of non-realistic conflict (stigma) and a realistic conflict (deviant behaviour) is indeed a violent one. Coser says, ". . . the reinforcing effect of non-realistic elements, in realistic conflict situations, led to the hypothesis that the intensity of conflict will be likely to increase through such admixture".[54] We are in a position now to offer a causal model of the genesis of delinquent and deviant groups incorporating stigma as an aetiological link. We shall proceed with our analysis by presenting the complete model itself, stigma being the last link in the formation of the criminal and deviant subculture:

A Model
of Social Factors of Criminal and Deviant Groups in Israel

Predisposition Configuration

The Family Unit
1. Criminals in the family.
2. Broken family.
3. Inadequate family.
4. "Masculine" protest.
5. Post-adolescence maladjustment.
6. Conspicuous consumption.
7. Malcohesion of family unit.
8. Slackening of parental control.

Ecological Factors
1. Urban areas.
2. High rate of delinquency areas.

Economic Factors
Relative need, as defined by individual,

Culture Conflict
1. A tangential proximity of different cultural areas.
2. Social change by industrialization, urbanization and immigration.
3. Conflict between levels of migrant youth and the norms of absorbing culture.

THE PREDISPOSITION CONFIGURATION

The Family Unit

In the case of the criminal family the differential association begins at home. The primary socialization itself contains criminal and deviant patterns to varying degrees. This ranges from the criminal tribes or castes in India, where the primary criminal socialization is normative,[55] to families one or more members of which has a criminal or deviant history or is actively engaged in crime. Research findings have indicated that the chances of another member of the family becoming delinquent are overwhelmingly higher in these families than in controls which do not have any criminal member.[56] This is also apparent in the significant number of cases with more than one prisoner from the same family in the Israel prison population which is rather small, both absolutely and relatively.[57]

Homes broken by divorce, separation, death and prolonged incapacitation have also been found to be significantly linked with juvenile delinquency.[58] Inadequate families marked by unhappy, conflict-ridden homes, tension, irritation, quarrels and friction

191

between parents which displayed itself by inconsistent treatment of the children, ambivalence and violent alternating attitudes were also found to be strongly linked with delinquency. These findings, by Burt, Shaw and McKay, Ivan Nye, Healy and Bronner and many others, have been also replicated in Israeli studies.[59] The "masculine protest", post-adolescent maladjustment and conspicuous consumption which have been hypothetically linked by many theorists to the genesis of delinquency have also been found by our studies to apply to Israel.[60]

The last two predisposing factors which are directly related to the family and linked with delinquency have been found to apply very strongly to the second generation youth of immigrant parentage. The native-born of immigrant parentage, or those who came very young, are the most prone to suffer from the effects of their parents' immigration.[61]

Ecological Factors

These factors, the study of which was initiated by Shaw, Mackay and others of the Chicago school of criminology in the U.S.,[62] Terence Morris in England[63] and Christiansen in Denmark,[64] have also been found to apply to Israel. The rates of juvenile delinquency have been found to increase with a higher degree of urbanization as measured by density of population and the volumes of commerce and industry.[65]

The delinquency rates in the Tel-Aviv-Jaffo area tend to decrease from the highest concentration in the older central business zone outwards. Exceptions are the new housing projects whose dwellers are rather heterogeneous demographically, and the Jaffo area, which is totally populated by "new" immigrants who arrived in Israel after the establishment of the State.[66]

Economic Factors

Economic factors are associated with the type and the manifestation of crime in a given community. Modern criminological

192

theory no longer vacillates between the two extremes of the ancient controversy: whether crime is caused by need[67] or by greed.[68] The hypothesis here is that want *per se* and even sheer hunger are very rarely linked to crime and delinquency. Thousands of people are dying of hunger in India but they would not dare slaughter a holy cow and fry themselves a steak, because the norm against eating meat has been deeply internalized by them and no degree of hunger and want would be strong enough to infringe it. Certain inmates of concentration camps would suffer extreme hunger and not think of stealing the bread rations of their fellow inmates, whereas others would.

Economic want or need is a subjective state of mind which is determined by the socio-cultural milieu; want is comparative, and is felt by an individual when his possessions or achievements are found lacking when compared with the money, power and gadgets of others. Need is therefore relative and subjective, and not absolute and objective. Most human beings, including those who dwell in the worst slums of the U.S., Latin America, Southern Europe and Asia, are not criminals; those who become delinquents are a small portion only of this population.

The crucial factor is the social context, which can induce a person to define his situation as needy if he is not able, for instance, to buy a third car, a mink coat and a diamond ring for his mistress or a swimming pool for his family.

The opportunity for committing property offences or embezzlement is present in most trades and professions. The needs of a person (in the present case, relative economic needs) and affluence are, for our purposes, subjective, and are determined by the relevant cultural contexts. The latter may exert varying degrees of pressure to consume. This pressure may be regarded by an individual as forceful enough and the consumption vital enough to risk breaking the law. It should be pointed out, however, that economic conditions as predisposing factors are regarded as subjective pressures which may raise the probability of a person entering the dynamic process of association with criminal patterns of behaviour.

Culture Conflict

The phenomenon of culture conflict on the social level may be observed no doubt in the general growth of civilization and especially in the clashes of norms and values resulting from industrialization and urbanization. But the study of the conflict process in these instances is highly problematic from the methodological point of view, and the length of time involved makes the possibility of comprehensive research highly remote. Most research on culture conflict and crime has therefore dealt with the clashes among divergent cultural codes and especially the conflict between the conduct norms of immigrant groups and the norms prevailing in the receiving country.[69]

The criminality of adult "new" immigrants in Israel exceeds the criminality of the native-born (and the "old" immigrants) at the rate of 4 to 3 (or 10 to 7.5). [70] We may conclude that the rate is quite high if we bear in mind Van Vechten's findings concerning the relevant rate in the United States, which was 10 to 9.[71]

An interesting comparison may be made among the rates of serious offences committed by immigrants from the various continents. The rates were computed from data collected in 1957, the best data available. These rates were, for serious offences per 1,000 immigrants from Africa, 13; Asia, 10; and from Europe and America, 5.

It should be mentioned that the overwhelming majority of immigrants from Africa have come from North Africa. They belong to the "Moghrabi" community, and they have as a rule a cultural background quite distinct from that of the rest of the oriental Jews. The Asian Jews belong mostly to the category of "oriental" Jews, whereas the relatively few American immigrants are mostly of European origin or parentage. The clue to these differential crime rates may quite possibly be found in the culture-conflict hypothesis, because, as we have already mentioned, the general cultural, economic, and educational standards of the North African and Asian immigrants are relatively low. It may be that the clash between cultural codes, norms, and values of these

194

immigrants and those of the receiving community causes a relative increase in the crime rate of these immigrants. [72]

The third item in the culture conflict group is related to Cohen's theory of the formation of delinquent groups. This theory, which is class centred, hypothesizes that delinquent solutions with lower-class boys are linked to the discrepancy between middle-class norms and their performance level. [73]

If we consider the case of Israel, classes (in the sense attributed to this concept in England and the United States) have not yet been formed; there are, of course, many criteria of social stratification, but these are not very distinct, and their effect is not decisive enough to justify a whole theory of criminal subculture formation (e.g., Cohen's theory on the delinquent gangs) on the discrepancies between middle-class norms and the actual achievement of lower-class boys. A mass immigration country like Israel, the Jewish population of which has trebled in the last fourteen years, could be fruitfully studied for the purposes of determining the pressures towards juvenile gang formation as an arena of "culture conflict" between the conduct norms of the various ethnic groups, and the new immigrants holding the underprivileged position which the lower classes held in Cohen's scheme. [74]

Social Disorganization and Anomie

Anomia, Anomy or Anomie was considered by Durkheim as a state of "normlessness" in society, the antithesis of social solidarity, a state of ideological disintegration, of collective insecurity where the regulating forces of social norms have been impaired or destroyed altogether and no distinction can be made between the feasible and the impossible, between the just and the unjust. [75]

The causes of social anomie are traced by Durkheim mainly to sudden social change: "when society is disturbed or disorganized, whether by a painful crisis or by a fortunate but too sudden turn of events, it is temporarily incapable of exercising (normative control) and influence upon the individual." [76] Anomic trends in societies are indeed universal and the real problem is, as De Grazia justly puts it, a matter of scaling and degrees. A society might suffer from simple anomie characterized by conflict among the various "belief systems" (ideologies) or be plagued, at the other extreme of the continuum, by acute anomie, the decline of religious, political and other ideological duties, a severe deterioration of the "belief systems" which result in the ultimate disintegration of a society's normative structure. [77] Social anomie is almost by definition a predisposing factor to crime and delinquency. We may assume that an anomic process is operating in Israel and it may even have far advanced on the continuum away from the mild form of anomie.

The types of "Personal Anomie" which are considered to be predisposing factors to crime stem from Merton's theoretical expositions. Merton's Typology of Modes of Individual Adaptation[78] is based more on the structure of behaviour and its discernible symptoms than on the inner motivations of the actor and the mechanism of his personality system; Merton also displays in his typology the relationship between the anomic behaviour and the social norm, i.e., the latter's acceptance or rejection as manifest in the socially deviant act itself.

It should be stressed that the personal anomic patterns are the final end-product. The predisposing factors are personal anomic *trends*—pressures to innovate, to retreat and to rebel; the *causa-causans,* however, would have to be the dynamic association process which is the subject of the second part of our model.

THE DYNAMIC PROCESS OF ASSOCIATION

Delinquent Solutions of Conflict Situations in the Primary Socialization Process

This closest link of the chain of association to the predisposition configuration deals with the crucial problem: What are the causes on the *personal level* for the fact that some adults and children are caught in the differential association process, which may lead them ultimately to membership in the criminal subculture, while other

196

persons are not? This link relates to the attitude of the individual toward the restraining norm, to the degree the individual internalized the restraining norm as a personality element, and to what process is necessary to overcome or "neutralize" the restraining force of the norm or norms (in case these have been internalized) on the personality level.[79]

The hypothesis in the present context is, therefore, that the first link in the dynamic process of association, bridging it with the predisposition configuration, lies in the area (hitherto scantily explored by criminologists) of social psychology which tries to explain the conformity (or nonconformity) of an individual to group norms. The degree of conformity to legal norms, that is, the extent to which the norm has been internalized by a certain individual (because of the pressures which enhance or injure the legitimacy imputed by the individual to the internalized norm), and the efficacy of the sanction to enforce compliance by a certain individual is determined on the group level by the efficacy of the norm-sending process with its three components (statement of the rule, surveillance, and application of sanctions) and on the personal level by the norm-receiving process with its three stages (compliance, identification and internalization).

The norm-sending process may be plagued by conflict situations, two or more inconsistent rules governing the same factual situation (as defined by the individual). These conflict situations may appear in all three stages of the norm-sending process. The extent and the severity of these conflict situations (which could be eventually expressed quantitatively) may determine the weakness or strength of an individual and indicate thus the extent to which this individual is ready and ripe for the differential association and differential identification processes which may lead him to crime or deviance as a way of life. This hypothesis, if found to be correct by empirical proof, might afford a useful clue to the crucial question in criminological theory, that even in the worst of slums plagued by poverty, bad living conditions, criminal gangs, prostitutes, and dope peddlers, only some boys become delinquent whereas a far greater number remain law-abiding.

Differential Identification

A theoretical step further, but still before the actual association with the criminal group, is identification with criminal images and playing of criminal roles. Daniel Glaser, who actually formulated this premise,[80] stated that prior to a person's actual criminal behaviour he becomes criminal valuewise and rolewise. *He sees himself as a criminal or law violator.* When his self-image is deviant he is ripe for the association with actual criminal behaviour. The delinquent image of being smart, as Miller remarks, "involves the capacity to outsmart, outfox, outwit, dupe, 'take', 'con' another or others and the concomitant capacity to avoid being outwitted, 'take' or duped oneself".[81] The status one aspires to and the image one identifies with is the "big-shot" with the big car, flashy suits, green wads and swell dames.

Differential Opportunity Structure

After the conflict situations in the primary socialization process have paved the way for delinquent solutions, there must be access to illegitimate structures and means for the actual criminal association and behaviour to take place. Cloward and Ohlin, who formulated this link in the causal chain,[82] hypothesize on how the limited access to legitimate opportunity may press an individual to be aware of the availability of illegitimate opportunities and try to find access to them.[83]

Differential Association

The actual initiation into criminal or deviant behaviour by means of association with a criminal group and learning the criminal techniques and patterns of behaviour has been proved to take place in many studies carried out in Israel. Our studies of juvenile delinquency in Israel have shown that the "lone wolf" does not exist either in lower-class or in middle-class delinquency. Unless a boy is mentally deranged and the manifestations of his mental

198

aberration constitute the offence, delinquency is a group phenomenon, the delinquent patterns of which are transmitted to new members by learning and association.[84]

This has also been the case in a follow-up study of the institutions for juvenile delinquents in Israel[85] and a follow-up study of the young adult prison in Tel-Mond, Israel.[86] Our small explorative study of a group of vagabonds who "followed the sun to Israel" from all over the world and built up a shanty-quarter on the sunny and pebbly shore of Eilath also revealed that the actual vagrancy of an individual started by association with other vagabonds, beatniks and hippies and learning their patterns of behaviour.[87]

The Social Stigma

The genesis of criminal and deviant groups receives its final tagging and identification by the groups' attitude toward a given behaviour, i.e., the stigma, or the Mark of Cain which it attaches to an act or individual.

Some initial empirical support for the major role of stigma in the genesis of delinquent and deviant subcultures is also available.

We have already mentioned the findings of Porterfield and Andry[88] as to the significantly higher probability of a lower-class boy being branded as delinquent than a middle or upper-class boy who committed the same deeds. We have also noted that the Beatles and similar groups in England might have become street-corner, deviant or even delinquent gangs if the British public did not choose to accept them and make national celebrities out of them. Also Miller's theory, by itself, is a demonstration of how the stigmatizing mechanism could be attired in an academic gown. Another appropriate support for our thesis may be found in the following statement of one of Israel's most renowned psycho-analysts: "To the psychopathic phenomena we could also add the multitudes of young delinquents all over the world. It would be sufficient if we mentioned the Rock 'n' Roll dance which excites to wild psychopathic states, to violence and orgies."[89]

We have the assertions of Harari and Chwast as to a marked class bias in psychodiagnosis of delinquents which operates against the lower-class boy.[90] Israeli data also indicate that middle-class delinquents were described by the probation officer as appealing and likeable significantly more frequently than were those of the lower class[91] This could be linked to a greater tendency to stigmatize lower-class boys as delinquents.

The positive feed-back cycle would become a closed circle: the stigmatizing effects induce and implant a corresponding self-image in the individual.

These mechanisms have been described by Sullivan as follows: "If the significant people in a child's life are derogatory and hateful, he will acquire a derogatory and hateful attitude toward himself (if the child learns) that it is highly disadvantageous to show any need for tender cooperation from authoritative figures about him, in which case he shows something else—the basic malevolent attitude, the attitude that one really lives among enemies."[92]

This tagging by society with the ensuing self-branding by the juvenile is the circle that isolates, defines, tightens and hardens the subculture, and ultimately signs it with the Mark of Cain of crime, delinquency or social deviation.

200

CHAPTER X

JEAN GENET: A CRIMINAL MANIFESTO

> *I shall allow myself a certain coquetry and say that I was a clever thief. Never have I been caught red-handed in* flagrante delicto. *But the fact that I know how to steal admirably for my earthly profit is unimportant. What I have sought most of all has been to be the consciousness of the theft whose poem I am writing.**

THE SET

Jean Genet, the thief-playwright-philosopher, can be considered the mouthpiece of the brotherhood of criminals. The aim of our analysis is to delineate patterns in Genet's writings which illustrate the genesis and mechanisms of stigma, crime and social deviation. In a devastatingly sincere manner, Genet has succeeded in portraying his self-image as a criminal and the ideology of the criminal group. Genet the thief, deviant and outcast will serve as the prototype illustrating the stigma theory of crime and deviation expounded in the previous chapters. He professes to be a perfectionist: "It is because an action has not been completed that it is vile." [1] He records in minute detail his self-image as a criminal, and vividly describes the underworld, its norms and values. He establishes a diametric negativity to the legitimate world and its institutions.

Genet proclaims the criminal manifesto with the voice of authority and experience; as Sartre says: "Genet the novelist speaking of Genet the thief, is more thief than a thief." [2] Genet is an exaggerated instance—almost a parody of the stigmatized criminal and his self-image; but it is precisely this extremeness and exaggeration which makes him invaluable to us. He illuminates every step of the stigmatization process and delineates

---

* Jean Genet. *The Thief's Journal*

the borders of a seemingly amorphous theoretical premise. An exaggerated case is invaluable for highlighting features, but it gives a very poor image of the middle-ranges. We should therefore bear in mind that Genet is far from being a model of the common thief, and is many standard deviations from the mean, mode or median type of the underworld.

Moreover, we must take into account Genet's obsessive and ideological homosexuality, which prevents us from trying to generalize from his self-image and his view of his own group and society at large to other members of the criminal subculture.

Genet's pederasty can be attributed to his satanic orthodoxy in behaving in a manner diametrically opposed to that prescribed by cultural mandates: If most men are heterosexual he is homosexual. In addition, homosexuality is part and parcel of the criminal world: ample evidence exists that most prisoners who are incarcerated for prolonged periods have, to a varying extent, homosexual experiences. Close proximity with a totally male world, long abstinence from heterosexual contact, and the grim, loveless routine, press most prisoners to some kind of relationship with their fellow convicts. The intensity of these relationships ranges from the profound homosexuality of a Genet to the anxiety and fears of pederasty that are a mild form on the same continuum of homosexuality. Homosexuality is an organic part of the criminal's world, his folklore and value system, though Genet creates an obsession of it.

The angle of vision of the observer is all-important in the social and behavioural sciences. Psychology, sociology and mental health devoid of values do not exist. Conclusions, observations, hypotheses and concepts are inevitably dependent on one's point of observation. An industrial psychologist studying "conflict" and "strain" with a view to finding the best ways and means of preventing them is obviously opposed to conflict and strain in worker-management relationship. A sociologist or criminologist studying the criminal and his group is clearly against crime. On the other hand a habitual criminal like Genet, who spent a considerable part of his life in prison, describes himself, his

202

colleagues and "the other" legitimate society as they are seen from his side of the barricade and in the shades perceived by his criminal group. This legal and social barricade between "our" criminal world and "your" legitimate world is institutionalized by Genet; he perceives it—as indeed he should, according to our stigma theory,—as a normative iron curtain. The criminal is, of course, aware of this barricade, because he bumps into it, to his detriment, almost continuously. Genet, however, perceives the individuals on the "legitimate side" of the barricade as equally preoccupied with being normatively opposite the criminals. The guard in *Death Watch* assures Lefrance that he has to be the very opposite of the criminals and thugs,[3] not good or bad, but the very opposite. This is the recurring theme in our stigma theory: that the law-abiding person is defined by exclusion as a non-criminal, and vice versa; definition by opposites contrasting "good" with the "not-good".

The central idea of Genet's play *The Blacks* is this definition by tagging: the blacks, who are the non-whites, are on the opposite side of the "right" side of the barricade. The blacks are the tainted and have been assigned by society the roles of prisoners, criminals and outcasts. In the words of Archibald: "On this stage, we're like guilty prisoners who play at being guilty."[4] Genet is no doubt "the foremost prince in the lineage of the French *poètes maudits*".[5] He is more profound than Villon, and more outspoken and sincere than de Sade. However, the present analysis is solely concerned with Genet's work insofar as it illustrates the stigma theory of crime and deviation. Sartre[6] has established Genet as a saint of existentialism, unearthing new vistas of art and philosophy.

SELF-IMAGE

Genet's self-image is, no doubt, one of a thief, an "ex-con", a member of the criminal sub-culture. His writings are very personal. Although fact and fiction intermingle, most of the episodes happened in one way or the other with Genet as participant, resulting in a *melange* of personal experience, feelings and reminiscences.

Genet was born out of wedlock. His mother abandoned him in his cradle and he was cared for in his formative years by the orphanage of the *Assistance Publique*. He never succeeded in finding out anything about his background. Later he imagined his mother as a thief just out of prison, "an old thief with a pale, shifty-looking face."[7]

The state orphanage in due course entrusted him to a foster-home—a peasant family in Le Morvan. At first he was happy there. He lived the peaceful life of a village youngster; as a child he was led to believe, as Sartre says, that his soul was white, without sin, without malice; he therefore saw himself as white, as innocent.[8]

However, he soon realized that he was not like the other village youngsters. He was a foundling, he had no mother, no father, and therefore no clear identity to internalize. The village was a closed community and he soon found out that in the peasant family he was "Jean, the little bastard". The other children in the family found a simple solution in attributing any mishap or misdeed to "the little bastard" from the orphanage. He thus became the receptacle for all the residuary, unwanted and despised attributes of the family and small peasant community: his self-image or inner anchor of identity consisted of definitions, images and characteristics tagged on him by the relevant others. Young Genet, in a state of "other-directedness" of *alteracion,* complied with the image built for him by his immediate surroundings. The branding and tagging in Genet's case derived from a non-existent, inner-directed alternative image—from his need to become what he was accused of being: "I owned to being the coward, traitor, thief and fairy they saw in me."[9]

We are, in fact connecting links in a chain which are not necessarily linked together in a causal sequence—what we are doing could be more described in drawing imaginary lines between the visible peaks of an iceberg. The gaps in our analysis are to be attributed to a lack of information or to the fact that Genet's accounts do not necessarily correspond to the actual process which took place. We have the facts of illegitimacy, the initial stay in the orphanage and the upbringing at Le Morvan. We then encounter a youth in an extreme state of other-directedness, who does his utmost to comply with the negative images branded on him by the peasant family and the village community. We do not have enough information to formulate a comprehensive account of the process, but we may describe it, from the facts we do know, as a typical positive feed-back cycle of being rejected by a group and rejecting it in turn; this could be traced to the initial stigmatizing process triggered by the primary fact of being born illegitimate. Genet says:

"The uncertainty of my origin allowed me to interpret it. I added to it the peculiarity of my misfortunes. Abandoned by my family, I felt it was natural to aggravate this condition by a preference for boys, and this preference by one for theft, and the preference for theft by one for crime. I thus resolutely rejected a world which had rejected me."[10]

This is the perpetual vicious circle. The cognitive rejection and counter-rejection could be more of a rationalization by Genet of his inner compliance with the image with which he has been tagged. The "other-directedness" of Genet being branded illegitimate, as "bad" and as a thief, and consequently obliging the alters by realizing their image of him—is a display of acquiescence and submission. He wilfully, almost joyfully, plunges into depths of negativity. He finally knows who he is, he has been given an image he never had—and if the image is that of a pederast and a thief, it has to be honed to perfection. This subconscious process is one phase of a cyclic ambivalence towards the stigmatizing group. The acceptance phase of submitting to the image and being compulsively overconforming towards it alternates with the cognitive counter-rejection of the painful rejection by the group. This, incidentally, might afford a partial explanation of the "outsider's dilemma", the agonizing, unsuccessful efforts of the outsider to be accepted by society. Our

205

thesis is that the outsider striving to be accepted and acclaimed by society fails because he never wishes to adjust, conform or integrate himself normatively into the group—all he wants is to be accepted as an outsider, thereby asking for the impossible.[11] Such an expectation is somewhat naive and undoubtedly shallow. The stigma premise seems to afford a deeper insight into the "outsider's dilemma".

Outsiders like Genet, who comply with the images of evil imputed to them by the surrounding 'alters', feel that by assuming the role they serve the group; by being evil because they have been defined as evil the outsider feels that he has fulfilled a mandate—he has been submissive, has conformed to the tagged image, and society owes him, if not acclaim, at least acceptance; disillusionment is bitter if he is not accepted. Many convicts have personally reported a similar feeling to the author. They are accused of committing a crime and against all common prudence they are seized with an urge to confess, a wish to expiate themselves, to turn over a new leaf, to repay the debts in order to be reaccepted—and all this by one magic act of admission, of compliance, of redemption. Some confess even when the prosecution has scant evidence against them, and subsequently feel a sense of ease, for they have been "good" for once by admitting their badness: "You, judge, jury, attorneys, the world at large, you say I am evil; right, I am, but now we are quits. You have to accept me—you owe it to me." The inevitable rejection quickens the cycle of stigma and counter-stigma; this is the meaning of the "outsider's dilemma".

After being rejected by society despite his compliance with the image cast on him, Genet feels cheated. He has what seems to him a justified grievance and he becomes thoroughly negativistic with a dual purpose. The first is to perfect the vile image; perhaps his contrariness was not thorough enough, maybe he has not yet achieved the requirements of the relevant others, so that he has to pursue more evil and greater vileness. "When I undertook to accomplish Evil," Genet writes, "I knew it was the only thing that had sufficient power to communicate enthu-

206

siasm to my pen, a sign in this case of my perfect allegiance . . . that will, that daring to pursue a destiny that is against all rules."[12] Genet's other purpose is his cognitive rationalization of his rejections and counter-rejections of "your world". This has more than a tinge of *ressentiment* in it because he never really relinquished his desire to be accepted by conventional avenues rather than through sordidness and crime. "I wanted," he says, "to give my body and arms an opportunity to assume conventionally beautiful poses which might integrate me into your world,"[13] but to no avail!

Nor was his normative transformation instantaneous; he had his inner struggles with the remnants of conventional morality he had managed to internalize. "I had to combat, . . . to abolish what is called remorse."[14] These may have been intermediate stages of an incomplete negation of the normative system of the "legitimate society". The exaggerated reaction-formation against these "square" norms indicates an inner struggle, an ambivalence, towards the attacked norms. However, these stages were passed very quickly, and from his first proclamation as thief he seems to pursue his inner identity and salvation furiously. His inner identity longs to fulfil an image: "In children's hells, in prisons, in bars, it was not heroic adventures that I sought, I pursued there my identification with the handsomest and most unfortunate criminals."[15] This identification with criminal images and the desire to play criminal roles are in line with a current theory of criminal behaviour,[16] which presupposes an inner identification with the criminal image prior to an outward delinquent behaviour, but does not try to explain why some people identify with criminal images and others with non-criminal ones. The stigma premise can provide a partial explanation: a person tagged with the stigma of a thief will eventually seek the proper criminal images with which to identify in order to comply inwardly with the image thrust upon him. For Genet, this crystallization of his identity with the ultimate in crime, the perfection in vileness and the Satanism in evil became his personal idea of salvation.

207

"The greater my guilt in your eyes, the more whole, the more totally assumed, the greater will be my freedom. The more perfect my solitude and uniqueness. By my guilt I further gained my right to intelligence. Too many people think, I said to myself, who don't have the right to. They have not paid for it by the kind of undertaking which makes thinking indispensable to your salvation."[17]

Genet would pursue his salvation through the gutters together with his mother, who, he hopes, would be more degraded than himself—proof of her higher saintliness in the dimension of sanctity through degradation: "Had I met my mother and had she been humbler than I, we would have pursued together the ascension: though language seems to call for the word 'fall' or any other that indicates a downward movement—the difficult, painful ascension which leads to humiliation."[18] This saintliness through filth would be quite similar to St. Jerome's sense of the Medusan beauty in the observation that the filthier a penitent is, the more beautiful he is.[19] In his striving for a diametric reversal of everything which belongs or relates to "your (legitimate) world" Genet even advocates an inversion of connotations. He realizes by intuition the gist of our stigma theory that name-calling, defining, tagging is not stimulating reality, *it is reality itself.* He therefore builds a novel and reversed system of adjectives to exchange the derogatory meaning of theft, cowardice and fear in "your world" with their commendable opposites in "our" world of crime and sin.[20]

Treachery, theft and homosexuality are Genet's sacred trinity. He raised these three inverse elements to the rank of a theology,[21] contrasting the cherished bourgeois virtues of loyalty, the sanctity of private property and heterosexuality.

An entire, splendidly inverted *Weltanschauung* is constructed to serve both as an internal mirror and as a negation of "your world". Beauty is of the Medusan genre—the more an object is ugly, dirty and disfigured the more it is magnificent, attractive and lovely.[22] Genet revels in and adores filth[23]—he reveres it as the counterpart of "cleanliness is next to godliness". Shame is great, marvellous and magnificent; he applies these adjectives to the Carolinas, the transvestites of Barrio Chino in Barcelona whom he lovingly calls the Daughters of Shame.[24] He would have accepted with shame (an emotion he cherishes) that his soul was rotten "since it emitted the odour that makes people hold their noses".[25] He takes pleasure in it not out of a "sour-grapes" resentment but as the inevitable corrollary of stigma. He is for others "Jean, the young bastard, we gave him shelter, cared for him like for our son, and the thankless treacherous thief started to steal from us." "That filthy degenerate, he is a conscientious pederast, a shameful fairy." Genet has been branded with all these tags, and he internalized alter's image of him as conveyed to him very often and very clearly. Whatever they said became reality, and more so: the plain truth and the only reality known to Genet himself. By complying with this image of himself he also obeyed the others. He fulfilled their wish, he accomplished his duty. By becoming the deserved receptacle of their scorn he earned their praise. If "your world" is delaying the payment of commendable recognition and acceptance, something is apparently wrong with the system of values, the adjectives are upside-down, and connotations should be reversed. Eventually we shall trace this reversal of the normative system of "your world", as the basic link which unifies the stigmatized, the rejected, into underworld groups and initiates the processes of association into criminal subcultures.

Young Genet is sent to a reform school, and this is the corner-stone of a career, which included begging in Spain, thieving in France, deserting from the Foreign Legion, being a male prostitute and smuggling drugs all over Europe. After several years of this, Genet and "your world" have no love for each other; their contacts are belligerent ones through the gaps in the legal and social barricade which separates them. Genet, the little bastard, who obliged his relevant alters by becoming what he was tagged as being, gives way to a belligerent outsider whose own cherished evil is contrasted with the fake evil of "your world". The prime meaning of theft for Genet is its being diametrically opposed to the legitimate world: "For half an hour I shall be operating (while committing a burglary) in a world which is the reverse of the customary world. I do not think specifically of the proprietor of the place, but all my gestures evoke him."[26]

The adroitness and literal-mindedness of the criminal world is contrasted with the hypocrisy, smoothness and double standards of "your world". Apparently the two different brands of evil, the personal satanism of Genet and the monstrosity of "your world", were conceived by him as force-fields combatting and repelling each other. He likens himself to the mother who reared and guarded her monster daughter. "Within herself she ordained an altar where she preserved the idea of the monster. She set herself up against the world, and against the world she set up the monster, which took on the proportions of the world and its power. It was on the basis of the monster that new principles were ordained, principles constantly combatted by the forces of the world which came charging into her, but stopped at the walls of her home where her daughter was confined."[27] Here we have a consecrated inner monstrosity to offset the monstrosity of the world. The world of evil is taken for granted. The relationship between the ego and the generalized alter is constant war and combat. The way to defend oneself against the greater evil is by an internal shield of evil. This is something quite different from the Hobbesian *Homo homini lupus* and the Sartrean "Hell is other people." For Genet the foundation, the very heart of the human society is evil in every possible sense, and the individual's inner evil is a writhing, struggling part of it. This is no controversy involving ethical judgment, of good or relative good against evil. It is a fight between a greater evil and a lesser one.

We shall deal later with Genet as a member of the criminal group; at this stage we wish to analyse the state of mind of Genet, the individual criminal. He professes to be happy in his despair, and his ecstatic adoration of destruction borders on a love affair with Thanatos. Perhaps this is proof of the psychoanalytic contention that crime is fuelled by a self-destructive urge, by a wish to be punished for unresolved subconscious guilt. This

210

does not seem to be the case if we rely on the evidence gleaned from the present study. The act of crime for Genet means vigour, freedom and fulfillment. Vigour, because one puts a lot of energy and concentration into an act of stealing; it has a "terminal oneness", a combination of sacrifice and damnation which, for Genet, is the epitome of moral vigour.[27] Freedom, because the commission of a crime or a betrayal gives one a sense of ease without any moral preoccupation, a feeling of expiatory detachment.[28] Fulfillment, because the inner violence of the act of theft gives it a ritualistic and religious aura—a sacrifice, an offering; Genet literally used to dedicate his crimes to various persons and objects. Crime is therefore an expiating sacrifice, a black satanic sacrifice. This is borne out by the fact that the flowers seemed black to him when he laid them on the altar of a church whose collection box he had stolen that morning.[29] This is a black mass offering at night in a dark and empty church. The ritualistic black offering inherent in a crime brings expiation and fulfillment. This combination of vigour, freedom and fulfillment associated with the act of crime seems to fit the stigma premises rather than the "guilt—quest for punishment—crime" formula.

When Genet commits a crime he acts according to the image cast on him. He complies first of all with the expectations of his immediate environment and this in itself is satisfying. He is no longer Jean, the nameless bastard; he is Jean, the thief. This newly found self-image is a source of strength and achievement. Genet, in a state of "ego-diffusion", to borrow Erikson's concept,[30] of unknown origin, no parents, no past, or a precarious present and uncertain future, at last finds his coveted ego-identity; one that is not only cast upon him, but is his alone; nobody is going to challenge him to it or take it away from him as they did with other things. The compliance with the image of a criminal not only gives him an individual ego-identity but also makes him eligible for entry into the group of other thieves and homosexuals, thus affording the opportunity for group identity and a sense of belonging.

Empirical confirmation of this hypothesis was provided by Lewin, who showed that the emotional tension of adolescent youths was greatly diminished when they finally became members of a criminal gang where they presumably found their coveted "ego-identity".[31] The crucial point, however, is that every new act of crime reinforces this ego identity with a resultant feeling of accomplishment, elation and energetic vigour. But the sense of fulfillment accompanying a criminal act is more complex and conjectural, possibly owing to the sense of pollution ingrained into the criminal stigma. He was chosen as scapegoat, as a receptacle of abuse and vileness. The black religiosity of Genet induces him to apply ritual to each step in his evil transformation. Each negation is a triumph. Murder should be performed as a human sacrifice to the accompaniment of a black mass. Being a criminal as a vicarious obligation to others, as a sacrifice to others, insofar as one complies with an image tagged on him by others, is a sacrifice worthy of fulfillment. The salvation through the gutters here is apparently not confined to Genet himself but is a sort of cleansing vehicle for the pollution of others. He is the scapegoat, the damned. As with stoning, all the evils of the community are cast off and transferred symbolically to him. By receiving these stigmatizing stones he is ritually expiated: he cleanses them of their sins by taking them upon himself. This is the basis of his claim for ritualistic fulfillment—the beatitude of a thief. However, there is no hope of resurrection for him;—he knows by now that his vicarious expiation of the evil of others by being their scapegoat will not be paid by social acceptance in this world or by heavenly love in the hereafter. The dilemma of the outsider emerges again in full force. Genet once had a gaze filled with love which did not perceive "the striking features which cause individuals to be regarded as objects".[32] He ceased to love because he felt cheated; he played the role required of him, conforming to the overt and covert wishes of others, but when coming to receive his desert—reciprocal love and acceptance—he is treated with abuse and scorn befitting the scapegoat whose role he was forced to play.

Genet, the existentialist criminal saint, ceased to love because other people invariably became objects incapable of giving love, and apparently of receiving it. The fulfillment, therefore, is to destroy this love which is built on sin.[33] This previous love of others should be transformed into ritual of destroying "your world". The previous joyful obedience is transformed into fires of hatred of "your world". Love of others is carnivorous and greedy.[34] It should be feared and destroyed. Eros should be transformed into a ritual of Thanatos, for which every new crime against "your world" is an act of expiatory fulfillment. A thief actually appears to Genet in the image of the destroying angel.[35] For the psychoanalysts punishment is the subconscious delegate of guilt which presses the individual towards crime.[36] The present case study does not uphold this hypothesis. For Genet the primary essence lies in the act of crime and the existence of a criminal in the group. Punishment is a dreary drudgery, a necessary evil regarded as a professional risk. It has no grandeur, nor is it desired; all it evokes in him are the reminiscences of prison smells, paint, formaldehyde and urine.[37]

THE GROUP

Genet describes the structure of the criminal group as a loosely organized band. The leaders, the "directors", choose the location of the "job", draw the plans, supervise the performance and sell the stolen property for a considerable commission.[38] Social stature within the gang is difficult to determine, because criminals usually magnify their exploits and their importance. Thieves have an innate need to boast of their successes after a theft, and they persist doing so even if they know that their bragging is frequently the cause of their apprehension. The main assets of a leader are not unlike those of a company executive: "brains", know-how, charisma, or, in Genet's words, mysterious brilliance and scintillating magnetism.[39] The younger members of the group are the bold performers and the daring lackeys

213

who carry out the job; the old-timers offer advice, professional hints and reassurance.[40] The criteria for upper vertical mobility in the group include the reputation of a "bruiser", a tough-guy", a record of spectacular jobs involving dare-devil stunts, a rich criminal career, and many years in prison.[41]

The king of them all, however, is the murderer. A thief is a beginner; if somebody is called the "slasher" and has a dozen armed robberies to his name he is fine, but in order to reach the top, to achieve the peak of status and prestige, "you need a murder with all the trimmings. Nothing else'll do".[42] The group is held together by a crude but severe normative system, "a rough-and-ready morality", which regulates relations between the members of the group and very often determines their fate by prescribing sanctions. There is a strong norm for comradeship and mutual help among the members of the group. "Squealing" and "ratting" to the police are the two unpardonable sins. Pimps and queers often betray their mates to the police and are therefore despised and considered the scum of the criminal group.[43]

Certain norms are actually rules of professional ethics, thus one should never commit murder without a financial motivation; a burglar who killed a mate "to settle an old score" took a five-franc note from the scene of the murder so "nobody'll say I committed murder without getting something out of it".[44] The techniques of crime and the pressures to join the criminal group, as described by Genet, uphold some of the sociological theories as to criminal subculture formation and the manner of operation of its members. These sociological pressures to join the group of criminals and deviants serve as an appropriate ground for the stigma premises. They afford a perspective as to the place of stigma in the other social pressures towards crime and deviation. The planning of an operation and its execution by the group involves collaboration by several individual functions and complex skills. This would support Sutherland's basic tenet of crime as largely a group phenomenon transmitted and acquired by association with the criminal group and the learning of patterns of criminal behaviour and criminal techniques.[45] The operation

214

is conceived first of all by information from "the intelligence service". A night watchman tips the gang as to worthwhile places for burglaries. The operation must be carefully planned, in order to allocate the right tasks to the right gang members, and to allow for the unforseen, the surprise element.[46] The techniques of crime are many and varied, and success depends mostly on applying the right method to the right "mugs". For instance, when stealing from queers one "should let the guy come up to you, keep him dangling, act a little surprised when he suggests that you do it."[47] One should recognize the right time to strike and with whom to act dumb. An example of the complicated and elaborate technique employed in property offences is the method of stealing from jewellers' showcases. This involves team work; one distracts the attention of the detective, another flirts with the salesgirl while the third examines a piece of jewellery and quickly replaces it with a similar counterfeit piece. A "quick snatch" of goods on display is more dangerous but more spectacular and daring.[48]

The actual initiation of group members into the life of crime fits the three theoretical components of the sociological exposition as to the pressures towards criminal behaviour which we have mentioned previously. These are:

a. *Differential Identification:* Daniel Glaser[49] contended that prior to a person's actual criminal behaviour he adopts criminal values and roles. He sees himself as a criminal or law-violator. When his self-image is deviant he is ripe for the association with criminals.

b. *Differential Opportunity Structure:* After the identification with criminal images there must then be access to illegitimate social structures for the actual criminal association to take place. Cloward and Ohlin[50] describe the way in which an individual becomes aware of the availability of illegitimate opportunities and finds access to them.

c. *Differential Association:* This is the process of actual initiation into criminal or deviant behaviour by association with a criminal

215

group and learning the criminal techniques and patterns of behaviour. Unless an individual is mentally deranged and the manifestations of his mental aberration constitute the offence, delinquency is deemed to be a group phenomenon, the patterns of which are transmitted to new members by learning and association.[51] The differential identification process is illustrated in the role-playing of Stilitano, one of Genet's criminal mates. He used to invent roles of criminals and "big shots"; he also invented gangster attitudes and cherished his role of a dangerous outlaw. He constantly acted the role of his ideal-typed hero.[52] Darling, one of the thieves-pimps-homosexuals of *Our Lady of the Flowers,* dresses up as a "big shot" to impress his mates, to appear as the "big-time" criminal he imagines himself to be and to impress the prison inmates. Darling actually dresses up for prison. He imagines the effect of each new purchase on his past or future prison mates at Fresnes or La Sante.[53]

"... Darling, wearing a glen plaid suit, a felt hat over one eye, his shoulders stiff and he walks so as to resemble Sebastopol Pete, and Pete holds them like that so as to resemble Teewee and so on, a procession of pure, irreproachable pimps leading to Darling ... for although he was a genuine crook, nevertheless he did not know how to be at ease in original postures and imitated the gangsters of Chicago and Marseilles.[54] Access to the illegitimate structures is sought at a tender age, members of juvenile gangs who for the time being are engaged in petty pilfering while they wait for the chance and look for ways to join the big fellows, whom they revere and who commit real crimes. The young beginner longs to be accepted by the "real man" of the criminal group and to win his friendship; then he feels that he "has made it".[56]

The differential association process is clearly depicted by Genet when he describes the learning process by which the more experienced criminal, the "chief", the "liege lord", would divulge the secrets of the trade to the novices. The bosses instruct the new recruits how to steal from churches, the techniques of robbing villas and the ways of prostituting themselves with

216

sailors.[57] In one of the prisons, where school for pick-pockets had been organized, the "pupils" had to practise on sleeping prisoners; they had to empty all their pockets and replace the contents without waking them. The gist of the operation was to tickle the victim in the right places so that he would turn over in his sleep to reveal the required pockets.[58]

Having studied some of the sociological processes leading to crime and deviation which may serve as a background for our main concern with the stigma of elements inherent in Genet's work, we shall proceed to analyse the latter as reflected by Genet's criminal menagerie.

The exclusive function of stigma, definition by negatives, operates, according to Genet, by the label "thief" itself. It determines a man's identity, the chief essence of which is theft. An antisocial label simplifies the image of a person: by calling a person a thief, you reduce to irrelevance all his other roles and attributes.[59]

Stigmatization by tagging, defining by symbolic elements of dress and behaviour, is the starting point of the process of segregating the criminal from the rest of society. Even a seemingly unimportant detail, a single pocket on the left side for convicts in Devil's Island, can suffice to distinguish these convicts from the rest of the world.[60]

A more basic element of the stigma premise is the classic instance of a child's behavioural compliance with the image branded on him. This is the pressure exerted by the group on an individual. Genet the child became a thief because he was stigmatized as such. When the child was caught stealing by the mother superior in charge of the school and was asked by her why he had stolen, all he could answer was: "Because the others thought I was a thief."[61]

Once an individual has been labelled a thief, many other derogatory attributes stick to him quite easily. The label of outlaw and outcast makes him more susceptible to other tags: he becomes a sort of "fly-paper attracting offensive adjectives. First they'll say that he's a thief, therefore his feet stink, and his teeth and his mouth; that he sucks his thumb, that he talks to himself when he's alone."[62] If somebody has been cast out of the community, he must be made as different as possible; a thief, an outsider cannot possibly remain a normative or legal outcast, and the stigma process piles on him label after derogatory label in order to make his apartness more and more conspicuous. Once this process has really pushed the stigmatized out of all possible legitimate roles and statuses, the thieves and outsiders actually have no choice but to operate within the confined boundaries of stigma. If we have been painted black we might as well act as complete cannibals. In the words of Archibald, a masterful combination of satanic preacher and black Muslim: "I order you to be black to your very veins. Pump black blood through them. Let Africa circulate in them. Let Negroes negrify themselves. Let them persist to the point of madness in what they're condemned to be, in their ebony, in their odour, in their yellow eyes, in their cannibal tastes. Let them not be content with eating Whites, but let them cook each other as well. Let them invent a criminal painting and dancing. Negroes, if they charge toward us, let it not be out of indulgence, but terror."[63] The whore in *The Screens* is another instance of stigma portrayed by Genet. She points out that the real essence of prostitution is compliance with the image cast on her by her clients.[64] The particular role of a whore is demanded of her by her patrons and this is what she gets paid for; whims, unfulfilled desires and perversions are projected onto the prostitute who caters thus to her stigmatizer's frustrations.

One cannot run away from the stigma with which one is branded. Green-Eyes, the handsome murderer in *Death Watch,* tried at first to shake off his Mark of Cain, but to no avail. "I didn't want mine", he said, "It chose me. It fell on my shoulders and clung to me. I tried everything to shake it off,"[65] but it neither fell off nor rubbed off, it just stuck and there is no choice but to accept it with the predetermined finality of a Calvinist priest. The stigmatized person has very little choice but to mould himself according to the cast set by his entourage of alters. The mother

218

of the thief, for example, knows that if he goes to jail, it is not just to pay for his crimes in the past or in the present but to receive his desert for the thefts he is sure to commit in the future. The judges and the public[66] have already determined his future for him: "once a thief always a thief". He stops being an individual, and becomes a prototype, the archetype of the thief roaming the collective mind of "public opinion".[67] Genet proceeds to rely on his peculiar brand of gutter psychoanalysis when describing the safety-valve function of stigma: The thief receives all the soddy, slimy and larcenous cravings of "your world", of good, law-abiding citizens. "Your world" projects it onto him and he has to accept this transference. You have to be thankful to the thief for taking your criminal cravings upon himself, albeit without choice, but complacently, otherwise you respectable folks "will steal cutlets and chickens in your dreams every night".[68] The finality of stigma, the pressure to act like the murderer one has been branded as being, has the power of destiny and the totality of Greek Fate.

Green-Eyes was crazed at first: he tried to back out, to adopt any other image but that of a murderer, he tried to be a dog, a cat, a horse, a tiger, even a rose, but he could not; even his body was tuned to the act of murder.[69] Murder was for him as inevitable as it has been for Oedipus. Concerning the stigma of conviction, Genet is even more final, almost disinterested. The stigma of conviction is the prime mover towards more and more crime and further deviation. Proof of guilt of subsequent offenses is unnecessary. Having already been convicted of theft, one is guilty as far as the stigmatizing public is concerned, forever and ever. The presumption of innocence is mere make-believe, and every casual accusation results in a conviction. If one has been convicted it means that one is capable of the deed[70] and will perform it again and again. A man may come out of prison, having served his sentence, but he is still a thief.[71] He may even be innocent, but if people think that he is guilty, guilty he is. "With a mug like mine, I can do anything I like. Even when I am innocent, people think I'm guilty."[72] This segregation and definition, tagging and separating the stigmatized criminal and deviant from the rest of "your world" results in a class of outcasts who must unite for sheer survival and creates a normative system of its own. This system is based on the common denominator of apartness but it also needs a common value system and an apology.

Criminals and deviants must find a justification for being criminal, "otherwise how could one live?"[73] Like everyone else, they must create a coherent self-image and determine for themselves the essence of their reference and membership groups. Criminals and deviants envelop themselves in a garment woven of rationalizations and explanations used to build and define their image as members of a criminal and deviant group, and to protect themselves from the corroding attacks of "your world".

The criminal novice looks for value rationalizations to account for his criminal deeds; not so the hardened professional—he has no illusions, his ambivalence towards the legitimate norms is a thing of the past and he knows that the immediate aim of his crime is gain, pure and simple. The trinity of moral vigour, freedom and fulfillment imputed by Genet to his own crimes is inevitably related to the criminal and deviant existence of the group as a whole. Moral vigour is also inherent in the acceptance of its destiny.[74] In terms of stigma we may interpret this feeling of right and propriety as the group's fulfillment of the role forced on it. They have finally become what "your world" has destined them to be, an isolated group for whom a certain space has been allocated outside the borders of the legitimized norms. By accepting the roles of criminals or outsiders in a special group, they have been institutionalized within the social structure, albeit the "wrong" part of it. They have performed the functions expected of them and are therefore "entitled" to a feeling of rectitude, propriety and moral vigour. The liberating ecstasy of the act of killing[75] is also described. Green-Eyes feels calm and relaxed after the murder that would eventually lead him to the guillotine,[76] because the confusion as to his identity and self-image has been clarified; he is a murderer now—how could

220

it be otherwise? Nobody had ever doubted that he would eventually end up under the guillotine. The liberating sense of freedom is incidental to the dispersion of the confusion as to one's self-image. Being a criminal clarifies every subsequent criminal act which reinforces the resolution of inner conflicts. The thief in the group defines himself by his crime, he delimits his social contours, liberates himself from confusion and sets himself in order.[77]

The fulfillment inherent in the criminal existence of the group is the consequence, the ritualistic nature of their crimes. Murder should be performed by a "noble gesture".[78] The ritual of a murder should have the solemnity of a Black Mass, it should be a ceremony, a rite of hatred.[79] The fulfillment in murder also stems from the pollution "earned" by it; this is the final and irremediable "badness", the point of no return—social damnation. The positive feed-back cycle of mutual rejection and counter-rejection has culminated in the sacrificial flow of blood.[80] The polluted have passed judgment both on themselves and on "your world". Murder is considered to be the most noble of crimes because more than any other crime it has the ritualistic finality of severing its perpetrator from "your world",[81] the society of legitimized fakes. The murderer holding the knife, the gun or the poison phial is in the super-human and extra lucid state of the damned.[82] He has begun the descent (or ascent). The outcast pollutes himself for the sake of others. A self-willed scapegoat, he hurls himself to the bottom of the pit. He has ritualistically damned and polluted himself in full compliance with his stigma and thereby achieves expiation and fulfillment. For good measure he dreams that he ejaculates into the toothless mouth of the old man he has just strangled.[83] Members of the criminal group quite often do not mind and are sometimes even glad to go to prison. This is not, as the psychoanalysts claim, because of an inner urge to be punished which makes prison the *raison d'être* of their crimes, but because they feel a sense of belonging to the inmate world and/or have high status within the prison community.[84] Genet himself displayed many traits of "prisonization"—prison being for him a place of relative

221

security where lovers could be procured in abundance and with ease. The members of the criminal group, through Genet their spokesman, felt a morbid affection for the world of prisons and penal colonies. They would not have wanted to transform them into "your world" kind of life. The disheartening message to penologists would be that the hard core of the underworld retain their nostalgic affection for the world of criminals and prisoners; this world is a part of "our world", and is not a tool for reforming the criminal into a boring and nauseating member of "your world".[85]

Genet feels that the prison leaves an imprint on the convict's external features, the signs of the penal colony being the cropped hair and heavy muscles; the personality of the convict also radiates hypocrisy, violence and fierceness.[86] These signs, which have been taken by many criminologists, from the archaic Lombroso to the modern Sheldon, as casual factors in the genesis of crime, are identified by Genet from his own experience as the traits acquired from prolonged incarceration and violent interaction with the society of inmates.

"YOUR WORLD": THE IMAGE OF SOCIETY

To the members of the criminal group "your world" is surrounded by a glass wall. This is the wall of laws, norms and mores for the outsiders and criminals to crash against and smash their faces.[87] The overwhelming image of "your world" is one of a field of force, a branding and degrading mechanism which operates by brute force and whose prime movers are geared to everything except the so-called morality and justice as defined by "your world".[88]

Another feature of legitimate society, as it is perceived by the criminal group, is its preoccupation with forms, outer shells, empty gestures rather than content and inner meaning. "Your world" consists of image-makers for whom the picture of an object is more important than the object itself.[89] External appearance above all is cherished by Mr. Blankensee in *The Screens*

222

who is a bizarre cross between a Bourgeois Gentilhomme and Babbit. He is very upset about losing his padded clothes: "without my pad on my belly, what would I look like? My pad is the chief element of my glamour. So are my boots..."[90] "Your world" renders impossible any sincere and open-hearted communication between its individuals: it is mortally afraid of any direct flow of emotions among its individuals, who rely heavily on the separating effects of pomp and insolence.[91]

The outwardly righteous and scrupulous bourgeois conceals within his murky brain "treasures of duplicity, hatred, meanness, cruelty and lust."[92]

A paradox and a dilemma result: If "your world" on the legitimate side of the legal and social barricade consists largely of a bunch of thieves who are hypocritical as well, how can an "honest" thief assert his criminal identity? He is, alas, inside the normative boundaries of "your world" when he steals. A conscientious thief, laments Genet, is bound to be forever frustrated because in a society of thieves, he conforms to the norm, he commits a model act when stealing. "If I steal here," Genet eulogizes, "I perform no singular deed that might fulfill me. I obey the customary order, I am not committing evil. The outrageous is impossible, I am stealing in a void."[93] The confusion here might stem, if we ignore Genet's vitriolic sarcasm, from an overlapping of roles; a thief's role of complying with the expectations of his stigma is marred by the fact that the stigmatizers themselves are thieves. The conspicuity inherent in the stigma is levelled down by the comradeship in larceny between criminal and victim. Genet leaves no doubt as to the criminal group's attitude and his own towards various social institutions.

The one institution close to Genet's heart and to the welfare (or misfortune) of the underworld is, of course, the police, which represents the legitimate society and its institutions. As the official delegates of "your world" they are crooked by definition: they are always willing to have "their palms greased"[94] and collaborate, for a consideration, with the underworld. Genet himself feels a certain affinity with the police. This admiration for them stems from his belief that they are trained to kill.[95] Their profession is a corrupting agent and the realization of this fills him with a spiteful pleasure. "The search bulletins posted on the walls, the photos and descriptions of wanted criminals, the contents of the registers, the objects under seal, create an atmosphere of foul infamy and it gives me pleasure to know that these big strapping fellows are breathing it in and that it is corrupting them, that it is evilly corroding their minds."[96]

The criminal group as a whole is less enamoured of the police: they know that the real game here is dog eat dog and the only relationship is unending warfare. The stakes are the confession or conviction of the criminal. The police try to achieve their ends by means of interrogations which often include violence.[97] But the criminal has a trump card—he can withhold his confession. The crucial point is that members of the criminal group believe that the police do not really care whether someone has actually committed a crime or not. Guilt and innocence are beyond their interest—all they are after is a conviction to enter in their files. The prominence of stigma in determining their brand of guilt is portrayed by the following conversation between two police officers apprehending a suspect: "Let him go, come on, Gaubert. After all, he hasn't committed a crime." "Him with that baby-doll mug of his? He's capable of it, all right."[98] Looking capable of committing an offence is proof.

Another aspect of stigma emerges from the dialogue between the policeman and the flute-player in *The Screens*. The flute-player is accused of confusing the order of things, of infringing every decent rule and legal norm; the policeman declares that he was ordered to intervene on behalf of everybody concerned, every enraged citizen and irritated peddler in the market-place, who observed the outrage, the accused playing two flutes with his nostrils. The flute-player, in the best tradition of innovators, tried to explain to the judge that it took him two years to perfect the art of playing with nostrils, but he did not realize that the mere conspicuity, difference, strangeness and irregularity inherent in his innovation were the necessary evidence to prove his guilt.

224

The policeman, in the best tradition of the righteous law-enforcer, deplores the thanklessness of the criminal; "we"—the legitimate society which he as a policeman represents—"give to you everything: schools, hospitals and police-stations." We try to be humane to you, but the better we treat you scum of the earth, the worse you become.[99] This is reminiscent of the "give them hell" school of criminal science and of the well-known speeches by J. Edgar Hoover on the "vermin of the underworld" and the "sewer-rats spawned by prisons." The policeman takes it as a personal affront if the criminal fails to confess, or, even worse, tries to escape. This, he feels, is a scheme, a plot against him: the criminals are trying to ruin his career. This is what comes of being decent to this scum, the politicians and policy-makers up there are full rights for the criminals and nothing but duties for us policemen. "They even advice us to talk to you politely, . . . you little louse," laments the gendarme in *The Screens* in front of the thief. "They have really funny notions, the boys up there at the top, with their politeness: I'd like to see them in close contact with you, like us little blokes."[100] The prison governors, the turnkeys and the guards are the other echelon of the administration of justice. "They are not all fools," decides Genet condescendingly, "but they are purely indifferent to the game they play."[101] They are neutral in this war between "our world" and "your world". They are like keepers of tombs totally disinterested in the identity of the corpses they guard. Racketeers, crooks, pimps, fences, forgers, killers, are all the same to them, cell-fodder to fill the prison. All they ask is to leave them alone; and if you do they won't bother you. The judicial system more than any other branch of the administration of justice yields the branding tools of formalized stigma. However from the stigmatized side of the barricade it appears that the judge needs the criminal much more than the criminal needs the judge. The phony judge in *The Balcony* realizes that his whole entity depends on his being able to declare thieves to be thieves and treat them accordingly: "My being a Judge," he tells the prostitute-thief, "is an emanation of your being a thief." The judge illustrates the main theme of Chapter One by declaring that stigma can divide the bad from the good by declaration. Stigmatizing is therefore one of the main functions of the judge: "if I no longer had to divide the Good from the Evil, what use would I be?"[102] In this phony world, Genet believes that, being a thief, he gives an ethical anchor to the world. He does a wonderful service to the "legitimate" world in providing the criterion (a false one, of course) for dividing the black from the white. As the judge says to the thief: "A judge! I'm going to be judge of your acts! On me depends the weighing, the balance. The world is an apple; I cut it in two: the good, the bad. And you agree, thank you, you agree to be the bad."[103] Without criminals there are no judges, no punishment and no condemnation; yet to condemn is the essence of judges and justice. It is as if the criminals owe the judges their crime so that by meting out just desert they perform their function. Here again the criminal has all the trump cards. What if he does not wish to confess, does not choose to play the game of "your-world" by committing the kind of crime that "your-world" judges can condemn, if he refuses to take upon himself the projected guilt of the judge? How is the judge going to assert his righteousness? The judge in *The Blacks* is horrified by this prospect. If there is no corpse at all (that is, no crime), he exclaims in fright, "why, that could kill us."[104] The judge reproachfully implores the criminal not to rock the boat, not to shatter the order of things. The show must go on, and if the criminal becomes somewhat sick of his role, the judge accuses him: "It's you who keep stalling, you promised us a re-enactment of the crime so as to deserve your condemnation."[105]

So the judges need a criminal; he can be defaced, can have no identity, anyone at all would be enough to comply with the forms and spirit of justice, whether or not he has committed a crime matters least of all. If he comes before us we shall decide his guilt for him; after all, the function of the judge is to declare guilt and innocence. Objective innocence does not exist and if we declare someone guilty, he is guilty or becomes guilty.

226

This is the way judicial stigma operates. The following is the image of justice in "your world" as portrayed in *The Blacks*: "The Judge: Who's the culprit? You won't answer? I'm offering you one last chance. Now listen: it doesn't matter to us which of you committed the crime. We don't care whether it's X, Y, or Z. If a man's a man, a Negro's a Negro, and all we need is two arms, two legs to break, a neck to put into the noose, and our justice is satisfied. Come, be decent about it."[106]

The dilemma here is expressed by the Qadi in *The Screens*; being branded by the judge reinforces the criminal's self-image. His identity has been clarified for him, which is literally essential for his coherent self-perception. Genet presents Said, the defendant, as actually pleading to the Qadi to convict him, otherwise "you'd be killing me,"[107]—his ego-identity is in danger of diffusion. But if the problems of the criminal are solved by the Qadi, who is out to solve his own problem, what criteria should be used for branding the stigma of conviction which he is actually obliged to do? God? Yes. "God knows all . . . but he is no longer here . . . God has lit out, skidaddled, scrammed. God has gone away."[108] Justice does not exist, it is an illusion. Morality is a nursery rhyme, a fairy-tale; both "your world" and "our world" are rife with larceny, false pretences, dishonesty and even murder. How should a judge, Qadi, decide whom to brand with a stigma and whom not to brand? We have tried to answer these questions as to the criteria for stigmatization in the previous chapters, but, as we have seen, these problems are very rarely related to the cognitive material issue, or to the offence of which the defendant is accused. Genet and his Qadi may not have the inclination to look for those symbolic links between the personality of the stigmatized, his behaviour and the actual tag branded on him. What they did sense is the absence of any clear-cut scales or measuring rods to define the criminal and the deviant. They reject the conventional criteria of religion, morality and justice. The gist of the dilemma is summarized by the Qadi himself: "It is all right for you, Said, because you have me to tag you, to identify you for yourself. I see very well," he says, "what you gain by each new condemnation." Said, the defendant, receives a reinforcement of his ego identity with each new condemnation; but who is going to define the judge for the judge? "But what about me," cries the Qadi, "to where does each new condemnation lead me?"[109] Apparently nowhere: without saintliness and sin, without right and wrong, without good and evil, there can be no criminals, and without criminals there are no judges, and the circle is complete. Of the five major objectives of criminal justice: retribution, expiation, deterrence, prevention and reformation, Genet imputes to his judge the first two only. It is not surprising that he does not impute any utilitarian purposes to the judiciary. A sentence that intended to reform an offender would obviously seem to him a contradication in terms. Prevention or social defence against crime is purely a "your world" affair. The primary purpose of judicial punishment is talionic retribution. The Roman Tables brand of *talio* seems too sophisticated for Genet. His Qadi interprets retribution with the crude symmetry[110] of the Code of Hammurabi. Expiation as a purpose of punishment has been the perennial escort of retribution. From the point of view of the bench, expiation is achieved when the defendant submits to the judicial powers of the court; objective guilt is not enough; subjective recognition of guilt, submission, humility, and in our terms, willing acceptance of the stigma of guilt and conviction not only lower the retributive drive of the court but also amount to expiation. In *The Blacks*, Archibald urges his fellow defendants to squat, and humbly asks the judge if they may whimper. The judge then orders the defendants to tremble: "Tremble! Harder! Tremble! Come on, shake!" This is the proper courtroom atmosphere for the judge to carry out his judicial duties. The defendant by his confession of the crime, experiences an expiatory release of tension a sensation of liberating fulfillment ensuring the acceptance of stigma. Our Lady of the Flowers actually has no control over the confession which keeps surging in his chest, upwards and outwards:

"First, there came from his liver, right up against his teeth,

228

the confession of the old man's murder. He didn't make the confession. But the confession was rising, rising. If he opens his mouth, he'll blurt it all out. He felt he was lost. Suddenly he gets dizzy. He sees himself on the pediment of a not very high temple. 'I'm eighteen, I can be sentenced to death,' he thinks quickly. If he loosens his fingers, he fails. He pulls himself together. No, he won't say anything. It would be magnificient to say it, it would be glorious. No, no, no! Lord, no! Ah! he's saved. The confession withdraws, withdraws without having gone over. I killed an old man."[111]

This is the masterful portrayal of a modern Orestes driven to his destiny by the Erinyes. For inner identity, salvation and expiation lay in murder, and to be worthy of one's Moira a murder has to be apparent, to be confessed, so that one complies finally with the image everyone has cast on him. Our Lady of the Flowers has arrived; he is somebody now, he has fulfilled himself. He has become what everybody had meant him to be— a murderer. After the confession comes the expiated relaxation. Our Lady of the Flowers falls asleep, spent, exhausted and contented.[112] As a direct corollary of Genet's conception of the courts as organs of retribution and expiation, he visualizes the criminal procedure as a festive ritual of a religious offering. Not the rite of bleeding an animal, but a human sacrifice—the Molloch of "your world" has to be pacified from time to time by an execution. There must be wide participation; the courtroom should be as packed as the arena of a public stoning, so that the expiation engulfs everyone present. After the human scape-goat is sacrificed, the men of religion proclaim the absolution of crimes (the scapegoat has carried them away with him) and everybody present prays, cleansed and purified.[113] The courtroom crowds certainly do come for a release of aggression. This, as we have seen, is one of the basic sources of stigma: a struggle goes on between the prosecution and the defence over the accused; here the process is more refined than in the public hangings and stoning but the crowds come for the same trophy—the defendant's head. "The public comes here (to the courtroom)," says Genet, "insofar as a word (the confession of the accused or the court's pronouncement of sentence) may result in a beheading and so that it may return, like Saint Denis, carrying its severed head in its hands."[114] The severed head carries away with it the combined aggression and projected guilt of righteous members of "your world" so that their righteousness is reinforced until the newly accumulated aggressiveness and frustration call for another head. The jury system seems vile to Genet because it makes judges—their job is evil, by definition—out of decent men. The court psychiatrist is depicted as an amorphous diagnostician throwing around words such as the following:

"Unbalanced . . . psychopathy . . . interrelation . . . splanchnic system . . . schizophrenia . . . unbalanced . . . unbalanced, unbalanced, unbalanced, unbalanced."[115] One term is repeated in this flow of verbosity: "unbalanced". We demonstrated in chapters one and two that the adjustment-centred approach to mental health takes the modal, mean or median values of behaviour in a given group to denote the "ins" and to exclude the "outs". This statistical construct to measure adjustment is quite hopeless in real situations, because nobody seems to know what kinds of behaviour and personality traits should be included in the eclectic, multi-dimensional concept of adjustment and which traits should be taken to denote the opposite, maladjustment. Even more amorphic than the term "adjustment" is the adjective "unbalanced", it is as though the psychiatrist had a means to determine who is and who is not. It comes down, therefore, to a conclusion which we have reached by deduction and Genet by intuition: that this sort of psychiatric diagnosis is no more than a tool of social control, a stigma, to keep in line those who leave the herd or are conspicuous in any other way not necessarily related to the crimes or deviations which are imputed to them.

As an appropriate summary of the stigmatizing function of the court we have the following observation made by Our Lady of the Flowers:

"The Court smiled, that is, with the smile imparted to the

face by the austere choice (already made) between the just and the unjust, the royal rigour of the brow that knows the dividing line—that has seen clearly and judged—and that condemns."[116]

Genet's court of justice comes to the bench with a predetermined decision. It smiles benevolently at the innocent and glares darkly at the obvious depravity of the guilty. With his branding powers, the judge divides, but not the just from the unjust, because for this he has neither the ability nor the inclination; he makes a formal extrinsic distinction between the acquitted and the condemned.

Genet's view of religion is put forth in *The Balcony*. This play is the ultimate in derision against "legitimate" society and its institutions. The play takes place in a brothel where illusion and reality are intermingled. The clients, who come to purchase temporary make-believe (or maybe real) status and power, represent the main institutions of society. The fake bishop realizes that all his power stems from the deep symbolism of the cloth. He therefore worships this source of his power: "Mitre, bishop's bonnet, when my eyes close for the last time, it is you that I shall see behind my eyelids, you, my beautiful gilded hat, ... you, my handsome ornaments, capes, laces."[117]

Apart from the mitre, lace, gold-cloth and glass trinkets, there is only one function which is important (the others are irrelevant—"The hell with the functions!"[118])—to forgive sins. The bishop is horrified at the idea that this function loses its *raison d'être* because in a world of evil (which Genet wholeheartedly believes our world is) you cannot commit sins. He realizes that "here there's no possibility of doing evil," and the whore teases him: "Reality frightens you, doesn't it?" Of course, it does, without real sins, where "good is only an illusion and Evil is a nothingness which arises on the ruins of Good."[119] There is no need for mitres, for gold cloth or for bishops.

The sham general in *The Balcony* is overjoyed to hear his exploits described by the prostitute: "Splinters of shell had gashed the lemons. Now death was in action. She moved nimbly from one to the other, deepening a wound, dimming an eye, tearing off an arm, opening an artery, discolouring a face, cutting short a cry, a song. Death was ready to drop. Finally, exhausted, herself dead with fatigue, she grew drowsy and rested lightly on your shoulder, where she fell asleep."[120]

War is waged in order to conquer; so the conquerors may win a war but die "or half-die . . . return crippled, armless, legless, broken and bent, balls torn off, noses eaten away, faces blasted."[121] "And the vanquished—who are the conquered? Conquer what? Or whom? You've seen them dragging in the mud, living on peelings. . . conquer that!"[122] These are the lethal games played by politicians and generals. The following the image conceived by our philosopher of the "respectable" employer-employee relationship. The domestic relations in Madame's household are not exactly puritan, and, as seen by Genet, Madame's most ardent desire is to be the prostitute kneeling at the feet of her lover, the thief.[123] The respectable Madame not only practises promiscuity, but is a whore; apparently Genet agrees with his criminal brethren that the false respectability in domestic relations is less palatable than a common whore who has no illusions about her profession. Of crucial importance to our present context is that Genet imputes actual criminality to Madame's lover, while making it clear beforehand that he has been falsely accused. This shows the importance of stigma in Genet's eyes; like a typical professional criminal, he knows that what one does is not as important as what one is reputed to have done. A professional criminal is horrified by a false accusation because he knows that he cannot defend himself; he would rather have a true charge, so that at least he knows what to expect. Genet, the professional criminal, knows that the actual results of a true and a slanderous accusation are very similar. The decision as to guilt or innocence is dependent not so much on acts as on social stigma; for Genet, "guilt comes to the offender from without. It is a collective image, a taboo that settles upon him."[124] Genet's image of the legitimate society is extreme. To varying degrees, this would be the trend of common rationalization among criminals, being a countering force to

232

the isolating and segregating pressures of stigma. This again quickens the pace of the positive feed-back cycle—the criminals' scorn and resentment.

We have examined the images of society's most important institutions: the priest, the judge and the warrior as portrayed by the philosopher-thief. As for the respectable bourgeoisie as a whole, the Madame in *The Balcony* has a real (not illusory this time) message. "Dress up . . . judges, generals, bishops, chamberlains, rebels, . . . You must go home now, where everything—you can be sure—will be even falser than here."

The adjustment problems of the criminal would have to be solved, as we have mentioned in the previous chapters, within the areas of occupation, domestic relations and social image. Reverting back to crime, patronising prostitutes and developing a *ressentiment* rationalization towards society is the active phase of the solution. However, the criminal value-structure regarding these three adjustment areas is masterfully expounded in another play by Genet: *The Maids.* Claire and Solange, the criminal maids, try to murder their mistress, falsely accuse her lover of the crime and denounce him to the police. Meanwhile, Genet lets us know how the criminal regards legitimate occupation, domestic relations and "respectable society".

Legitimate occupation is degrading slavery: to be an employee, any employee, you are just scum, at worst you are regarded (and therefore are) filth . . . "everything, yes, everything, that comes out of the kitchen is spit."[125] At best you are regarded by your employer as a useful chattel: "Madame loves us the way she loves her arm-chair. Not even that much: like her bidet, rather. Like her pink enamel lavatory seat."[126] To our employers we are invariably neuter, devoid of any recognizable "respectable" love and passion because "filth doesn't love filth";[127] criminals cannot have "noble" emotions. They (the criminal maids) smell like animals, they have the foul odour of the attic, the garret, the maids room where lackeys visit them at night.[128] As we have mentioned above, Genet refers to "your world", "your laws", "your norms", "your salvation" as denoting a diametrically opposite world to the distinct universe of the underworld of "our laws", "our man" and "our morals", the world of thieves, pimps, whores and homosexuals. "Your world employs stigma and tags with which labelled criminals are to provide a contrast, and thereby define its own virtues.[129] The complaisance of "your world" is a corollary, albeit an inverse one, of the wretchedness conferred on the criminals and deviants. The wretchedness of all outsiders is reinforced by "your world" by means of the vicious circle of stigma and counter-rejection. Criminals and deviants owe their social identity to your world" which was instrumental in defining it, and by "repudiating the virtues of 'your world' criminals hopelessly agree to organize a forbidden universe."[130] It may be no more than conjecture whether the attitude of the criminal world towards "your world" is filled mainly by resentment, reaction-formation, straightforward negation or satanic salvation. The attitude itself is expressed in unequivocal terms by Bobo in *The Blacks:* "What we need is hatred. Our ideas will spring from hatred." Diouf adds in agreement: "I've suffered too much shame not to want to befoul their [your world] beauteous soul."[131] The unique and universal hatred of the criminals for "your world" would frequently be expressed, according to Genet, by a symbolic act of defiance by defecating after a burglary at the site of the crime.[132] As to the victims or the "mugs" who are the most useful segment of "your world" to "our [criminal] world", they were invariably ugly: "and the only thing they made me feel was a cruel pleasure."[133] This pleasure was augmented by the awkward plight of the victim: "When he stole a car Guy would manage to drive off just when the owner appeared. He got a kick out of seeing the face of the man watching his car, docilely, going off with the thief."[134] "Your world" and "our world" are connected by a two-way lane. The crime and deviation of the criminal group is used by "your world" to define its own righteousness; in exchange it punished the criminal thereby giving him pardon and absolution.[135] At first this looks like a "heads I win, tails you lose" arrangement between "your world" and the underworld, where the latter is permanently the loser. On closer scrunity, however, the stigma cast on the criminal and internalized by him identifies him for himself just as his crimes define by exclusion the legitimacy of "your world". This is why the mother thief preaches to her son the thief in *The Screens* (Genet himself always imagined his mother as an old thief) that "you should choose evil . . . and irrevocable grief", the evil and vileness should be complete "without the brilliance of darkness, the softness of flint and the honey of thistles", all this for the tranquillity and peace of mind of those in "your world" who are sending the criminals to prison and the outcasts to their social damnation. The mother thief knows that "we're here so that those who are sending us here realize that they're not here," and her son Said, the thief, realizes his usefulness to "your world": when he reaches the abyss of depravity those on the legitimate side of the barricade will be able to say: "Compared to Said, it's a cinch."[136] The best lines, however, are thrown at us by Felicity, the whore, in *The Blacks*. The righteous Queen of "your world" threatens Felicity: "I'm going to have you exterminated," to which Felicity answers ironically: "You fool, just imagine how flat you'd be without that shade to set you off in high relief."[139]

What are the various uses that "your world" finds for the criminals and outcasts? One can start from the aesthetic pleasure that "your world" derives from "slumming". They find poverty picturesque. The miseries of the beggars and their shabby rags remind them of the Goyas and Dores adorning their walls: "There's a perfect harmony between the tonalities of the sky and the slightly greenish shades of the rags," remarks one over-clad matron to her overweight escort. "We've seen them when they all are frozen," answers her escort with the air of a connoisseur, "they have to be seen in the right weather."[140] They take pictures of the *clochards*.[141]

The mechanisms of projection and transference make the criminal an appropriate receptacle for the primitive urges of society which stem from its own aggressiveness: "I wanted to oppose society, but it had already condemned me, punishing

235

not so much the actual thief as the indomitable enemy whose lonely spirit it feared . . . an anxiety—a wound from which flowed its own blood which it dared not shed itself."[142] This release of pent-up aggression is the fuel which kindles the fires of stigma. The inner aggressiveness is generated by the various normative proscriptions, moral, social and legal, which riddle man's life. The constant inner struggle and especially the desire to act against these morals and laws create guilt feelings which are eased by righteously punishing the criminal. The overflow of guilt is then absorbed by the criminal trial and punishment. The other outcasts carry the condemnation of "your world" by moving along its edges, out of its bounds and in its shadows.[143] This is why the grief and misery of the criminal and deviant are perpetuated by "your world" so that they may continue to bear the cross of its condemnation. The dull, routine lives of the bourgeois are tinged with excitement as they vicariously identify with the daring exploits of the criminal.[144] But the criminal's is actually a self-condemnation because it stems from his complying with the judgment of "your world". Archibald, in *The Blacks,* even talks about deserving the reprobation of "your world", its judgment and subsequent condemnation.[145] This is the need for ego-identity—fulfillment and salvation through stigma. We, the criminals, the deviants, the queers, the rejects, the blacks, regard ourselves in "our world" the way we have been, tainted and tagged. As Archibald continues gloomily: "We are what they wanted us to be. We shall therefore be it to the very end."[146] The force of the stigma is portrayed by the judge who proclaims that as from a given date, God being dead, the colour of black ceases to be a sin, it becomes a crime.[147] One of "our world" who has been tainted and branded does not have to do anything in order to be a criminal, his stigma alone suffices to define him as such, both to "your world" and to "our world". Once stigmatized, the road back is hazy, uncertain and sometimes blocked. The blacks, the criminal and deviants must deface themselves; to discolour themselves by eradicating stigma, an impossible task anyway, is not enough.

236

"Go join them," concludes the satanic Archibald, pointing to the audience, "if they'll have you, and if you succeed in winning their love, come back and let me know." [148]

So arise, ex-cons of the world, and tell of the acceptance and love offered you by "your world" after you were released from prison: or, for that matter, tell of the success of the little bastard, Genet, how he regained the love of the peasant family in Le Morvan after he was proclaimed a thief.

NOTES

INTRODUCTION

[1] J. G. Frazer: *Psyche's Task.* pp. 114, 115.
[2] H. Wright: *Physical Disability—A Psychological Approach.*
[3] M. Greenblatt, D. Levinson and R. Williams: *The Patient and the Mental Hospital.*
[4] E. Goffman: *Stigma.*
[5] Fritz Heider: *The Psychology of Interpersonal Relations.*
[6] A. Morris says: "Perhaps it is time that we faced the fact that the generally used concept of 'crime' is altogether too broad to be of much use to the serious investigator of criminal behaviour. I am suggesting that if we are to get on with the business of learning to deal more effectively with crime we had better stop talking about crime and begin to identify and study with as much care and thoroughness as is possible the nature and workings of the significant factors essential to each type of criminal behaviour." *Homicide: An Approach to the Problem of Crime* cit. by M. E. Wolfgang: *Patterns in Criminal Homicide,* pp. 3, 4.
A similar view is stated by R. S. Cavan who says:"Crime, as legally defined, includes so many different types of behaviour that it would be unreasonable to expect all of them to have the same aetiology." *Criminology,* p. 20.
[7] For a comprehensive statement of this dilemma *vide* C.R. Jeffery: "The Structure of American Criminological Thinking," *Jour. of Criminal Law, Criminology and Police Science.* No. 46, p. 658.
[8] R. Garofalo: *Criminologie,* pp. 46, 47.
[9] *Crime, Law and Social Science.*
[10] M. Adler: *Art and Prudence*
[11] Marshall B. Clinard: *Sociology of Deviant Behaviour.*
[12] Sutherland realizes that the stigma of crime following a conviction at the end of a criminal process has social significance, but then he fails to reach the logical conclusion from his observation, viz. that the criminal law norm becomes therefore a special social reality. See: Is "White-Collar Crime" Crime?
[13] Jerome Hall adds some other distinguishing factors on the social

238

level between the social norms and legal ones: "Coercion in such situations (i.e., compliance to non-legal norms) is surely different from that wholly one-sided inexorable operation of legal sanctions, and this basic fact rather vaguely signified in the assertion that the State has "monopoly" of force. It is also noteworthy that the force thus employed is approved by the society generally, and that the condition of its exercise requires that it be deferred until after a more or less standardized procedure, necessitating deliberation, has been employed. Accordingly, it may be concluded that those supreme norms which symbolize social interests and apply to the entire community, whose sanction is force that operates rather specifically as prescribed and in total disregard of the offender's volition, can be distinguished from other norms and may properly be designated "rules of Law". *General Principles of Criminal Law,* 1947, p. 545.

CHAPTER 1

[1] J. W. Thibaut and H. H. Kelley: *The Social Psychology of Groups,* p. 239 ff.
[2] H. C. Lea: *A History of the Inquisition in the Middle Ages.*
[3] Konrad Heiden: *Der Fuehrer.*
[4] H. Arendt: *The Origins of Totalitarianism,* p. 229.
[5] R. Kretschmer: *Physique and Character.*
[6] W. James: *Principles of Psychology,* p. 28.
[7] W. H. Sheldon: *Varieties of Delinquent Youth.*
[8] Sheldon and E. Glueck: *Physique and Delinquency.*
[9] The term offender in the present chapter is not confined to denoting infringers of legal norms in the modern sense but includes also infringers of religious and social norms.
[10] Genesis: 4:12.
[11] S. Ranulf: *Moral Indignation and Middle-Class Psychology.*
[12] J. G. Frazer: *Folklore in the Old Testment,* Chapter III.
[13] Thucydides: *The Greek Historians.* p. 683.
[14] Aeschylus: *The House of Atreus,* pp. 83, 84.
[15] J. G. Frazer: *Psyche's Task,* pp. 114, 115.
[16] Malinowsky: *Crime and Custom in Savage Society,* p. 79.

[17] J.G. Frazer: *Psyche's Task*, p. 115.

[18] *ibid.* p. 127.

[19] P.H. Fawcett: *Lost Traits, Lost Cities, an Explorer's Narrative.* pp. 220, 221.

[20] Von Hentig: *Punishment*, p. 117 ff.

G. Ives: *A History of Penal Methods*, p. 78 ff.

[21] *The Code of Hammurabi*, sec. 127.

[22] *The Laws of Manu*, sec. 237–239.

[23] J. Darmesteter: *The Zend-Avesta.*

[24] Wolff: *The Roman Law.*

[25] W. W. Buckland: *A Manual of Roman Private Law*, p. 53.

[26] *ibid.* p. 54.

[27] G. O. W. Mueller: "Tort Crime and the Punishment," *J. Crim. L. Crimin. and Police Science*, No. 46, p. 309.

[28] W. Ullmann: *The Medieval Idea of Law*, p. 145.

[29] M. E. Wolfgang: "Crimes and Punishment in Florence," *J. Crim. L. Crimin. and Police Science*, No. 47, p. 323.

[30] G. Ives: *History of Penal Methods*, p. 56.

[31] P. Klein: *Prison Methods in New York State,* p. 23, cited by Sutherland and Cressey: *Principles of Criminology*, p. 266.

[32] J. G. Frazer: *The Golden Bough, op. cit.* p. 266.

[33] *ibid.* p. 270.

[34] W. G. Sumner: *Folkways*, p. 43.

[35] E. E. Evans-Pritchard: *Witchcraft, Oracles and Magic Among the Azande.*

[36] Buckland: *A Manual of Roman Private Law.*

[37] J.G. Peristiany: *The Institutions of Primitive Society.*

[38] W.G. Sumner: *op. cit.* p. 219.

[39] *Social Science Research Council*, N.Y. 1938, p. 219.

[40] "The Significance of Control in the Treatment of the Antisocial Person: Crime in America," p. 74.

[41] W. C. Reckless, S. Dinitz and E. Murray: *Self Concept as an Insulator against Delinquency, Society and Self*, p. 43.

[42] D. Lee: *Freedom and Culture*, p. 64.

[43] E. Durkheim: *The Division of Labour in Society*, p. 398.

[44] G. Nettler: "Antisocial Sentiment and Criminality, *Am. Soc. Rev.*, No. 28, p. 208

[45] *L'être et le nèant*, p. 23.

[46] L. Coser: *The Functions of Social Conflicts*, pp. 20–21.

[47] S. Kierkegaard: *The Present Age*, p. 38.
[48] M. Heidegger: *Sein Und Zeit.*
[49] K. Jaspers: *Man in the Modern Age*, p. 41.
[50] H. H. Hyman: *The Value Systems of Different Classes*, in *Class, Status and Power.*
[51] W.F. Whyte: *Street Corner Society: the status of an Italian slum.*

CHAPTER 2

[1] H. D. C. Lewis: *A Short History of Psychiatric Achievement.*
[2] G. Zilboorg: *History of Medical Psychology.*
[3] M. Guttmacher: *Psychiatry and the Law*, pp. 24–25.
[4] K. Menninger: *The Vital Balance.*
[5] T. S. Szasz: The Myth of Mental Illness, *Amer. Psychol.* (1960), pp. 113–116.
[6] A. R. Lindesmith: *Opiate Addiction.*
[7] Fisher and Mendel: *The Communication of Neurotic Patterns over Generations,* in Vogel and Bell: *The Family.*
[8] M. E. Giffin, A. M. Johnson, and E. M. Litin: *The Transmission of Superego Defects,* in Vogel and Bell, *ibid.*
[9] Menninger: *ibid.*
[10] G. E. Partridge: Current Conceptions of Psychopathic Personality *American Journal of Psychiatry,* 10, (1938) p. 53 ff.
[11] J. C. Pritchard: *Treatise on Insanity.*
[12] H. Cason: "The Psychopath and the Psychopathic" *J. of Criminal Psychopathology,* (1943) pp. 522–527.
[13] D. Stafford-Clark: *Psychiatry Today*, p. 118.
[14] M. Frym: "The Treatment of Recidivists," *J. Crim. L. Crimin. and Police Science,* (1956).
[15] *ibid.*
[16] W. Bromberg: *Crime in the Mind*, p. 36.
[17] R. W. White: *The Abnormal Personality*, p. 397.
[18] H. Cason: "The Symptoms of the Psychopath," *Public Health Reports,* vol. 61, (December 1946), p. 1883.
[19] Lind: *Knowledge for What?* Chapter III.
[20] *ibid.*

[21] G.M. Calhoun: *The Growth of Criminal Law in Ancient Greece.*

[22] A. Camus: *The Myth of Sisyphus.*

[23] *Genealogy of Morals,* First Essay, Sect. 14.

[24] H. Weihafen: *The Urge to Punish,* p. 198. See also J. C. Flugel: *Man, Morals and Society,* p. 205 ff.

[25] At least, according to the conception of Judaism.

[26] Job: 9:24.

[27] See E. Cahn: *The Moral Decision,* p. 9 ff.

[28] *The Division of Labor in Society,* cited by C. W. Mills: *Images of Man,* p. 477.

[29] A. Camus: *The Plague.*

[30] H. H. Goddard: "Who is a Moron?" *Scientific Monthly,* No. 24, (1927) pp. 24–41.

[31] Y. G. Gasset: *The Revolt of the Masses,* p. 14.

[32] M. Heidegger: *Sein und Zeit.*

[33] *L'être et néant,* p. 399.

[34] L. Fiedler: *Waiting for the End.*

[35] A. Toynbee: *A Study of History,* p. 438.

[36] Legge: Tao Te King, Chapter 34.

[37] *Tintern Abbey.*

[38] *Social Structure and Anomie* in *Social Theory and Social Structure.*

[39] *Topaze.*

[40] E. Fromm: *The Art of Loving.*

[41] A. Cohen: *Delinquent Boys: The Culture of the Gang.*

[42] *L'être et le Néant.*

[43] P. M. Blau: *Exchange and Power in Social Life.*

[44] *The Lonely Crowd.*

[45] *The Art of Loving, op. cit.* p. 64.

[46] *Civilization and Its Discontents,* pp. 87–91.

CHAPTER 3

[1] D. Stafford-Clark: *Psychiatry Today,* p. 106.

[2] R. W. White: *The Abnormal Personality,* p. 548.

[3] A. C. Bouquet: *Comparative Religion,* p. 128.

[4] *The Sankorscharya of Kanchi Kamakoti Peetam,* quoted by A. Koestler: *The Lotus and the Robot,* p. 64.

[5] The Sir Edwin Arnold translation, Book VI. p. 35.

[6] J. Finegan: *The Archaeology of World Religions*, pp. 210–211.

[7] E. J. Thomas: *The Life of Buddha as Legend and History*, p. 87.

[8] E. Durkheim: *Suicide*, p. 81.

[9] H. Silving: *Suicide and Law* in H. S. Shneidman and N.L. Farberow: *Clues to Suicide*, p. 81.

[10] T. Reik: *The Compulsion to Confess*.

[11] R. K. Merton: *Social Theory and Social Structure*, pp. 153–154.

[12] R. A. Cloward and L. B. Ohlin: *Delinquency and Opportunity*, pp. 180–182.

[13] R. R. Dynes, A. C. Clarke and S. Dinitz: "Level of Aspirations; Some aspects of Family Experience as a Variable." *Am. Soc. Rev.* (April 1956) pp. 212–214.

[14] S. Shoham, N. Shapiro and J. Spiegel: *The Vagabonds of Eilath*.

[15] D. Riesman: *Individualism Reconsidered*.

[16] *ibid.* p. 155.

[17] A. Salomon: *The Tyranny of Progress.* pp. 27–28

[18] *ibid.* p. 26.

[19] S. Shoham and M. Hovav: "'*B'nei Tovim.*', Middle and Upper Class Delinquency in Israel." Report, second stage of the research project.

[20] Metaphysische Anfangsgruende der Rechtslehre (Hastic's Translation), p. 191.

[21] D. R. Taft: *Criminology*, p. 63.

[22] E. H. Sutherland: *White, Collar Crime*.

[23] Uniform Crime Report for the U.S., Washington 1958.

[24] The Challenge of Crime in a Free Society. U.S. Government Printing Office, Washington D. C., February 1967. pp. V–VIII.

[25] Crunhut: *Statistics in Criminology*. pp. 139–157.

[26] The Annual Reports of the Israeli Police for the years 1961–1962.

[27] C. Foote: "The Bail System and Equal Justice," *Federal Probation*. (September 1955) 19:43–48.

[28] I. F. Gaudet: "Individual Differences in the Sentencing Tendencies of Judges," 1938, *Archives of Psychology*.
II. S. Shoham. The Sentencing Policy of Criminal Courts in Israel." *J. Crim. L. Crimin. and Police Science.* Nov.-Dec. 1959.
III. R. Hood: *Sentencing in Magistrate's Courts*.
For a different view, see E. Green: "Sentencing Practices of Criminal Court Judges in Philadelphia," *Am. J. Correction*, 1960, No. 22, pp. 32–35.

[29] A. L. Porterfield: "Delinquency and Its Outcome in Court and College," *American Journal of Sociology,* Nov. 1943, pp. 199–208.

[30] P. Van Nye: *Family Relations and Delinquent Behaviour.*

[31] R.G. Andrey: *Delinquency and Parental Pathology.*

[32] R. D. Schwartz and J. H. Skolnick: "Two Studies of Legal Stigma," *Social Problems,* Fall 1962, p. 133 ff.

[33] This statement is attributed to Daniel Drew, a pious old fraud cited by Sutherland; "White-Collar Crime," *Am. Soc. Rev.,* Feb. 1940, p. 10.

[34] A. Cohen: *Delinquent Boys: The Culture of the Gang.*

[35] A. W. Green: "Culture, Normality and Personality Conflicts," *The American Anthropologist,* April/June 1968, p. 228.

[36] Albert Camus: *The Myth of Sisyphus.* p. 61.

[37] Ryall Book A.5.

[38] R.K. Merton: "Anomie, Anomia, and Social Interaction," *Contexts of Deviant Behaviour,* p. 226.

CHAPTER 4

[1] See Svend Ranulf: *The Jelousy of the Gods and the Criminal Law in Athens,* p. 122.

[2] Ranulf: *op. cit.* p. 147.

[3] O. Borger: *Vedel.* p. 55.

[4] W. C. Reckless: *The Crime Problem.*

[5] *The Revolt of the Masses.*

[6] The author is indebted to Mr. J. Zahavi for bringing this comparison to his attention.

[7] Nineteen Eighty-Four, pp. 241 ff.

[8] *The Image,* p. 19.

[9] H. Garfinkel: "Research Note on Inter- and Intra-Racial Homicides," *Social Forces,* May 1959, pp. 369–381.

[10] *No Exit,* p. 47.

[11] S. Ranulf: *op. cit.* p. 267.

[12] W. Sombart: *Luxus und Kapitalismus,* p. 66.

[13] H. C. Lea: *A History of the Inquisition in the Middle Ages,* Vol. III, p. 625 ff.

[14] *The Power Elite.*

[15] *ibid.* p. 267.

[16] *Stigma, op. cit.* p. 141.

[17] *White-Collar Crime.*

[18] Sutherland and Cressey: *Principles of Criminology.* p. 11. Parenthetical remarks, mine.

[19] A Report on the Incidence of Criminal Behaviour, Arrests and Conviction in Selected Groups.

[20] "Delinquency and its Outcome in Court and College," *Am. J. Soc,* 1943, pp. 199–208.

[21] 82nd. U.S. Congress, 1st Session, Report 307.

[22] *The Power Elite, op. cit. p.* 345.

[23] C.W. Mills: *Op. cit.* pp. 339–348.

[24] *Anthropology,* pp. 159–160.

[25] *A Study of History, op. cit.,* Vol. I, p. 9.

[26] S. Ben-Dov: *Israel in the Crisis of Statehood,* p. 12.

[27] A. Camus: *The Myth of Sisyphus,* p. 17

[28] *The Present Age,* p. 38.

[29] J. P. Sartre. *Self Deception* in *'L'être et le Néant,* p. 259.

[30] Cited by Camus: *The Myth of Sisyphus.*

[31] *The Fall.*

[32] A. Camus: *The Myth of Sisyphus.*

[33] Howard S. Becker: *Outsiders, op. cit.* p. 20 ff.

CHAPTER 5

[1] *Man, Morals and Society,* pp. 206–207.

[2] *The Golden Bough, op. cit.* p. 753.

[3] H. Brunner: *Grundzüge der Deutschen Rechtsgeschichte,* p. 68. See also Haim Cohen: *On Stoning.*

[4] J. Steinbeck: *Travels with Charley,* p. 143.

[5] Speeches of Adolf Hitler cited by Konrad Heiden: *Der Fueher,* p. 118 ff.

[6] Modern China: *Ha'aretz Weekly,* January 1965.

[7] Sumner: *Folkways,* p. 27.

[8] Aristotle, *Politics.*

[9] Aeschylus: *Prometheus Bound.*

[10] Scholiast on Pindar's Olympian Odes 1. 97.

[11] S. Ranulf: *The Jealousy of the Gods and the Criminal Law.*
[11] *Herodotus in Athens,* VII, 10, p. 47.
[12] Aeschylus: *Oresteia.*
[11] *ibid.*
[14] A. B. Drachmann: *Undvalgts, Afhondlingers,* p. 42.
[15] Frazer: *The Golden Bough,* p. 294.
[16] Evans-Pritchard: *Witchcraft Among the Azande,* p. 114.
[17] Lea: *Inquisition,* Vol. I, p. 110.
[18] M. E. Goodman: *Learning Who is Nice and Who's Not* in *Man and Society,* p. 168.
[19] Levy-Bruhl: *La Mentalite Primitive,* p. 310 ff.
[20] Karen Horney: "Culture and Neurosis", *American Soc. Rev.* (1936 pp. 227–229.)
[21] Tenenbaum: *Race and Reich,* p. 12.
[22] P.G.P. Pulzer: *The Rise of Political Anti-Semitism in Germany and Austria,* p. 284.
[23] *The Authoritarian Personality,* p. 611.
[24] J. Chwast: "Value Conflicts in Law Enforcement," *Crime and Delinquency,* pp. 151–160.
[25] S. Shoham, R. Keren and G. Shavit: "Pimps and Prostitutes, A Criminal Dyad."
[26] Hafetz-Haim: *On Defamation and Slander,* p. 16.
[27] Rosenzweig: "The Experimental Measurement of Types of Reaction to Frustration" in H. A. Murray: *Explorations in Personality,* pp. 585–99
[28] Tenenbaum: *op. cit.* p. 11.
[29] W. W. Buckland: *A Manual of Roman Private Law,* p. 53
[30] Plato: *The Republic,* 338–340.
[31] Sumner: *Folkways: op. cit.* p. 72.

CHAPTER 6

[1] Zelditch in T. Parsons and R.F. Bales: *Family, Socialization and Interaction Processes.*
[2] J.P. Spiegel: "The Resolution of Role Conflict," in Vogel and Bell: *The Family.*
[3] Vogel and Bell: "The Emotionally Disturbed Child as the Family Scapegoat," in *The Family, ibid.*

246

[4] M. Seeman: "On the Meaning of Alienation," *American Sociological Review*, No. 24, 1959, p. 183.

[5] A. Kuhn: *The Study of Society*.

[6] S.E. Asch: "Effects of Group Pressures upon Judgement" in Newcomb, Heartly, and Swanson: *Readings in Social Psychology* and Krech, Crutchfield and Ballachey: *Individual in Society*.

[7] *Individual in Society, ibid.*

[8] E. Frenkel-Brunswick: "Intolerance of Ambiguity as an Emotional and Perceptual Variable, *Journal of Personality* and "A Study of Prejudice in Children," *Human Relations*.

[9] E. Frenkel-Brunswick: *ibid.*

[10] G. Saenger: *The Social Psychology of Prejudice*, p. 124.

[11] E.H. Erikson: *Childhood and Society* and "The Problem of Identity," *Journal of American Psychiatric Association*, 1956.

[12] Rosenzweig: "Types of Reaction to Frustration" and "Study of "Repression" in H.A. Murray: *Explorations in Personality*.

[13] M. Sherif and H. Cantril: *The Psychology of Ego-Involvement*.

[14] Sutherland and Cressey: *Principles of Criminology*.

[15] R. Cloward and L. Ohlin: *Delinquency and Opportunity*.

CHAPTER 7

[1] The Author wishes to acknowledge with thanks the assistance given to him by Mr. Yehonotan Livine, L. L. M. in the collection of source material for this chapter.

[2] Buckland: A manual of Roman Law.

[3] J. G. Frazer: *Folklore in The Old Testament*, p. 80.

[4] Punishment stems from the Sanskrit to cleanse.

[5] C. K. Ogden and I. A. Richards: *The Meaning of Meaning*, p. 11.

[6] J. G. Frazer: *op. cit.* p. 93 ff.

[7] H. Von-Hentig: *Die Strafe*, p. 423 ff.

[8] Buckland: *A Manual of Roman Law*, p. 91 ff.

[9] M. Wolfgang: "Socio-Economic Factors Related to Crime and Punishment in Renaissance Florence," *J. Crim. L. Crimin. and Police Science*. No. 47 pp. 322, 323.

[10] S. Ranulf: *Moral Indignation and Middle-Class Psychology*, p. 19.

[11] S. Assaf: *The Penalties after the Talmud.*

[12] *ibid.*

[13] J. B. Bury: *A History of Greece,* pp. 249, 250.

[14] S. Ranulf: *The Jealousy of the Gods and Criminal Law in Athens, op. cit.* Vol. 1. p. 147.

[15] *ibid.* p. 134.

[16] G. O. W. Mueller: *Tort Crime and Primitive,* J. Crim. Law Crimin. and Pol. Science Vol 46, p. 312.

[17] S. Ranulf: *op. cit.*

[18] Maimonides: Mishna. *Midot* B.2.

[19] S. Pines: *Be'emek Habbacha.*

[20] Ezra 10, 7, 8.

[21] G. O. W. Mueller; Tort, Crime and the Primitive, *J. Crim. L. Crimin. and Pol. Science,* vol. 46, p. 309.

[22] F. Pollock and F. W. Maitland: *The History of English Law Before the Time of Edward I,* pp. 450, 451.

[23] *ibid.* p. 449.

[24] J. Lipkin: "The Punishment of Karet," *Hamishpat,* Vol. 3, p. 9.

[25] Maimonides: Talmud-Torah; 7; 4–5.

[26] Wolfgang: *op. cit.*

[27] F. J. Feldbrugge: *Soviet Criminal Law.* pp. 209, 210.

[28] See Alexander and Staub: *The Criminal, The Judge and the Public, op. cit.* p. 221. Also H. Weihofen: *The Urge to Punish,* p. 138 *et seq.*

[29] Royal Commission On Capital Punishment 1949–53, Minutes of Evidence, p. 207.

[30] W. N. East: *Society and the Criminal,* p. 161.

[31] Files Nos: J/64/31 and J/67/31 which are now at the State of Israel Archives.

[32] N. Timashef: "The Retributive Structure of Punishment," *J. Crim. L. Crimin. and Police Science,* 1937–38, p. 400.

[33] See S. Shoham: "The Sentencing Policy of Criminal Courts in Israel," *J. Crim. L. Crimin. and Police Science,* Vol. 50, pp. 327–337.

[34] S. Shoham. "The Sentencing Policy of Criminal Courts in Israel," *op. cit.*

[35] *J. Crim. L. Crimin. and Police Science,* Vol. 47. p. 413.

[36] Criminal Case; *Jerusalem District Court,* 125/54.

[37] Criminal Case; *Jerusalem District Court,* 20/55.

[38] Criminal Appeal 105/56, Piskey-Din of the Supreme Court of Israel Vol. 11. p. 1297.

[39] Criminal Appeal; *The Supreme Court of Israel,* 251/53.

[40] Criminal Appeal; *The Supreme Court of Israel*, 238/54.

[41] Criminal Appeal; *The Supreme Court of Israel*, 127/57.

[42] Motion; *The Supreme Court of Israel*, 275/57.

[43] S. Shoham: The Sentencing Policy of Criminal Courts in Israel.

[44] Wolfgang: *op. cit.* p. 325.

[45] S. Assaf: *op. cit.* p. 40.

[46] *The French Penal Code of* 1810, as amended in 1959 *Articles* 9, 28, 29 34, 36, 37, 42, 43.

[47] *Penal Code of the German Federal Republic of May* 15 1871, as republished August 25, 1953, corrected 1954, as of January 1, 1961; sec. 31, 32, 33, 34, 35.

[48] *The Penal Code of* 1930, sec. 38, 30, 32, 34, 35.

[49] L. Radzinowicz: *A History of English Criminal law,* p. 313.

[50] N. E. Napier: Florentine History, cited by M. Wolfgang: "Socio-Economic Factors related to Crime and Punishment in Renaissance Florence," *J. Crim. L. Crimin. and Pol. Science,* pp. 315–316.

[51] Arts, 6 and 8.

[52] ELECTORAL, CIVIL AND SOCIAL RIGHTS OF PRISONERS 1962.

The Committee of Ministers,

Having regard to Recommendation 195 (1959) of the Consultative Assembly of the Council of Europe on penal reform; Having regard to the resolution adopted in Paris on 6th June 1961 by the Ministers taking part in the Conference of European Ministers of Justice; Having regard to the necessity of promoting in member countries of the Council of Europe a prison system which, while protecting society, nevertheless upholds respect for human dignity; Considering that the 'Standard Minimum Ruler for the Treatment of Prisoners' adopted on 30th August 1955 by the first United Nations Congress on the Prevention of Crime and Treatment of Offenders, should be supplemented to this end, defining by common agreement the limits which a regime of detention may legitimately set to the exercise by the prisoner of rights pertaining to him as an individual;

Recommends that member Governments of the Council of Europe should apply the following provisions so far as is consistent &ith their constitutional principles and international undertakings.

A. General Principles

1 The rules set out herein define the effect of detention on the electoral, civil and social rights which the prisoner, untried or convicted

would enjoy if he were free. They constitute examples of the application of common minimum rules.

2 When, in a given State, a person is deprived by law of the rights referred to at Point 1, it is desirable that these rules be taken into consideration, should the relevant legislation be modified.

In the absence of any national law on a particular point, these rules should be regarded as expressing European legal conscience in that respect.

3 These provisions are founded on the principle that the mere fact of detention does not affect the possession of these rights, but that their exercises may be limited when it is incompatible with the purpose of imprisonment or the maintenance of the order and the security of the prison.

4 Under no circumstances shall the rules set out in this resolution be interpreted as restricting or derogating from the rights and freedoms recognised in the Convention for the Protection of Human Rights and Fundamental Freedoms and the Protocol thereto.

B. Electoral Rights

5 If the law allows electors to vote without personally visiting the polling-booth, a detainee shall be allowed this prerogative unless he has been deprived of the right to vote by law or by court order.

6 A prisoner permitted to vote shall be afforded opportunities to inform himself of the situation, in order to exercise his right.

7 (a) Except as stated at Point 8 below, the mere fact of imprisonment shall not impede a prisoner from exercising his civil rights in person or through a representative acting on his behalf;

(b) If a prisoner finds it impossible to exercise his rights in person, he shall be allowed to be represented.

8 The prison administration may forbid a prisoner to exercise his civil rights:

(a) if the exercise of such rights is incompatible with the aims of imprisonment or the treatment of the offender;

(b) if, in the case of a convicted person, the exercise of such rights may be postponed without prejudice to his interests until his release.

D. Social Rights

9 When a prisoner has acquired the right to social security benefits before his imprisonment, this shall not be annulled by the mere fact of imprisonment.

10 A prisoner shall as far as possible preserve his right to social security benefits during imprisonment; all appropriate arrangements to that effect shall be made.

11 With the exception of pensions to which the prisoner is entitled by virtue of contributions paid only by him, the payment of benefits to the prisoner may be suspended or reduced during the period of imprisonment, but family allowance for his dependants should continue to be payable directly to the beneficiaries with or without the the consent of the prisoner.

E. Protection of Rights

12 A prisoner may at all times defend a legal action. As a plaintiff he may continue proceedings which were pending at the time he was imprisoned, if the requisite action cannot conveniently be postponed until his release.

13 He may likewise institute new proceedings if such action cannot conveniently be postponed until his release and is compatible with the aims of the imprisonment or the treatment of the offender.

14 A prisoner shall not have the right to appear in person before the competent court, unless the law or the court require his presence.

15 In civil and administrative proceedings to which the prisoner may be a party under the rules now set out, he shall have the right to communicate orally or in writing with the person empowered to defend his interests.

16 Subject to the special regulations governing communications with lawyers, visits and correspondence received by a prisoner may be supervised by the competent authority.

17 A prisoner shall have the right to make prompt written application to government departments or similar bodies, in order to safeguard his interests. All correspondence from such departments or bodies shall be transmitted to the addressee without delay.

54 Ezra 10, 8.
55 Art. 34.
56 Art. 34.
57 Arts 32, 34 and 35.

[1] R.K. Merton: "The Self-Fulfilling Prophecy," *The Antioch Rev.*, Vol. 8 (1948), p. 194 ff.

[2] F. Tannenbaum: *Crime and the Community,* p. 21.

[3] P. Tappan: *Crime, Justice and Correction,* p. 139.

[4] J. Kelner: *A Treatment Diary.*

[5] D.C. Reitzes: "The Effect of Social Environment Upon Former Felons," *J. Crim. L. Crimin. and Pol. Science,* 1955–56, p. 226.

[6] J.P. Martin: "Sociological Aspects of Conviction," *Advancement of Science,* Mar. 64.

[7] *ibid.* p. 14.

[8] R. K. Merton: *Social Theory and Social Structure,* p. 357 ff.

[9] *ibid.* p. 362.

[10] C.W. Mills: "The Professional Ideology of Social Pathologists" in *Power, Politics and People,* pp. 551–552.

[11] A. K. Cohen: "The Sociology of the Deviant Act; Anomie Theory and Beyond," *American Sociological Review,* (Feb. 1965) pp. 5–14.

[12] L. Coser: *The Functions of Social Conflict.*

[13] A.K. Cohen. "The Sociology of the Deviant Act," *op. cit.* p. 7.

[14] Genet. The Balcony.

[15] S. Runciman: *The Medieval Manichee,* p. 2.

[16] H.C. Lea, *A History of the Inquisition in the Middle Ages,* pp. 373 ff.

[17] *ibid.* p. 453.

[18] S. Ranulf: *Moral Indignation and Middle-Class Psychology, op. cit.* p. 134.

[19] Georg Simmel: *Conflict,* p. 43.

[20] *ibid.* pp. 47–48.

[21] L. A. Coser: *The Functions of Social Conflict,* pp. 70–77.

[22] *ibid.* pp. 48–55.

[23] S. Schachter: *The Psychology of Affiliation.*

[24] K. Back: "Influence through Social Communication," *J. Abnorm. Soc. Psychol.,* No. 46, 1951, p. 23.

[25] L. Festinger: "Informal Social Communication," *Psychol. Rev.* No. 57 (1958) pp. 271–282.

[26] S. Schachter: "Deviation, Rejection and Communication." *J. Abnorm. Soc. Psychol.,* No. 46, pp. 190–207.

27 L. Berkowitz and R.C. Howard: "Reactions to Opinion Deviates as affected by Affiliation Need and Group Member Interpendence" *Sociometry,* 1959, p. 22.

28 L. Weller: "The Effects of Anxiety on Cohesiveness and Rejection," *Human Relations,* 1963, pp. 189–196.

29 M. Scheller: *Ressentiment,* pp. 155–156.

30 E. Park: "Human Migration and the Marginal Man," *Am. J. Sociology,* 1927–28, pp. 881–893.

31 E.V. Stonequist: "The Problem of the Marginal Man," *Am. J. Sociology,* 1935–36 pp. 1–12.

32 Sophocles: *Phoenician Women,* p. 501.

33 S. E. Asch: "Studies of independence and conformity." A minority of one against a unanimous majority. *Psychological Monographs.*

34 D. Krech, R. S. Crutchfield and E. L. Ballachey: *Individual in Society,* p. 519.

35 R. S. Crutchfield: "Conformity and character." *Amer. Psychologist,* 1955, pp. 191–198.

36 H.B. Linton: "Dependence on External Influence: Correlates in Perception, Attitude and Judgement," *J. Abnorm. Soc. Psychol.,* No. 51, pp. 502–507.

37 R. R. Blake, H. Nelson and J. Mouton: "The Generality of Conformity Behaviour as a Function of Factual Anchorage Difficulty of Task, and Amount of Social Pressure," *J. Pers.,* 1957 pp. 294–305.

38 I.A. Berg: "Response Bias and Personality: The Deviation Hypothesis," *J. Psychol.,* 1955 pp. 61–72.

39 E. Frenkel-Brunswick: "A Study of Prejudice in Children," *Human Relations,* 1948, pp. 295–306.

40 Crutchfield: *op. cit.*

41 S. Schachter: Deviation, Rejection and Communication," *J. Abnorm. Soc. Psych.,* 1951 pp. 190–207.

CHAPTER 9

1 A. K. Cohen: *Delinquent Boys.*

2 W. F. Whyte: *Street Corner Society.*

3 W. B. Miller: "Lower Class Culture as a Generating Milieu of Gang Delinquency" *Journal of Social Issues,* Vol. 14, No. 3 (1958) p. 9.

[4] R. A. Cloward and L. E. Ohlin: *Delinquency and Opportunity.*

[5] F. M. Thrasher: *The Gang.*

[6] T. Parsons: *Essay in Sociological Theory.* pp. 304–305.

[7] H. Bloch and A. Niederhoffer: *The Gang: A Study in Adolescent Behaviour.* pp. 7–9, 15, 17.

[8] E. Erickson: "The Problem of Identity", *Journal of American Psychiatric Association,* 4 January, 1956.

[9] S. Shoham: "Conflict Situations and Delinquent Solutions"; *J. of Social Psychiatry,* 1964, 64 pp. 85–215.

[10] R. K. Merton: *Social Theory and Social Structure.*

[11] F. Tannenbaum: *Crime and the Community.*

[12] H. W. Zorbaugh: *The Gold Coast and the Slum.*

[13] J. Landesco: *Organized Crime in Chicago, The Illinois Crime Survey,* Ill. Assoc. for Criminal Justice, part 3, 815–1090.

[14] W. C. Kvaraceus: *Dynamics of Delinquency.*

[15] L. Yablonsky: *The Violent Gang.*

[16] C. Sykes and D. Matza: "Techniques of neutralization: A theory of delinquency," *Amer. Social Rev.* D. Matza: Delinquency and Drift.

[17] D. Downes: *The Delinquent Solution.*

[18] A. K. Cohen: "The Sociology of the Deviant Act: Anomie Theory and Beyond", 30 American Soc. Dev. Feb. 1965 pp. 5–14.

[19] W. H. Sutherland and D. H. Cressy: *Principles of Criminology.*

[20] Cloward and Ohlin *op. cit.* p. 127.

[21] Miller *op. cit.* p. 68.

[22] *ibid.* pp. 813.

[23] *ibid.*

[24] *ibid.*

[25] *ibid.*

[26] Thrasher *op. cit.* p. 68.

[27] *ibid.* p. 31.

[28] *ibid.* p. 339.

[29] *ibid.* p. 332.

[30] Bloch and Niederhoffer *op. cit.* pp. 709.

[31] Erikson: *op. cit.*

[32] K. Lewin: *Field Theory in Social Science* p. 272.

[33] T. Parsons *op. cit.* p. 405.

[34] A. Cohen, *op. cit.*

[35] N. Shoham *op. cit.*

[36] T. W. Newcomb: *Social Psychology.*

[37] R. K. Merton: "Social Structure and Anomie" in *Social Theory and Social Structure*.

[38] S. Shoham: "The Norm, The Act and the Object of Crime as Bases for the Classification of Criminal Behaviour" *The International Journal of Social Psychiatry*, Vol. XI No. 4, 1965.

[39] *ibid.*

[40] R. K. Merton: "Contributions to Theory of Reference Group Behaviour" in *Social Theory and Social Structure, op. cit.* pp. 225 *et seq.*

[41] *ibid.* p. 269.

[42] *ibid.* p. 269.

[43] H. Zorbaugh: *op. cit.* p. 176.

[44] Landesco *op. cit.* p. 1043.

[45] F. Tannenbaum *op. cit.*

[46] W. C. Kvaraceus *op. cit.* p. 4.

[47] D. Downes *op. cit.* p. 258.

[48] D. Matza: *Delinquency and Drift*, pp. 27–30.

[49] T. Veblen: *The Theory of the Leisure Class*, pp. 237–28.

[50] T. R. Fyvel: *The Insecure Offenders*, 1961.

[51] Kvaraceus *op. cit.* p. 4.

[52] Muzafer Sherif: *The Psychology of Ego Involvement, op. cit.*, p. 288.

[53] D. Matza *op. cit.* p. 52.

[54] Coser *op. cit.* p. 68.

[55] P. W. Cressy, "The Criminal Tribes of India": *Sociology and Social Research*, Vol. 20, pp. 503–511, and Vol. 21, pp. 18–25, 1936.

[56] C. Burt, *The Young Delinquent*, S. and E. Glueck, *Unravelling Juvenile Delinquency*, The Commonwealth Fund, 1950.

[57] The total population of prison inmates for the whole country at the beginning of 1964 was 1158. *Annual Report of the Israeli Prison Service*, 1964.

[58] S. Shoham and M. Hovav, "Social Factors, Treatment Aspects and Criminal Career of "B'nei-Tovim", Middle and Upper Class Juvenile Delinquency in Israel", *Human Relations* 1966.

[59] L. D. Joffe, *Delinquency Proneness and Family Anomie* (in Hebrew) Jerusalem, Megamot, 1962. S. Shoham and M. Hovav, " "B'nei-Tovim"—Middle and Upper Class Delinquency in Israel," *Soc. and Social Research*, Vol. 48, No. 4, July 1964.

[60] S. Shoham and M. Hovav, *"B'nei-Tovim" op. cit.*

[61] In Israel these hypotheses were upheld in: S. Shoham, N. Shoham and Abd-El-Razek: "Immigration Ethnicity and Ecology as Related

to Juvenile Delinquency in Israel" (in press), *British Journal of Criminology;* in the U.S. see the following. As to the possible impact of these factors on juvenile delinquency see Shaw and McKay, *Report on Social Factors in Juvenile Delinquency* (Report No. 13, 2 Report on the Causes of Crime, National Commission on Law Observance and Enforcement 1937); Drucker and Hexter, *Children Astray* (1923); 1 Thomas and Zsaniecki, *op. cit.; J. Crim. L. and C.* 330 (1949); Korbin. "The Conflict of Values in Delinquency Areas", *Am. Soc. Rev.* 653 (1951).

[62] C. B. Shaw and H. D. McKay: *Juvenile Delinquency and Urban Areas,*

[63] T. Morris, *The Criminal Area.*

[64] K. O. Christianson, "Industrialization and Urbanization in Relation to Crime and Juvenile Delinquency," *International Rev. of Criminal Policy* 1960.

[65] S. Shoham, N. Shoham and A. Abd-El-Razek, *op. cit.*

[66] S. Shoham and M. Hovav; "B'nei-Tovim", *op. cit.*

[67] Adhered to by Harrists; see: Ronger, *Criminality and Economic Condition.*

[68] E. Ferri: *Criminal Sociology,* N. Plascowe, "Some Causative Factors in Criminality; Report on the Causes of Crime", in *Report of the National Commission, Law Observance and Law Enforcement* (Vol. 1), Washington D.C.; Government Printing Office 1931, pp. 114–116.

[69] C. Van Vechten: "Criminality of the Foreign Born," *Proceedings of the Seventieth Annual Congress of Correction of the Am. Prison,* 505 (1940).

[70] The rates have been computed from "raw" data received from the Central Bureau of Statistics, Israel.

[71] Van Vechten, op. cit., at 505–516. The short-comings of this comparison are obvious, because Van Vechten compared the criminality of all the foreign born with that of the native born. If we had done the same, and based our comparison on the corresponding age groups, the criminality of our foreign born would have been much higher than that of the native born, but for our present purposes the rate as computed above is adequate because our main concern is with the criminality of immigrants who entered the country after 1948.

[72] S. Shoham: "The Application of the 'Culture-Conflict' Hypotheses to the Criminality of Immigrants in Israel," *J. Crime Law. Criminal and Pol. Science,* Vol. 53, No. 2 June 1962.

256

[73] A. K. Cohen: *Delinquent Boys: The Culture of the Gang.* New York, The Free Press of Glencoe (1955).

[74] S. Shoham, Ruth Erez and Walter C. Reckless: "Value Orientation and Awareness of Differential Opportunity of Delinquent and Non-delinquent Boys in Israel", The British Journal of Criminology, July 1965.

[75] E. Durkheim: *Suicide,* Free Press (1951), p. 247.

[76] ibid.

[77] The Political Community: *A study of Anomie* (Chicago, 1948), pp. 71, *et seq.*

[78] R. K. Merton: "Social Structure and Anomie" in *Social Theory and Social Structure.* p. 133.

[79] J. W. Thibaut and H. W. Kelly: *The Social Psychology of Groups,*

[80] W. B. Miller: *Delinquent Behaviour, Culture and the Individual* (Washington D.C. National Education Association, 1959), pp. 74–75.

[81] R. A. Cloward and L. E. Ohlin: *Delinquency and Opportunity.*

[82] See S. Shoham, R. Erez and W. C. Reckless: "Value Orientation and Awareness of Differential Opportunity of Delinquent and non-Delinquent Boys in Israel," *Brit. J. of Crim.,* July 1965.

[83] S. Shoham and M. Hovav: *"B'nei-Tovim,"* *op. cit.*

[84] Carried out by the author under the auspices of the Ministry of Welfare, Israel.

[85] Carried out by the author under the auspices of the Prison Commission, Israel.

[86] S. Shoham, J. Spiegel and W. Shapiro-Libai.

[87] See bibl. items 178, 8.

[88] Dr. M. Wolf: "Psychopathy a Modern Symptom"; *Ofakim,* Vol. 14, p. 238.

[89] J. Chwast: "The Malevolent Transformation"; 54 *J. Crim. L. Crimin. and Pol. Science,* 1963, p. 42.

[90] Shoham and Hovav: "B'nei-Tovim"; *op. cit,* p. 10.

[90] Cited in Crime and Delinquency: April 1964, p. 145.

CHAPTER 10

[1] *The Thief's Journal.*

[2] *Saint Genet, Actor and Martyr.*

[3] *Death Watch.*

[4] *The Blacks.*
[5] A. Szogyi: *The N.Y. Times Book Review.*
[6] *Saint Genet: Actor and Martyr.*
[7] *The Thief's Journal*, pp. 21, 167.
[8] *Saint Genet*, p. 15.
[9] *The Thief's Journal*, p. 176.
[10] *ibid.* p. 87.
[11] C. Wilson: *The Outsider.*
[12] *L'Enfant Criminel.*
[13] *The Thief's Journal*, p. 101.
[14] *ibid.* p. 81.
[15] *ibid.* p. 86.
[16] Daniel Glazer: "Criminality Theories and Behavioural Images," *Amer J. Sociol.*
[17] *The Thief's Journal*, p. 84.
[18] *ibid.* p. 91.
[19] H. C. Lea: *A History of Auricular Confession and Indulgences in the Latin Church.*
[20] *The Thief's Journal*, p. 109.
[21] *ibid.* p. 149.
[22] *ibid.* p. 91.
[23] *ibid.* p. 24.
[24] *ibid.* p. 65.
[25] *ibid.* p. 72.
[26] *ibid.* p. 155.
[27] *ibid.* p. 28.
[28] *ibid.* p. 215.
[29] *ibid.* p. 79.
[30] *ibid.* p. 101.
[31] E. Erikson: "The Problem of Identity," *J. Amer. Psychiat. Assoc.*
[32] K. Lewin: *Field Theory in Social Science.*
[33] *The Thief's Journal*, p. 101.
[34] *The Screens*, p. 77.
[35] *Our Lady of the Flowers.*
[36] *The Thief's Journal*, p. 58.
[37] See T. Reik: *Gestaendniszwang und Strafbeduerfnis, Probleme der Psychoanalyse und der Kriminologie.*
[38] *Our Lady of the Flowers*, p. 25.
[39] *The Thief's Journal*, p. 25.

40 *ibid.*

41 *ibid.* p. 59.

42 *Death Watch*, p. 10.

43 *ibid.* p. 35.

44 *Our Lady of the Flowers*, p. 82.

45 *The Thief's Journal*, p. 212.

46 E. Sutherland and D. Cressey: *Principles of Criminology.*

47 *The Thief's Journal*, p. 226.

48 *ibid.* p. 14.

49 *Our Lady of the Flowers*, p. 244.

50 D. Glazer: "Criminality Theories and Behavioural Images," *Am. J. Sociol.*

51 R. A. Cloward and L. B. Ohlin: *Delinquency and Opportunity.*

52 E. Sutherland and D. Cressey: *op. cit.*

53 *The Thief's Journal*, p. 125.

54 *Our Lady of the Flowers*, p. 83.

55 *ibid.* pp. 82, 124.

56 *Death Watch.*

57 *The Thief's Journal*, p. 29.

58 *Our Lady of the Flowers*, p. 300.

59 *The Thief's Journal*, p. 243.

60 *Our Lady of the Flowers*, p. 214.

61 *ibid.* p. 211.

62 *The Screens*, p. 33.

63 *The Blacks*, p. 52.

64 *The Screens*, pp. 18–20.

65 *Death Watch*, p. 40.

66 *The Screens*, p. 39.

67 *ibid.* p. 40.

68 *Death Watch*, p. 23.

69 *The Thief's Journal*, p. 211.

70 *The Screens*, p. 38.

71 *Death Watch*, p. 20.

72 *The Thief's Journal*, p. 246.

73 *ibid.* p. 12.

73 *ibid.* p. 12.

74 *ibid.* p. 101.

75 *Death Watch*, p. 23.

76 *The Thief's Journal*, p. 243.

[77] *The Blacks.*
[78] *ibid.* p. 85.
[79] *The Thief's Journal,* p. 107.
[80] *ibid.* p. 107.
[81] *Our Lady of the Flowers.*
[82] *ibid.* p. 120.
[83] *The Thief's Journal,* p. 51.
[83] *The Thief's Journal,* p. 51.
[84] *ibid.* p. 111.
[85] *ibid.* p. 136.
[86] *ibid.* p. 252.
[87] *ibid.* p. 88.
[87] *ibid.* p. 88.
[88] *The Screens,* Grove Press, p. 85.
[89] *The Blacks,* p. 12.
[90] *The Thief's Journal,* p. 123.
[91] *ibid.*
[92] *ibid.* p. 230.
[93] *ibid.* pp. 196–197:
[94] *ibid.* p. 197.
[95] *Our Lady of the Flowers.*
[96] *ibid.*
[97] *The Screens,* p. 42.
[98] *ibid.* pp. 59–60.
[99] *ibid.* p. 58.
[100] *The Balcony.* p. 19.
[101] *ibid.*
[102] *ibid.* p. 20.
[103] *ibid.*
[104] *The Blacks,* p. 99.
[105] *ibid.* p. 25.
[106] *ibid.* p. 109.
[107] *The Screens,* p. 46.
[108] *ibid.* pp. 45, 46.
[109] *ibid.* p. 47.
[110] *ibid.* p. 44.
[111] *The Blacks,* p. 97.
[112] *Our Lady of the Flowers,* p. 165.
[113] *ibid.*

[114] *The Blacks,* p. 101.
[115] *Our Lady of the Flowers,* p. 269.
[116] *ibid.* p. 285.
[117] *ibid.* p. 189.
[118] *The Balcony.* p. 7.
[119] *ibid.* p. 11.
[120] *ibid.*
[121] *ibid.* p. 25.
[122] *The Screens,* p. 105.
[123] *ibid.* p. 105.
[124] *The Maids.* p. 17.
[125] *ibid.* p. 7.
[126] *ibid.* p. 16.
[127] *ibid.*
[128] *ibid.* p. 10.
[129] *The Thief's Journal,* pp. 9–10.
[130] *The Blacks,* p. 33.
[131] *The Thief's Journal.*
[132] *ibid.* p. 180.
[133] *ibid.* p. 227.
[134] *The Blacks,* p. 102.
[135] *The Screens,* p. 97.
[136] *The Blacks,* p. 104.
[137] *The Thief's Journal,* p. 164.
[138] *ibid.* p. 165.
[139] *ibid.* p. 244.
[140] *The Blacks,* p. 30.
[141] *Our Lady of the Flowers,* p. 51.
[142] *The Blacks,* p. 30.
[143] *ibid.* p. 126.
[144] *ibid.*
[145] *ibid.* p. 39.

BIBLIOGRAPHY

1. ABRAHAMSON, D. *Crime and the Human Mind.* Columbia University Press, 1945.

2. ABRAHAMSON, D. "Family Tension—Basic Cause of Criminal Behaviour," *Journal of Crim., Crim. Law and Police Science,* XL, (1949).

3. ADLER, M. J. *Art and Prudence.* New York: Longmans, Green and Co., 1937.

4. AESCHYLUS. *Prometheus Bound.* The Complete Greek Drama. New York: Random House, Vol. I, 1938.

5. AESCHYLUS. *The House of Atreus.* The Complete Greek Drama. New York: Random House, Vol. I, 1938.

6. ALEXANDER and STAUB. "The Criminal, the Judge and the Public," in Reiwald, P. *Society and its Criminals.* London: W. Heinemann, 1949.

7. ALLERTON, R. *The Courage of his Convictions.*

8. ANDREY, R. G. *Delinquency and Parental Pathology.* London: Methuen, 1960.

9. *Annual Reports of the Israeli Police,* 1961–1962.

10. ARENDT, H. *The Origins of Totalitarianism.* Meridian Books. New York: Harcourt, Brace and Co., 1951.

11. ARISTOTLE. *Politics.* The Basic Works of Aristotle. New York: Random House, 1941.

12. ASCH, S. E. "Effects of Group Pressures upon Judgement," in Newcomb, Heartly and Swanson. *Readings in Social Psychology.* New York: Holt, Rinehart and Winston, 1952.

13. ASSAF, S. *The Penalties after the Talmud.* Jerusalem: Janowitz Press 5682. (Hebrew).

14. BACK, K. "Influence through Social Communication," *Journal of Abnormal Social Psychology,* VIXL, (1951).

15. BAR-JOSEPH, R. "The Morrocans," *Molad,* Jerusalem: (July, 1959). (Hebrew).

16. BECKER, HOWARD S. *Outsiders.* New York: Free Press of Glencoe, 1963.

17. BEN-DOV, S. *Israel in the Crisis of Statehood.* Safed: Hamatmid, 1960. (Hebrew)

18. BERG, I. A. "Response Bias and Personality: The Deviation Hypothesis," *Journal of Psychology,* XL, (1955), pp. 61–72.

19. BERKOWITZ, L. and HOWARD, R. C. "Reactions to Opinion Deviates as affected by Affiliation Need and Group Member Interdependence," *Sociometry,* 1959.

20. THE BHAGAVADGITA. The Sir Edwin Arnold translation of *The Bhagavadgita.* London, 1925.

21. BLAKE, R. R., HELSON, H. and MOUTON, J. "The Generality of Conformity Behaviour as a Function of Factual Anchorage Difficulty of Task, and Amount of Social Pressure," *Journal of Personality,* XXV, (1957), pp. 294–305.

22. BLAU, P. M. *Exchange and Power in Social Life.* N. Y., London and Sidney: John Wiley and Sons, 1964.

23. BLOCH, H. and NIEDERHOFFER, A. *The Gang, A Study in Adolescent Behaviour.* New York: Philosophical Library, 1958.

24. BONGER, W. A. *Criminality and Economic Condition.* Boston: Little, 1916.

25. BOORSTIN, D. J. *The Image; What happened to the American Dream.* New York: Atheneum, 1962. Harmondsworth: Penguin Books, 1963.

26. BORGER, O. *Vedel.*

27. BOUQUET, A. C. *Comparative Religion.* Harmondsworth: Penguin Books, 1941. (Pelican books, A 89).

28. BRUNNER, H. *Grundzuge der Deutschen Rechtsgeschichte.* Leipzig, 1901.

29. BUCKLAND, W. W. *A Manual of Roman Private Law.* Cambridge: University Press, 1939.

30. BURT, C. *The Young Delinquent.* London: University of London Press, 1952.

31. BURY, J. B. *A History of Greece (to the Death of Alexander the Great).* New York: The Modern Library.

32. CAHN, E. N. *The Moral Decision, Right and Wrong in the Light of American Law.* London: Stevens, 1959.

33. CALHOUN, G. M. *The Growth of Criminal Law in Ancient Greece.* Berkeley, Calf.: University of California Press, 1927.

34. CAMUS, A. *The Fall.* New York: Vintage Books, 1963.

35. CAMUS, A. *The Myth of Sisyphus.* New York: Vintage Books, 1961.

36. CASON, H. "The Psychopath and the Psychopathic," *Journal of Criminal Psychopathology,* IV, (1943), pp. 522–527.

37. CASON, H. "The Symptoms of the Psychopath", *Public Health Reports,* LXI, (December, 1946).

38. CATZ, J. *Megamot,* X4, (March, 1960). (Hebrew).

39. CHRISTIANSEN, K. O. "Industrialization and Urbanization in Relation to Crime and Juvenile Delinquency," *International Review of Criminal Policy,* 1960.

40. CHWAST, J. "The Malevolent Transformation," *Journal of Criminal Law, Criminology and Police Science,* LIV, (1963).

41. CHWAST, J. "Value Conflicts in Law Enforcement," *Crime and Delinquency.* New York, (April, 1965).

42. CICERO. *De Legibus.* The Francis Basham translation, 1841.

43. CLOWARD, R. A. and OHLIN, L. B. *Delinquency and Opportunity.* Glencoe, Ill.: Free Press, 1961.

44. COHEN, A. K. *Delinquent Boys: The Culture of the Gang*. Glencoe, Ill.: Free Press, 1955.

45. COHEN, A. K. "The Sociology of the Deviant Act; Anomie Theory and Beyond," *American Sociological Review,* XXX, (1965).

46. COHEN, HAIM. *On Stoning*. Bar-Ilan University, 1962. (Hebrew).

47. COSER, L. A. *The Functions of Social Conflict*. Glencoe, Ill.: Free Press, 1956.

48. CRESSEY, P. F. "The Criminal Tribes of India," *Sociology and Social Research,"* XX, (1936) and XXI, (1936).

49. CRUNHUT, M. *Statistics in Criminology*. Publication of the Royal Statistical Society 114: Part II, 1951. pp. 139–157.

50. CRUTCHFIELD, R. S. "Conforming and Character," *American Psychologist,* X, (1955).

51. DARMESTETER, J. *The Zend-Avesta*. Oxford, 1895.

52. DE GRAZIA, S. *The Political Community: A Study of Anomie*. Chicago: The University of Chicago Press, 1948.

53. DOWNES, D. *The Delinquent Solution*. London: Routledge and Kegan Paul, 1966.

54. DRACHMANN, A. B. *Umdvalgte, Afhondlinger*. Copenhagen, 1911.

55. DREUCKER, S. and HEXTER, M. B. Children Astray. Cambridge, Mass. Harvard University Press, 1923.

56. DURKHEIM, E. *Suicide. A Study in Sociology*. Glencoe, Ill.: Free Press, 1951.

57. DURKHEIM, E. *The Division of Labour in Society*. Glencoe, Ill.: Free Press, 1947. p. 398.

58. DYNES, R. R., CLARKE, A. C. and DINITZ, S. "Level of Aspiration: Some Aspects of Family Experience as a Variable," *American Sociological Review,* April, 1956.

59. EAST, W. N. *Society and the Criminal*. London, 1949.

60. ERIKSON, E. H. *Childhood and Society*. New York: W.W., 1950.

61. ERIKSON, E. H. "The Problem of Identity," *Journal of American Psychiatric Association,* IV, (1956).

62. EVANS-PRITCHARD, E. E. *Witchcraft, Oracles and Magic Among the Azande.* Oxford: The Clarendon Press, 1937.

63. FAWCETT, P. H. *Lost Traits, Lost Cities, an Explorer's Narrative.* London, 1953.

64. FELDBRUGGE, F. J. *Soviet Criminal Law.* Leyden: A. W. Sythoff, 1964.

65. FERRI, E. *Criminal Sociology,* Boston: Little Brown, 1900.

66. FESTINGER, L. "Informal Social Communication," *Psychological Review,* LVII, (1950).

67. FIEDLER, L. *Waiting for the End: The American Literary Scene from Hemingway to Baldwin.* London: J. Cape, (1965 c. 1964).

68. FINEGAN, J. *The Archaelogy of World Religions.* Princeton: Princeton University Press, 1952.

69. FISHER and MENDEL. *The Communication of Neurotic Patterns over Generations,* in Vogel and Bell. *The Family.* Glencoe, Ill.: Free Press, 1960.

70. FLUGEL, J. C. *Man, Morals and Society.* Pelican Books, 1955.

71. FOOTE, C. "The Bail System and Equal Justice," *Federal Probation,* XXIII, (September, 1959), pp. 43–48.

72. FRAZER, J. G. *Folklore in the Old Testament.* London: MacMillan and Co., 1919.

73. FRAZER, J. G. *Psyche's Task:* a discourse concerning the influence of superstition on the growth of institutions. London: MacMillan and Co., 1920. pp. 114–115.

74. FRAZER, J. G. *The Golden Bough.* London: MacMillan, 1960.

75. FRENKEL-BRUNSWICK, E. "A Study of Prejudice in Children," *Human Relations,* London: Tavistock Publications, Ltd., (London, 1948), pp. 295–306.

76. FRENKEL-BRUNSWICK, E. "Intolerance of Ambiguity as an Emotional and Perceptual Variable," *Journal of Personality,* (1949).

266

77. FREUD, S. *Civilization and its Discontents,* in *The Complete Psychological Works of Sigmund Freud.* London: The Hogarth Press, 1960.

78. FROMM, E. *Escape from Freedom.* New York: Rinehart and Co., 1941.

79. FROMM, E. *The Art of Loving.* London: Union Books, 1964.

80. FRYM, M. "The Treatment of Recidivists," *The Journal of Criminal Law and Criminology and Police Science,* XXXVII, 1946/1947.

81. FYVEL, T. R. *The Insecure Offenders.* London: Chatto and Windus, 1961.

82. GARFINKEL, H. "Research Note on Inter and Intra-Racial Homicides," *Social Forces,* XXVII, (May, 1949).

83. GAROFALO, R. *La Criminologie, étude sur la nature du crime et la theorie de la pénalité.* Paris: F. Alcan, 1890.

84. GAUDET. F. I. "Individual Differences in the Sentencing Tendencies of Judges," *Archives of Psychology,* no. 230, New York, (1938).

85. GENET, J. *L'Enfant Criminel.* Paris: Morihien Paul, 1949.

86. GENET, J. *Death Watch.* London: Faber and Faber, 1961.

87. GENET, J. *The Blacks.* New York: Grove Press, 1960.

88. GENET, J. *The Balcony.* London: Faber and Faber, 1957.

89. GENET, J. *The Maids.* London: Faber and Faber, 1953.

90. GENET, J. *The Screens.* London: Faber and Faber, 1963.

91. GENET, J. *The Thief's Journal.* New York: Grove Press, 1964.

92. GENET, J. *Our Lady of the Flowers.* Bantam Books.

93. GIFFIN M. E., JOHNSON, A. M. and LITIN, E. M. *The Transmission of Superego Defects,* in Vogel and Bell.

94. GILLIN, J. L. *Criminology and Penology.* Rev. ed. New York: D. Appleton-Century Co., 1935.

95. GLASER, D. "Criminality Theories and Behavioural Images," *American Journal of Sociology,* LXI, (1956).

96. GLUECK, E. and S. *Physique and Delinquency*. New York: Harper, 1956.

97. GLUECK, E. and S. *Unravelling Juvenile Delinquency*. The Commonwealth Fund, 1950.

98. GODDARD, H. H. "Who is a Moron?" *Scientific Monthly, XXIV,* (1927).

99. GOFFMAN, E. *Stigma: notes on the management of spoiled identity.* Englewood Cliffs, N.J.: Prentice Hall, 1963.

100. GOODMAN, M. E. *Learning Who is Nice and Who's Not* in *Man and Society,* London: MacMillan. p. 168.

101. GREEN, A. W. "Culture, Normality and Personality Conflicts," *The American Anthropologist,* (April-June, 1948).

102. GREEN, E. "Sentencing Practices of Criminal Court Judges in Philadelphia," *American Journal of Correction,* XXII, (July-August, 1960).

103. GREENBLATT, M., LEVINSON, D. and WILLIAMS, R. *The Patient and the Mental Hospital.* Glencoe, Ill.: Free Press, 1957.

104. GUTTMACHER, M. and WEIHOFEN, H. *Psychiatry and the Law.* New York: W. W. Norton, 1952.

105. HAFETZ-HAIM. *On Defamation and Slander.* Wilno, 1873.

106. HALL, C. S. and LINDSEY, G. *Theories of Personality.* New York: Wiley, 1957.

107. HARARI, C. and CHWAST, J. in *Crime and Delinquency,* (April, 1964), p. 145.

108. HARPER, R. F. (ed.) *The Code of Hammurabi.* University of Chicago, 1904.

109. HEIDEGGER, M. *Being and Time.* New York: Harper and Row, 1962.

110. HEIDEN, K. *Der Fuehrer.* Boston: Houghton Mifflin Co., 1944.

111. HEIDER, F. *The Psychology of Interpersonal Relations.* New York: Wiley, 1958.

268

112. HERODOTUS. *The Greek Historians.* New York: Random House, Vol. I, 1942.

113. HOOD, R. *Sentencing in Magistrates' Courts.* London: Stevens, 1962.

114. HOOTON, E. A. *The American Criminal.* Harvard University Press, 1939.

115. HORNEY, K. "Culture and Neurosis," *American Sociological Review,* I, (1936), pp. 227–229.

116. HYMAN, H. H. *The Value Systems of Different Classes,* in *Class, Status and Power.* Glencoe, Ill.: The Glencoe Free Press, 1953.

117. IVES, G. *A History of Penal Methods.* London, 1914.

118. JAMES, W. *Principles of Psychology.* New York: Holt, 1890.

119. JASPERS, K. *Man in the Modern Age.* London: Routledge and Kegan Paul, 1966.

120. JEFFERY, C. R. "The Structure of American Criminological Thinking," *Journal of Criminal Law, Criminology and Police Science,* XLVL, p. 658.

121. JOFFE, L. D. "Delinquency Proneness and Family Anomie," Jerusalem: *Megamot,* (1962). (Hebrew).

122. KANT, I. *Metaphysische Anfangsgruende der Rechtslehre.* Frankfurt, 1797.

123. KAUFMANN, W. A. (ed.) *Existentialism from Dostoyevsky to Sartre.* New York: Meridian Books, 1957.

124. KELNER, J. *A Treatment Diary.* (unpublished)

125. KIERKEGAARD, S. *The Present Age.* London: Oxford University Press, 1940.

126. KLEIN, P. *Prison Methods in New York State.* New York: Columbia University Press, 1920.

127. KOESTLER, A. *The Lotus and the Robot.* London: Hutchinson, 1960.

128. KORBIN. "The Conflict of Values in Delinquency Areas," *American Sociological Review,* XVI, (1951), p. 653.

269

129. KRECH, D., CRUTCHFIELD, R. S. and BALLACHEY, E. L. *Individual in Society*. Mc.Graw-Hill, 1962.

130. KRETSCHMER, R. *Physique and Character*. New York: Harcourt, Brace and Co., 1956.

131. KUHN, A. *The Study of Society*. Irwin-Dorsey, 1963.

132. KVARACEUS, W. C. *Dynamics of Delinquency*. Columbus, Ohio: Charles E. Mercill, 1966.

133. LANDESCO, J. *Organized Crime in Chicago*. The Illinois Crime Survey, Ill. Association for Criminal Justice. Chicago: Blakeley, 1929, part 3.

134. LANGE, J. *Crime and Destiny*. New York: Berni, 1930.

135. LEA, H. C. *A History of Auricular Confession and Indulgences in the Latin Church*. Vol. I, London, 1896.

136. LEA, H. C. *A History of the Inquisition in the Middle Ages*. New York: Russel and Russel, 1958.

137. LEE, D. D. *Freedom and Culture*. Englewood Cliffs, N. J.: Prentice-Hall, 1959.

138. LEGGE. *Texts of Taoism,* Tao Te Ching. Chapter 34.

139. LEVY-BRUHL. *La Mentalité Primitive*. Paris: Presses Universitaires de France, 1922.

140. LEWIN, K. *Field Theory in Social Science*. New York: Harper and Brothers, 1951.

141. LEWIS, H. D. C. *A Short History of Psychiatric Achievement*. New York: Norton, 1941.

142. LILIENTHAL, D. E. *The Journals of David E. Lilienthal*. New York: Harper and Row, 1964.

143. LIND. *Knowledge for What?* Princeton: Princeton University Press, 1939.

144. LINTON, H. B. "Dependence on External Influence: correlates in Perception, Attitude and Judgement," *Journal of Abnormal Social Psychology,* LI,

145. LIPKIN, J. "The Punishment of Karet," *Hamishpat,* III, (1928). (Hebrew).

146. LOMBROSO, C. in Gillin, J. L., *Criminology and Penology.* New York: D. Appleton-Century Co., 1935.

147. MAIMONIDES. *Talmud Torah.* (Hebrew).

148. MARTIN, J. P. "Sociological Aspects of Conviction," *Advancement of Science,* (May, 1964).

149. MATRAS, J. *Social Change in Israel.* Chicago: Aldine Publishing Co., 1965.

150. MATZA, D. *Delinquency and Drift.* London: Wiley, 1964.

151. MENNINGER, K. *The Vital Balance.* New York: Vitkin Press, 1963.

152. MERTON, R. K. "Anomie, Anomia and Social Interaction," in Clinard, M. B. (ed.) *Contexts of Deviant Behaviour.* The Glencoe Free Press.

153. MERTON, R. K. *Social Theory and Social Structure.* Glencoe, Ill.: The Glencoe Free Press, 1957.

154. MERTON, R. K. "The Self-Fulfilling Prophecy," *The Antioch Review,* VIII, (1948).

155. MICHAL, L. and ADLER, M. J. *Crime, Law and Social Science.* London: Kegan Paul, 1933.

156. MILLER, W. B. *Delinquent Behaviour, Culture and the Individual.* Washington D. C.: National Education Association, 1959.

157. MILLER, W. B. "Lower-Class Culture as a Generating Milieu of Gang Delinquency," *Journal of Social Issues,* XIV, (1958).

158. MILLS, C. W. *Images of Man,* New York, 1960.

159. MILLS, C. W. *Power, Politics and People;* the collected essays. New York: Oxford University Press, 1963.

160. MORRIS, T. *The Criminal Area.* London: Kegan Paul, 1958.

161. MUELLER, G. O. W. "Tort Crime and the Punishment," *Journal of Criminal Law, Criminology and Police Science,* XLVI.

162. NAPIER, N. E. "Florentine History," Vol. V, London, cited by Wolf-
gang, M. "Socio-Economic Crimes and Punishments in Renaissance
Florence," *Journal of Criminal Law, Criminology and Police Science,*
XLVII, (Oct., 1956).

163. NETTLER, G. "Antisocial Sentiment and Criminality," *American
Sociological Review,* XXIV, (1959), pp. 202–208.

164. NEWCOMB, T. M. *Social Psychology.* New York: Henry Holt and Co.
1958.

165. NICHOLS "How Opiates changes Behaviour," *The Scientific
American,* (Feb., 1965).

165. NETTLER, G. "Antisocial Sentiment and Criminality," *American
Sociological Review,* XXIV, (1959), pp. 202–208.

166. OGDEN, C. K. and RICHARDS, I. A. *The Meaning of Meaning.*
London: Routledge and Kegan Paul, 1960.

167. ORTEGA, Y. G. *The Revolt of the Masses.* London: Unwin Books,
1961.

168. ORWELL, G. *Nineteen Eighty-Four.* Harmondsworth: Penguin Books
1961.

169. PAGNOL, M. *Topaze.* Paris: Fasquelle, 1958.

170. PARK, E. "Human Migration and the Marginal Man," *American
Journal of Sociology,* XXXIII, (1927/28).

171. PARSONS, T. *Essay in Sociological Theory.* New York: The Free Press
of Glencoe, 1954.

172. PARSONS, T. and BALES, R. F. *Family, Socialization and Interaction
Processes.* Glencoe, Ill.: The Free Press, 1955.

173. PARTRIDGE, G. E. "Current Conceptions of Psychopathic Personality," *American Journal of Psychiatry,* X, (1930), pp. 53–99.

174. PINES, S. *Be'emek Habbacha.* Jerusalem, 5243. (Hebrew).

175. PLATO. *The Republic: Dialogues of Plato.* New York: Random
House, 1937.

176. PLASCOW, M. "Some Causative Factors in Criminality; Report on the Causes of Crime" in *Report of the National Commission on Law Observance and Law Enforcement*, Vol. I, Washington D.C., 1931.

177. POLLOCK, F. and MAITLAND, F. W. *The History of English Law before the Time of Edward I*. Vol. I, Cambridge: University Press, 1932.

178. PORTERFIELD, A. L. "Delinquency and Its Outcome in Court and College," *American Journal of Sociology*, XLVIII, (Nov., 1943).

179. PRITCHARD, J. C. *Treatise on Insanity*. London: Gilbert and Piper, 1835.

180. PULZER, P. G. P. *The Rise of Political Anti-Semitism in Germany and Austria*. New York: Wiley, 1964.

181. RADZINOWICZ, L. *A History of English Criminal Law*, I, London: Stevens, 1948.

182. RANULF, S. *Moral Indignation and Middle-Class Psychology, a Sociological Study*. Copenhagen: Levin and Munksgaard, 1938.

183. RANULF, S. *The Jealousy of the Gods and the Criminal Law in Athens*. Copenhagen: Levin and Munksgaard, 1933.

184. RECKLESS, W. C. *The Crime Problem*. New York: Appleton-Century Crofts, 1961.

185. RECKLESS, W. C., DINITZ, S. and MURRAY, E. "Self Concept as an Insulator against Delinquency," *American Sociological Review*, XXI, (December, 1956), pp. 744–746.

186. REIK, T. "Gestaendniszwang und Strafbeduerfnis," *Probleme der Psychoanalyse und der Kriminologie*.

187. REITZES, D. C. "The Effect of Social Environment upon Former Felons," *Journal of Criminology, Criminal Law and Police Science*, VIXL, (1955–56).

188. RIESMAN, D. *The Lonely Crowd*. New Haven: Yale University Press, 1961.

189. RIESMAN, D. *Individualism Reconsidered and other Essays*. New York: The Free Press of Glencoe, 1964.

273

190. ROSENZWEIG, S. "The Experimental Measurement of Types of Reaction to Frustration," in Murray, H. A. *Explorations in Personality*. Oxford: University Press, 1938.

191. ROSENZWEIG, S. "Study of Repression," in Murray, H. A. *Explorations in Personality*. Oxford: University Press, 1938.

192. RUNCIMAN, S. *The Medieval Manichee*. Cambridge: University Press, 1955.

193. SAENGER, G. *The Social Psychology of Prejudice*. New York: Harper, 1953.

194. SALOMON, A. *The Tyranny of Progress*. New York: The Noonday Press, 1955.

195. SARTRE, J. P. *No Exit*. New York: Vintage Books, 1949.

196. SARTRE, J. P. *Being and Nothingness*. London: Methuen, 1957.

197. SARTRE, J. P. *The Present Age*. London: Oxford University Press, 1940.

198. SARTRE, J. P. "Saint Genet, Comedien et Martyr" in Genet, J. *Oeuvres Completes*. Paris: Gallimard, 1967.

199. SCHACHTER, S. "Deviation, Rejection and Communication," *Journal of Abnormal Social Psychology*, XLVI, (1951).

200. SCHACHTER, S. *The Psychology of Affiliation*. Stanford, Calif.: Stanford University Press, 1959.

201. SCHELLER, M. *Ressentiment*. Glencoe, Ill.: The Free Press, 1961.

202. SCHWARTZ, R. D. and SKOLNICK, J. H. "Two Studies of Legal Stigma," *Social Problems*, X, (Fall, 1962), pp. 133–142.

203. SEEMAN, M. "On the Meaning of Alienation," *American Sociological Review*, XXIV, (1959).

204. SELLIN, J. T. "Culture Conflict and Crime." New York, Social Science Research Council, Bulletin 41, (1938), p. 34.

205. SHAKESPEARE, W. *Julius Caesar*. Cleveland and New York: The World Publishing Co.

206. SHAW, C. and MC KAY, R. *Juvenile Delinquency and Urban Areas*. University of Chicago Press, 1942.

274

207. SHAW, C. and MC KAY, R. Report on Social Factors in Juvenile Delinquency. Report # 13, 2, Report on the Causes of Crime, National Commission on Law Observance and Enforcement, 1937.

208. SHELDON, W. H. *Varieties of Delinquent Youth.* New York: Harper, 1949.

209. SHERIF, M. and CANTRIL, H. *The Psychology of Ego-Involvement.* New York: J. Wiley, 1966.

210. SHOHAM, S., EREZ, R. and RECKLESS, W. "Value Orientation and Awareness of Differential Opportunity of Delinquent and Non-delinquent Boys in Israel," *The British Journal of Criminology,* (July, 1965).

211. SHOHAM, S, and HOVAV, M. "'B'nei Tovim,' Middle and Upper Class Delinquency in Israel." Report on the second stage of the research project, *Human relations,* (1966).

212. SHOHAM, S. "The Application of the 'Culture-Conflict' Hypothesis to the Criminality of Immigrants in Israel," *Journal of Criminal Law, Criminology and Police Science,* LIII, (1962).

213. SHOHAM, S. and HOVAV, M. "Social Factors, Treatment Aspects and Criminal Career of 'B'nei Tovim,' Middle and Upper Class Juvenile Delinquency in Israel," *Human Relations,* (1966).

214. SHOHAM, S. and HOVAV, M. " 'B'nei Tovim,' Middle and Upper Class Delinquency in Israel," *Sociology and Social Research,* first stage, XLVIII, No. 1, (July, 1964).

215. SHOHAM, S., SHOHAM, N. and ABD-EL-RAZED "Immigration, Ethnicity and Ecology as related to Juvenile Delinquency in Israel," *The British Journal of Criminology,* (1966).

216. SHOHAM, S. "Conflict Situations and Delinquent Solutions," *Journal of Social Psychiatry,* LXIV, (1964), pp. 85–215.

217. SHOHAM, S. "The Norm, the Act and the Object of Crime as Bases for the Classification of Criminal Behaviour," *The International Journal of Social Psychiatry,* XI, No. 4, (1965).

218. SHOHAM, S. "The Sentencing Policy of Criminal Courts in Israel," *Journal of Criminal Law, Criminology and Police Science,* L, (Nov./Dec., 1959).

219. SHOHAM, S. *The Sentencing Policy of Criminal Courts in Israel.* Tel Aviv: Am Oved, 1963. (Hebrew).

220. SHOHAM, S. "Psychopathy as Social Stigma: A Myth Revisited," *The Journal of Corrective Psychiatry.* (January, 1967).

221. SHOHAM, S., KEREN, R. and SHAVIT, G. "Pimps and Prostitutes, A Criminal Dyad," *Revue Absolutioniste Internationale,* (1964).

222. SHOHAM, S., SHAPIRO, N. and SPIEGEL, J. The Vagabonds of Eilath, (unpublished).

223. SHORT, J. F. A Report on the Incidence of Criminal Behaviour, Arrests and Conviction in Selected Groups.

224. SHUVAL, J. *Social Problems in Development Towns.* Jerusalem: The Institute of Applied Social Research, 1959.

225. SILVING, H. "Suicide and Law" in Shneidman, E. S. and Farberow, N. L. *Clues to Suicide.* New York: McGraw-Hill, 1957.

226. SIMMEL, G. *Conflict.* Translated Kurt H. Wolf. Glencoe, Ill.: The Free Press, 1955.

227. SOPHOCLES. Phoenician Women.

228. SOROKIN, P. A. "Sociology of Yesterday, Today and Tomorrow," *American Sociological Review,* XXX, (1965), p. 833.

229. STAFFORD-CLARK, D. *Psychiatry Today.* Pelican Books, 1951.

230. STEINBECK, J. *Travels with Charley.* New York: Bantam Books, 1963.

231. STONEQUIST, E. V. "The Problem of the Marginal Man," *American Journal of Sociology,* XLI, (1935/36).

232. SUMNER, W. G. *Folkways.* Boston: Ginn and Co., 1934.

233. SUTHERLAND, E. H. *White-Collar Crime.* New York: Dryden, 1949.

234. SUTHERLAND, E. H. and CRESSEY, D. R. *Principles of Criminology.* Chicago: Lippincott, 1960.

235. THE SUTHERLAND PAPERS Edited by Albert Cohen et al. Bloomington: Indiana University Press, 1956. P. 62.

236. SYKES, G. and MATZA, D. "Techniques of Neutralization: A Theory of Delinquency," *American Sociological Review,* XXII, (1957–58), pp. 664–670.

237. TAFT, D. R. *Criminology.* 2nd ed. New York, 1956.

238. TAHON, H. H. *Subgroups in Israel.* Jerusalem 1957. (Hebrew).

239. TANNENBAUM, F. *Crime and the Community.* New York: Columbia University Press, 1938.

240. TAPPAN, P. W. *Crime, Justice and Correction.* New York: McGraw-Hill, 1960.

241. TENENBAUM, J. *Race and Reich.* New York: Twayne Publishers, 1956.

242. THIBAUT, J. W. and KELLEY, H. H. *The Social Psychology of Groups.* New York: John Wiley and Sons, 1959.

243. THOMAS, E. J. *The Life of Buddha as Legend and History.* London: Routledge and K. Paul, 1960. p. 87.

244. THOMAS, W. and ZNANIECKI, F. *The Polish Peasant in Europe and and America.* New York: Dover Publ., 1958.

245. THRASHER, F. M. *The Gang.* Chicago: University Press, 1927.

246. THUCYDIDES. The Greek Historians, Vol. I, New York: Random House, 1942.

247. TIMASHEF, N. "The Retributive Structure of Punishment," *Journal of Criminal Law, Criminology and Police Science,* XXVIII, (1937–38).

248. TOYNBEE, A. *A Study of History.* Abridgement of Vols. I-VI by D.C. Somerwell, New York: Oxford University Press, 1947.

249. ULLMAN, W. *The Medieval Idea of Law.* London: Methuen and Co., 1946.

250. *Uniform Crime Report for the U.S.* Washington, 1958.

251. VAN NYE, P. *Family Relations and Delinquent Behaviour.* New York: Wiley, 1958.

252. VAN VECHTER, C. "Criminality of the Foreign Born," *Proceedings of the Seventieth Annual Congress of Correction of the American Prison, 1940.*

253. VEBLEN, T. *The Theory of the Leisure Class.* New York: The Modern Library, 1931.

254. VOGEL and BELL. *The Family.* New York: The Free Press, 1967.

255. VON HENTIG, H. H. *Punishment.* London, 1935.

256. WALKER, E. L. and HEYNS, R. W. *An Anatomy for Comformity.* Englewood Cliffs, N. J.: Prentice Hall, 1962. p. 23.

257. WELLER, L. "The Effects of Anxiety on Cohesiveness and Rejection," *Human Relations,* XVI, 1963.

258. WEIHOFEN, H. *The Urge to Punish.* New approaches to the problem of mental irresponsibility for crime. New York: Farrar, Straus and Cudahy, 1956.

259. WEINGROD, A. "Morrocan Jewry in Transition," *Megamot,* Jerusalem, (Jan., 1960). (Hebrew).

260. WHITE, R. W. *The Abnormal Personality.* New York: Ronald Press, 1956.

261 WHYTE, W. F. *Street Corner Society: The social status of an Italian slum.* Chicago: University of Chicago Press, 1943.

262. WILSON, C. H. *The Outsider.* London: V. Gollancz, 1964.

263. WOLF, M. "Psychopathy, a Modern Symptom," *Ofakim,* XIV, p. 238. (Hebrew).

264. WOLFF, *The Roman Law.* Norman, 1951.

265. WOLFGANG, M. E. "Socio-Economic Factors Related to Crime and Punishment in Renaissance Florence," *Journal of Criminal Law, Criminology and Police Science,* XLVII, (Oct., 1956).

266. WOLFGANG, M. E. *Patterns in Criminal Homicide.* Pennsylvania: University of Pennsylvania Press, 1958.

267. WORDSWORTH, W. *Tintern Abbey.*

278

268. WRIGHT, H. *Physical Disability—A Psychological Approach*. New York: Harper and Row, 1960.

269. WRIGHT, M. *The Power Elite*. Oxford University Press, Galaxy Books, 1959.

270. YABLONSKY, L. *The Violent Gang*. New York: Macmillan, 1962.

271. ZAMIR, R. *Beer-Sheva* 1958–9. Jerusalem: The Hebrew University Press, 1964. (Hebrew).

272. ZILBOORG, G. A. in collaboration with Henry, G. W. *A History of Medical Psychology*. New York: W. W. Norton, 1941.

273. ZORBAUGH, H. W. *The Gold Coast and the Slum*. Chicago: University Press, 1929.

NAME INDEX

A

Abrahamsen D   26
Ackerman N.W.   27
Adler M.   3
Adorno T.W.   117
Andeneas J.   148
Andry R.G.   66, 199
Asch S.F.   121, 172, 173

B

Back K.   168
Ben Dov S.   91
Berg I.A.   173
Berger E.M.   134
Berkowitz L.   168
Blau P.M.   42
Bloch H.A.   175, 182
Boorstin D.   78
Breuer   25
Bronner H.   26, 192
Burt C.   26, 192

C

Calhoun G.M.   33
Camus A.   33, 51, 72, 94, 114
Cason H.   28
Charcot J.   25
Chwast J.   16, 110, 200
Clarke J.   54
Clinard M.B.   3, 32
Cloward R.E.   54, 128, 175, 177,
    178, 181, 198, 215
Cohen A.   163, 175, 176, 177, 183,
    195
Coser L.A.   18, 163, 168, 190
Coulton   135
Crutchfield R.S.   121, 173

D

de Beze T.   107

de Grazia S.   195
Dinitz S.   54
Dostoyevski   40
Downes D.M.   176, 187, 188
Drachmann A.B.   105
Durkheim E.   17, 18, 37, 52, 72,
    102, 195
Dynes R.R.   54

E

East N.   140, 141
Eriksen E.H.   83, 122, 175, 182,
    211
Evans-Pritchard E.E.   14, 28, 30

F

Festinger L.   168
Fiedler L.   39
Fisher R.A.   27
Flugel J.C.   100
Frazer J.G.   10, 13–14, 102, 129,
    133
Frenkel-Brunswick E.   117, 121
Freud S.   25, 41, 42, 83
Fromm E.   40, 41, 43, 69
Fyvel T.R.   188

G

Garofalo R.   3
Genet J.   129, 163, 201–237
Giffin M.E.   27
Glazer D.   126, 198, 215

Goffman E.   86
Guttman L.   20
Glueck S. and E.   8, 26

H

Hafetz–Haim   111
Harari C.   200